# *Community Life*

# Community Life
# An Introduction
# to Local
# Social Relations

GRAHAM CROW AND GRAHAM ALLAN

*University of Southampton*

**HARVESTER
WHEATSHEAF**

New York   London   Toronto   Sydney   Tokyo   Singapore

First published 1994 by
Harvester Wheatsheaf
Campus 400, Maylands Avenue
Hemel Hempstead
Hertfordshire, HP2 7EZ
A division of
Simon & Schuster International Group

Typeset in 10/12pt Sabon
by Photoprint, Torquay, Devon

Printed and bound in Great Britain
by Biddles Ltd, Guildford and King's Lynn

British Library Cataloguing in Publication Data

A catalogue record for this book is available
from the British Library

ISBN 0–7450–1198–5

1  2  3  4  5          98  97  96  95  94

For our students

# CONTENTS

# FOREWORD

'Community' – a word which continues to resonate through our everyday lives, a totem of how we would like our lives to be, as opposed to the less-than-perfect reality. The notion of community therefore retains an enduring appeal, even though it becomes a somewhat empty vessel into which we can pour our images of the Good Life. Who does *not* wish to live in a 'community'? Who can resist its use as an omnibus label – the European Community, community care – applied as a veneer of sociability to otherwise somewhat impersonal public activities?

Social scientists who seek to analyse the concept of community therefore have to wade through thickets of sentiment and emotion. Even attempts to define the term have been fraught with difficulty, not least, one suspects, because almost any definition will do violence to a number of deeply held beliefs about its essential qualities.

Community studies have an honoured place in the history of British sociology and social anthropology. British sociology may be said to have its origins in the studies of Victorian and Edwardian poverty by Charles Booth and Seebohm Rowntree in London and York respectively. Less well known are the anthropological studies of English villages stimulated by the establishment of the Development Commission in 1909. But arguably the most famous community study of all – on which a whole generation of sociology students was weaned – was Michael Young and Peter Willmott's study of Bethnal Green, *Family and Kinship in East London*, first published in 1957. In these days of mass media, investigative reporting and newspaper supplements, it is easy to overlook the brilliance of Young and Willmott's social reportage. The book was a best-seller, in a manner scarcely conceivable today, and went on to inspire a whole genre of sociological study.

The rather self-conscious sense of the social scientist as intrepid investigator was to produce an inevitable reaction – 'the poor sociologist's substitute for the novel', sniffed one commentator, Ruth Glass, in a famously acerbic comment. And it was certainly true that at times it was difficult to disentangle the values and prejudices of the investigators from the empirical observations of everyday life in the communities which fell within their purview. This, together with the continuing disputes over definitions and methodologies, led to a decline in conventional community studies from the early 1970s onwards.

Looking back, we can see that something has been lost as a result. Community studies provided a method of integrating the study of various strands of contemporary life in an imperfect, but nevertheless holistic, account. As a result, our finger is perhaps less securely on the pulse of social change in Britain in the 1990s than it was in the early 1960s – and this despite the huge advances in information technology which have taken place over the intervening period. The tradition has not been lost, but it has become attenuated. This is a shame, and may well be an unintended consequence of the critique which Colin Bell and I set out in our book *Community Studies*, published in 1971.

Our book is now out of print. Graham Allan and Graham Crow have provided an excellent overview of the topic, which encompasses both the history of the sociology of community and its use in contemporary public debate. The study of community still provides an excellent entrée to the study of sociology, social policy and social anthropology. But the use – and misuse – of 'community' in recent public debates make this text invaluable to all who have an interest in understanding a *leitmotif* of our present discontents.

Howard Newby
ESRC, Swindon
July 1993

# PREFACE

The sociology of community is currently undergoing something of a revival, and this book has been written with the aim of contributing to this process in a number of ways. First of all, it has been our object as authors to draw attention to the burgeoning literature on sociological aspects of community life, since it is our belief that work in this field has been undeservedly neglected, and that the writings of sociologists of community merit more than the marginal recognition which they have tended to receive. In our view, the breadth and depth of much of their research makes it worthy of being brought before a wider audience, and to the extent that this book helps to do that then a primary objective will have been achieved. Secondly, we have sought to bring together the various studies considered here into a more coherent whole than they possess as simply a collection of separate pieces of research. This has inevitably involved arbitrary decisions on our part about which investigations ought to be included, and which aspects of those studies selected should be emphasised, but we are nevertheless confident that the book develops a systematic account of community life in modern Britain which goes beyond the limitations of time and place that historically have dogged individual studies, and says something about society more generally. This confidence stems in part from our view that 'community' is a key sociological variable, and one which adds an important dimension to the analysis of social relations in a variety of settings. The means by which sociologists in the field of community undertake their research tell us a good deal about the practice and purpose of the discipline more broadly, and presenting an account of how and why the various investigations were undertaken stands as a third strand to the thinking behind our decision to write this book. These three objectives – to report in one place what researchers have found, to develop a comparative analysis of these findings, and to show the relevance of this mode of analysis for an understanding of the current state of society – are at the heart of this book's rationale.

A good deal has happened since the last general surveys of the sociology of community in Britain were published (Bell and Newby, 1971; Frankenberg, 1969). To begin with, there have been numerous pieces of research into community life conducted in contrasting locations, pursuing a range of objectives and employing a variety of methodologies. These investigations include studies of ordinary people's everyday lives in the context of diverse social settings and policy initiatives, and collectively they provide a wealth of information on the ways in which local social life is structured. The dearth of research into community matters in the 1970s has been replaced in the 1980s and 1990s by studies stretching between the geographical extremes of Cornwall and north-east Scotland and between equally broad parameters in terms of topics of enquiry. If certain themes like the impact of unemployment or the effect of planning decisions are recurrent in the literature, it is also the case that sociologists have studied unique and unusual features of local social life such as the embeddedness of ritual celebrations and musical associations in community networks. The research projects included on the map on page xxiv are by no means all community studies in the classical sense of the term, but they are all studies of some aspect of community life, and their number and differences stand as convincing testimony of the enlivened state of the sociology of community in contemporary Britain.

The justification for writing this book does not lie simply with the volume of research which there has been, however, impressive though the number of studies is. There have also been important developments in both the theories and the methods employed by researchers. It is true that serious problems existed with the old tradition of community studies in the period up to and including the 1960s, and these problems have led to the call being made by some commentators for social scientists to abandon the use of the concept of 'community' altogether. This has not happened, and the fact that, in Day and Murdoch's words, ' "community" is a concept that just will not lie down' (1993, p. 85), suggests that it is unlikely to. On the negative side, the continued use by sociologists and others of the term 'community' indicates a dissatisfaction on their part with suggested alternatives such as 'local social system' and 'locality'. Whatever their other merits, these alternatives have run into conceptual difficulties of their own, not least their failure to capture the subjective dimension of community attachments and identities. More positively, theories of 'community' have developed in important respects since the time when community studies were rightly criticised for their tendency to be descriptive and atheoretical.

Much of the impetus for the 'rethinking' of community has come from other disciplines besides sociology. Anthropologists have directed attention to the importance of the symbolic boundaries around communities (Cohen, 1985), for example, and historians have also contributed to fresh thinking about how communities are created and sustained; the significance of this work is suggested by the comment that 'The concept of community has come to play an increasingly important part in historical writing' (Burke, 1992, p. 56). Similar points could be made about other related disciplines such as geography, demography, political science, psychology, women's studies and social policy analysis, in all of which areas the need has been recognised to go beyond the situation in which 'community' is used uncritically as a blanket term and 'means all things to all people' (Dalley, 1988, p. 48). The project of rethinking the concept of community has engaged the attention of a considerable number of people with a range of interests and disciplinary backgrounds.

It was never likely that this rethinking of the meaning of community would come up with the elusive definition around which a consensus could be built. Yet for all that community remains a contested concept, certain valuable conclusions have emerged. One is that community is a key part of the language which we use to describe and account for our lives and experiences, and as such it enters into the ways in which we express ideas of 'solidarity, interest and identity' (Bornat, 1993, p. 22) which are at the heart of community life. This language is not neutral, and it follows that representations of community are necessarily selective or partial. It does not follow that the term community is infinitely pliable, however, since its usage conforms to certain patterns which can be identified. For instance, it is clear that while community is often associated with place, it is by no means the case that all communities are territorial communities; occupational communities may be geographically dispersed, to cite just one example. Nor is there any straightforward relationship between places and the capacity to support particular types of social relationships. The abandonment of the idea that there are peculiarly rural and urban communities has led to renewed interest in the capacity of empirical social investigation to identify the conditions under which place, occupation and like variables 'have the potentiality to generate other forms of social solidarity' (Harris, 1990, p. 190). The thing which members of a community share in common may be a particular sense of place, but precisely how space structures social relationships is an empirical question which cannot be undertaken without reference to the findings of particular case studies.

It is of course true that places with strong physical boundaries are a potent base for territorial communities. Tiger Bay in Cardiff's dockland is one such place, bounded by a canal and a railway line, a road and a dock wall, all of which act as barriers to keep in members of the community and to exclude outsiders. This compact area has long had an ethnically heterogeneous population but this did not prevent the development of a strong local identity: 'Along with African and West Indian sailors, Tiger Bay also became home to Asians, southern Europeans, Filipinos and Chinese. In its heyday Tiger Bay was an exciting cosmopolitan community' (Dennis, 1993, p. 9). Mining villages provide another example of community ties being reinforced by physical isolation, but in modern society it is rare for the boundaries of place to coincide neatly with the sense of community which people hold (Harper, 1992). The symbolic boundaries of community relate to membership categories in which geographical presence may be a necessary but is usually not a sufficient condition for an individual's inclusion. Studies of remote and inaccessible locations such as Tory Island off Ireland (Fox, 1978) or Whalsay in the Shetland Islands (Cohen, 1987) demonstrate the impossibility of complete self-containment for communities, and point to the importance of recognising the social construction of communities and the negotiated nature of their terms of membership. Precisely what it takes to be accepted as 'one of us' varies enormously from place to place and also between different types of social groups, and the processes by which these social boundaries are constructed and maintained have become a key concern of community sociologists.

The potential for community identity to be constructed around certain symbols is now a well-established theme in the literature, but an important issue remains unresolved regarding Anderson's suggestion that 'all communities larger than primordial villages (and perhaps even these) are imagined' (1991, p. 6). Attention to the symbolic meanings of community benefits from being linked to an analysis of the content of the social relationships which are taken to make up 'community', since shared identities are unlikely to be sustained where professed loyalties fail to materialise in practical action. As Goodin has noted, 'Flag waving is just not enough. Symbolic acts implicitly promise subsequent action, and the symbolism will rightly be regarded as empty if the implied follow-up is never forthcoming' (1985, p. 157). The discrepancy between idealised, romantic representations of community and the more prosaic reality is readily apparent in the case of the middle-class commuters who move to the countryside in pursuit of 'the cosy community' (Strathern, 1981, p. 221) in which they believe everyone knows everyone else, only to find it necessary to adjust their model of how village life operates. Other contexts are marked by the reverse situation of the absence of imagined communities. In a part of south-east London dominated by large housing estates, for example, one study found that only two people in five felt that they belonged to a community, although research of this kind is hampered (as the authors recognise) by the difficulties of specifying 'what people mean by community spirit' (Clarke and Hedges, quoted in Foster, 1990, p. 12), and it is important to note that even here community traditions such as neighbourhood support networks among kinsfolk remained an important feature of the area's social structure.

Sociologists of community have become keenly aware of the danger of representations of community being one-sided, and have sought in particular to give voice to previously unheard accounts. Community publishing and oral history have been significant in this respect in allowing formerly invisible groups such as poor working-class people, especially working-class women, to speak for themselves about the ways they lived (Bornat, 1993). Such accounts in which the uglier side of life is not suppressed are sharply at odds with preconceived notions of past communities being characterised by supportiveness in adversity, of being poor but happy, yet such rethinking is necessary if we are to make sense of Damer's observation that 'Nobody in his or her right mind *wanted* to live in a slum tenement . . . The vast majority of slum dwellers wanted only one thing. Out' (1990, p. 90; emphasis in original). This conclusion squares with other reassessments of 'traditional' neighbourhood patterns celebrated in many of the older community studies. For Abrams, this type of community should not be romanticised, because 'when one considers the social conditions that made it possible one is forced to the conclusion that on balance it is rather undesirable' (Bulmer, 1986, p. 92). The comfortable images of traditional communities as social entities with strong collective identities and relations of reciprocity between members have to be tempered in view of what has also come to light concerning the poverty, insecurity, divisions and parochialism which also stand out as defining characteristics.

Rethinking community has challenged not only particular images of community life but also certain underlying ideas, such as the notion that communities are 'natural' phenomena. Abrams has noted how 'The so-called natural helping networks of the traditional neighbourhood [were] not actually natural at all . . . [but] developed as a response to certain highly specified social conditions' (Bulmer, 1986, p. 92). Abrams went on from this to suggest that the nature of community ties varies with different patterns of physical proximity, differences in the longevity of settlements and of people's residence there, different levels of resources (varying according to age, class and gender), and different senses of obligations between people. None of these factors has a 'natural' level, and recognition of this opens the way for identifying community types as products of sociological variables. It is clear that more work remains to be done in specifying the detailed contents of a general typology of communities, but the broad distinction made by Abrams between 'the traditional neighbourhood and modern neighbourhoodism' (Bulmer, 1986, p. 91) is one that subsequent writers have employed profitably, as is Wallman's (1985) contrast between 'homogeneous' and 'heterogeneous' areas. Attempts to develop typologies of communities have a long and contentious history

(Bailey, 1980; Bell and Newby, 1971; Poplin, 1979), but cautious optimism may be appropriate where the matter is approached not as a question of grand theory but as one requiring detailed empirical studies of the factors behind patterns of variation.

Methodological developments in the sociology of community have been complementary to these theoretical developments. The identification of the variables which lie behind community differences requires comparative research, and community sociologists have been mindful that the old tradition of community studies was seriously deficient in this respect. Two shifts in particular deserve mention. One important change has been the greater frequency with which individual studies have contained a comparative element, and have investigated two (or more) communities rather than one. Thus Coffield *et al.* (1986) investigated youth unemployment in three areas of north-east England, as did Hutson and Jenkins (1989) in South Wales, and in each case the comparative structure of the research allowed differences between communities to be accounted for in terms of variables such as social class and housing tenure. Similarly Gilbert's (1992) contrast between two coal-mining communities in Nottinghamshire and South Wales a century ago, Warwick and Littlejohn's (1992) study of four present-day West Yorkshire mining communities, St Leger and Gillespie's (1991) comparison of informal caring arrangements in three Belfast communities, Saunders' (1990) enquiry into owner-occupation in the three towns of Burnley, Derby and Slough, and Waddington *et al.*'s (1989) analysis of community disorders in six different settings are all examples of the comparative method being employed to good effect in individual research projects. In addition, comparative analysis has been assisted by greater consciousness on the part of researchers of the need to identify working hypotheses which are in principle testable in other settings. A good example of this is Pahl's (1984) hypothesis concerning economic restructuring and social polarisation which has been investigated in several other places besides the Isle of Sheppey, where his own research was conducted. Cooke's (1989) report on various locality studies was a more formally co-ordinated project but was founded on the same assumption concerning the value of comparative analysis.

The findings of research in the field of community indicate that the nature of community life is at one level almost infinitely diverse, and writing a book of this kind requires that some order be put onto the vast array of social relationships which have been identified. The logic of our argument dictated that we isolate a limited number of variables which research suggests play a key role in determining patterns of community life and subject them in turn to scrutiny. Thus following the introduction contained in chapter 1, chapter 2 is devoted to examining the idea that communities are shaped by their traditions, chapter 3 to the impact of economic restructuring, and chapter 4 to the effects of geographical mobility. Chapter 5 concentrates on race and ethnicity as a marked and enduring feature of patterns of residential segregation, while chapter 6 assesses the argument that involvement in community life is influenced by patterns of domestic life. Chapters 7 and 8 consider community as it relates to issues of planning and social policy, and chapter 9 draws these various strands together in making a case for treating the sociology of community as a field of research which has continuing importance and relevance.

This way of dividing up the subject has a coherence which will become clearer as the reader follows through the unfolding argument chapter by chapter. The accounts of the past contained in chapter 2 provide an historical benchmark which allows a more informed discussion of the impact of economic restructuring and geographical mobility in the subsequent chapters. The analysis of migration in chapter 4 in turn leads on directly to the focus in chapter 5 on race and ethnicity, since explanations of residential segregation along ethnic lines have always involved some reference to migration patterns, although such explanations are now widely recognised to be inadequate as accounts of continuing spatial inequalities. The spatial distribution of the population along ethnic lines also reflects inequalities in the housing market, and the fuller discussion contained in chapter 6 of the significance for community ties of the growth in owner-occupation and the marginalisation of the rented sectors follows on directly from this. In turn, housing patterns have themselves been the product of the activities of planners which are the subject of chapter 7, while chapter 8 echoes many of the points made about the impact of state bodies in relation to other social policies.

Over and above these factors such as economic restructuring and geographical mobility which have individual chapters devoted to them there are some more general themes which run throughout the book. Gender is one key variable which is prominent in a number of the discussions in the book, particularly in chapter 2 (where the significance of women's lives in traditional working-class communities is examined), chapter 3 (where the importance for economic activity of women's social networks is analysed), chapter 6 (where the debate about the gendered nature of home life is discussed), and chapter 8 (where the gendered assumptions underlying community-care policies are considered). In a similar way differences along lines of social class figure at various points of the argument, including the discussion of social polarisation in chapter 3, the analysis of the debate on housing classes in chapter 6, and examination of the idea of balanced communities in chapter 7.

In a rather different way the perennial sociological debate over how much the nature of our social life can be attributed to choice and how much of it is due to forces beyond our control is also to be found running through the discussions of community which follow. The residential segregation along ethnic lines considered in chapter 5 can be seen as either chosen or enforced, although recent contributors to the debate such as Sarre *et al.* (1989) have sought to go beyond this dichotomy. In like manner the growth of owner-occupation analysed in chapter 6 is interpreted by some commentators as an expression of people's choices while for others it indicates the paucity of alternatives. Similarly chapters 7 and 8 bring out the concentration of power which exists in the hands of state officials to influence and control ordinary people's everyday lives, but at the same time illustrate the limits to that power and the ability of community members either individually or collectively to subvert policies imposed upon them with which they do not concur. The historical record suggests that it is easier for planners to destroy communities than it is to create them, although community traditions are remarkably resilient even in the context of extensive geographical mobility and redevelopment, as the discussions in chapters 4 and 7 show. More generally the diversity, persistence and creativity of the local social life described in the pages which follow indicate that despite repeated pronouncements of its inevitable decline in the modern world, community life is still very much a part of our social existence.

# ACKNOWLEDGEMENTS

Many people have helped us in the writing of this book and we are grateful for their time and effort in sharing ideas, commenting on drafts, and generally providing a supportive environment. Colleagues in the Department of Sociology and Social Policy at the University of Southampton have helped in a number of ways, especially Martin Bulmer, who read through the whole manuscript and provided many useful suggestions for improvement. Similar thanks must go to Fiona Devine of the University of Liverpool for undertaking the same task, as did the publisher's (anonymous) reader, to whom an equal acknowledgement is due. We would also like to thank Clare Grist at Harvester Wheatsheaf for her prompt and efficient editorial guidance at the various stages of the writing of this book. And, finally, gratitude ought also to be extended to the several cohorts of students whose individual and collective responses to earlier versions of the arguments contained in the book have undoubtedly made it better than it would otherwise have been.

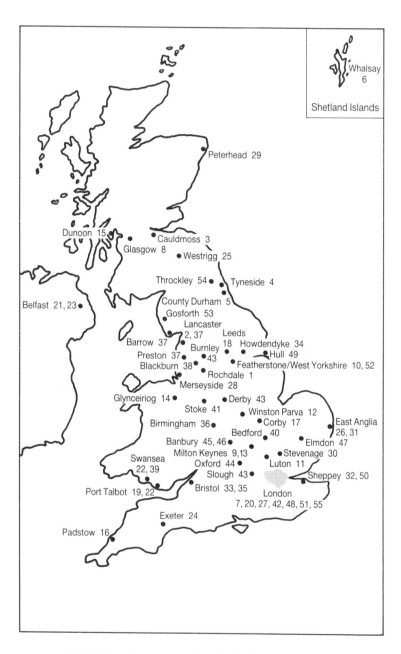

A Geography of Community and Locality Studies in the British Isles

## KEY TO MAP

1 M. Anwar (1985) *Pakistanis in Britain* Rochdale
2 P. Bagguley *et al.* (1990) *Restructuring* Lancaster
3 A. Bostyn and D. Wight (1987) 'Inside a community' 'Cauldmoss'
4 D. Byrne (1989) *Beyond the Inner City* Tyneside
5 F. Coffield *et al.* (1986) *Growing up at the Margins* County Durham
6 A. Cohen (1987) *Whalsay* Shetland Islands
7 J. Cornwell (1984) *Hard-Earned Lives* East London
8 S. Damer (1989) *From Moorepark to 'Wine Alley'* Glasgow
9 R. Deem (1986) *All Work and no Play?* Milton Keynes
10 N. Dennis *et al.* (1956) *Coal is our Life* Featherstone
11 F. Devine (1992) *Affluent Workers Revisited* Luton
12 N. Elias and J. Scotson (1965) *The Established and the Outsiders* 'Winston Parva', Leicestershire
13 R. Finnegan (1989) *The Hidden Musicians* Milton Keynes
14 R. Frankenberg (1957) *Village on the Border* Glynceiriog
15 G. Giarchi (1984) *Between McAlpine and Polaris* Dunoon
16 H. Gilligan (1990) 'Padstow' Cornwall
17 M. Grieco (1987a) *Keeping it in the Family* Corby
18 J. Hanmer and S. Saunders (1984) *Well-Founded Fear* Leeds
19 C. Harris (1987) *Redundancy and Recession* Port Talbot
20 A. Holme (1985) *Housing and Young Families in East London* East London
21 L. Howe (1990) *Being Unemployed in Northern Ireland* Belfast
22 S. Hutson and R. Jenkins (1989) *Taking the Strain* South Wales
23 R. Jenkins (1983) *Lads, Citizens and Ordinary Kids* Belfast
24 B. Jordon *et al.* (1992) *Trapped in Poverty?* Exeter
25 J. Littlejohn (1963) *Westrigg* Cheviot Hills
26 T. Lummis (1985) *Occupation and Society* East Anglia
27 P. Marris (1987) *Meaning and Action* Docklands, East London
28 R. Meegan (1989) 'Paradise postponed' Merseyside
29 R. Moore (1982) *The Social Impact of Oil* Peterhead
30 B. Mullan (1980) *Stevenage Ltd* Stevenage
31 H. Newby (1977) *The Deferential Worker* East Anglia
32 R. Pahl (1984) *Divisions of Labour* Isle of Sheppey
33 M. Porter (1983) *Home, Work and Class Consciousness* Bristol
34 J. Porteus (1989) *Planned to Death* Howdendyke
35 K. Pryce (1979) *Endless Pressure* Bristol
36 J. Rex and R. Moore (1967) *Race, Community and Conflict* Birmingham
37 E. Roberts (1984) *A Woman's Place* Barrow/Lancaster/Preston
38 V. Robinson (1986) *Transients, Settlers and Refugees* Blackburn
39 C. Rosser and C. Harris (1965) *The Family and Social Change* Swansea
40 P. Sarre *et al.* (1989) *Ethnic Minority Housing* Bedford
41 J. Sarsby (1988) *Missuses and Mouldrunners* Stoke-on-Trent
42 P. Saunders (1979) *Urban Politics* Croydon, London
43 P. Saunders (1990) *A Nation of Home Owners* Burnley/Derby/Slough
44 A. Shaw (1988) *A Pakistani Community in Britain* Oxford
45 M. Stacey (1960) *Tradition and Change* Banbury
46 M. Stacey *et al.* (1975) *Power, Persistence and Change* Banbury
47 M. Strathern (1981) *Kinship at the Core* Elmdon, Essex
48 J. Tivers (1985) *Women Attached* Merton, London
49 J. Tunstall (1962) *The Fishermen* Hull
50 C. Wallace (1987) *For Richer, for Poorer* Isle of Sheppey
51 S. Wallman (1984) *Eight London Households* Battersea, London
52 D. Warwick and G. Littlejohn (1992) *Coal, Capital and Culture* Yorkshire
53 W. Williams (1956) *The Sociology of an English Village: Gosforth* Cumbria
54 B. Williamson (1982) *Class, Culture and Community* Throckley
55 M. Young and P. Willmott (1957) *Family and Kinship in East London* East London

# 1

## INTRODUCTION:
## OLD AND NEW THEMES IN THE
## SOCIOLOGY OF COMMUNITY

'Community' figures in many aspects of our everyday lives. Much of what we do is engaged in through the interlocking social networks of neighbourhood, kinship and friendship, networks which together make up 'community life' as it is conventionally understood. 'Community' stands as a convenient shorthand term for the broad realm of local social arrangements beyond the private sphere of home and family but more familiar to us than the impersonal institutions of the wider society, what Bulmer (1989, p. 253) calls 'intermediary structures'. The diversity and spread of these structures helps to account for the bewildering variety of meanings associated with the term 'community'. Community ties may be structured around links between people with common residence, common interests, common attachments or some other shared experience generating a sense of belonging. In each case competing definitions of 'community' are constructed, yet while the numerous meanings of 'community' are contested (Plant *et al.*, 1980, ch. 9), there is no doubt that the communities of which we are members play a significant role in shaping our social identities and patterns of action. In this chapter we start by examining the different meanings of 'community'. We then turn to the many problems there are in investigating the character of different communities and end the chapter by indicating the continued significance of community matters in our personal and public lives.

It is possible to distinguish between several different types of community according to their contrasting features and characteristics, such as the density of their social networks, the degree of their openness, and their duration (St Leger and Gillespie, 1991; Scherer, 1972). A classic example of a close-knit community structure in which the various dimensions of community life overlap and interpenetrate is provided by the traditional working-class communities found throughout industrial Britain during the earlier part of the twentieth century. The term 'occupational communities' has been applied to these tightly knit settlements of workers and their families which grew up around the mines, factories, ports and other workplaces that left a heavy imprint on local social relationships. The subsequent decline of these occupational communities should not be treated as synonymous with the decline of community as such, however, since community life takes many forms. It will be the argument of chapter 5, for instance, that some ethnic minority communities in contemporary Britain have many of the same features of 'encapsulation' as those of the traditional working class. Other contemporary communities in which members lead more detached lives are closer to what Janowitz (1967) has called 'the community of limited liability'. The more restricted patterns of sociability found in such communities indicate that individuals here have more control over and are more selective about their involvement in local social networks, but the term 'community' remains applicable for all that. The sociology of community is concerned with the whole range of community relationships and not with only one particular form.

Investigating the nature of community life is not a straightforward matter. To begin with there is the problem faced by researchers of gaining access to local social networks, given that these networks are not necessarily open to outsiders, and may be quite effectively closed off. Communities are rarely so exclusive that researching them becomes impossible, however, and fieldwork reports testify to the variety of (often ingenious) ways in which access to information about the lives of insiders has been negotiated. A second methodological problem relates to the dangers of researchers romanticising community life, finding and reporting only solidarity and co-operation and ignoring the schism and conflict in local social life, highlighting the positive, celebrated sides of communities and neglecting their oppressive and coercive aspects. The community study method has been seen by some critics as particularly problematic in this respect, and such criticism has been responsible in part for the proliferation of other research methods employed in the field of community sociology in recent years.

The extent to which 'community' shapes our lives continues to be important, despite the frequently held belief that modern times have witnessed a 'decline of community'. Closer investigation reveals that the idea of society undergoing a 'loss of community' has a very long history, but that it is sustainable only if selective, romanticised views of the past are adopted. This is not to suggest that nothing has changed in the field of community relations, however, and it is as mistaken to portray contemporary community life uncritically as it is to romanticise the past. It is now widely acknowledged that a number of questionable and outdated assumptions about the nature of local social relationships have informed policies of community care, for example. This recognition was not automatic; it emerged in no small measure through sociological researchers highlighting the mismatch between theory and evidence relating to the caring capacities of relatives, friends and neighbours in 'the community'. The sociology of community thus has a bearing on matters of immediate, practical significance as well as raising important issues at a more abstract, theoretical level. The aim of this book is to explore both these facets of the subject and their interconnections, beginning with the question 'What is community?'

## THE MEANINGS OF 'COMMUNITY'

'Community' does not have one single meaning, but many. On the basis of research experience in the field over several decades, Willmott (1986, ch. 6) suggests that basically 'community' refers to people having something in common, and that this shared element is often understood geographically; he terms this 'territorial community' or 'place community'. In contrast to this sense of community as shared residence, Willmott identifies a second meaning where the basis of community is shared characteristics other than place, in which people are linked together by factors such as common ethnic origin, religion, occupation or leisure pursuits. Since such networks are structured around common interests, Willmott uses the term 'interest community' to describe them. He notes immediately that there is quite a strong possibility of place communities and interest communities coinciding (as they did in the traditional working-class communities which are the subject of chapter 2, for example), but the distinction allows recognition that interest communities may also be geographically dispersed. Willmott then goes on to distinguish a third sense of community relating to people's 'spirit of community' or community sentiments, which he labels 'community of attachment'. (This sense of community is most obviously expressed in the various forms of collective action which are the subject matter of chapter 7.) Again there exists the possibility of overlap between this and the other senses of community that Willmott identifies, but he argues that it is a legitimate distinction to make since communities of territory and interest do not necessarily involve the interaction with other people and the sense of shared identity which are the defining characteristics of communities of attachment.

A similar conclusion to Willmott's is arrived at in Lee and Newby's (1983, ch. 4) discussion of definitions of community. Again there are three senses of community identified, and although these are not identical to Willmott's, the broad similarity is striking. Lee and Newby suggest that the geographical sense of community is best termed 'locality', and argue that the concept of community is not being used sociologically here because, 'apart from the observation that they are all living together in a particular place, there is no consideration of the inhabitants at all, nor of how – or, indeed, whether – they interact with one another' (1983, p. 57). Lee and Newby's second sense of 'community', adopting Stacey's (1969) term 'local social system', retains a geographical referent in a way that Willmott's interest community does not, but it is comparable in the sense that it implies individuals are linked together in social networks, the patterns of which can be studied as objective social structures. People are not necessarily committed subjectively to the local social systems of which they are part, and for this reason Lee and Newby distinguish a third definition of community which involves a shared sense of identity and which they call 'communion'. Like Willmott's community of attachment, Lee and Newby's communion is conceptually distinct from their other definitions, although (again like Willmott) Lee and Newby note the tendency of sociologists in the field of community to run the different elements together, and to cause confusion as a result.

'Community' may thus be defined more or less extensively. In the extreme it is possible to conceive of all the above elements of community being present simultaneously, although a definition in which shared residence, interests and identity coincide has only limited value as a sociological tool since reality is always likely to fall short of such an idealized standard, and in consequence to appear somehow incomplete. It is from such idealized notions that the pervasive 'loss of community' thesis gains misplaced credibility. A more fruitful approach is to follow Stacey's proposition that 'Physical proximity does not always lead to the establishment of social relations' (1969, p. 144), and to go on to investigate the circumstances in which there is some such link, and those in which there is not. This approach focuses attention on variables like the degree of heterogeneity of a local population and rates of inward or outward mobility, with the result that certain social structures can be identified as likely to promote (and others to impede) community interaction and community solidarity. A settled, homogeneous population is more likely than a mobile, heterogeneous one to develop community in its more extensive sense, for example, although it is clear that these are not in themselves sufficient conditions for this to happen.

The emergence of community life in its broader sense requires not only favourable local social structures but also the active creation of 'community'. This positive involvement of people and organisations in the generation and reproduction of local social networks and identities is captured in the title of Suttles' (1972) study, *The Social Construction of Communities*. Suttles' argument highlights the importance of recognising the active involvement of individuals and groups in the construction of communities because common sense, embodied in what he calls 'folk models' (1972, p. 4), tends to play it down. There is a superficial attraction to the idea of the 'natural community' in which social order and integration emerge automatically, without direction or even intention, an idea summed up in the term 'planless stability' (1972, p. 9). Thinking of communities as 'natural' appeals to us, Suttles writes, because it suggests 'a process in which communities [are] more nearly the products of personal and human nature than the contrivances of planners, bureaucracies and depersonalized institutions' (1972, p. 9). Suttles is rightly critical of such romanticism for its neglect of the active, directive role of builders, developers and government agencies in the social process of the social construction of communities, a theme pursued further in chapter 7. Suttles' argument is sensitive to the point that the construction of communities may involve the imposition of artificial patterns of residential segregation which in time come to be treated as 'natural' by residents, outsiders and external organisations alike.

The idea of the naturalness of community is understandably attractive for all its falsity. Where community is perceived as a natural unity, community ties are at their most potent, as Bauman has noted: 'The community type of belonging is at its strongest and most secure when we believe just this: that we have not chosen it on purpose, have done nothing to make it exist and can do nothing to undo it' (1990, p. 72). Put another way, 'those who pursue community as an end in itself will be ... disappointed' (Greeley, quoted in Scherer, 1972, p. 120). The appeal of a community tends to be undermined when the things that are shared by its members are openly examined and debated, rather than being taken for granted, since the process of discussion is likely to unearth divisions and reveal the contrived, created character of the ties formerly considered natural. Bauman goes on to argue that the sharing of beliefs about the natural unity of community 'would be at its fullest among isolated people who conduct all their life-business, from birth to death, in the same company, who neither venture into other places nor are visited by members of other groups' (1990, p. 73). Insulation from contact with other styles of life discourages questioning of the bases of the current order, and allows the belief to be sustained that communities are natural entities.

The apparent naturalness of community in relatively isolated locations has attracted a large number of researchers to remote communities over the years (Frankenberg, 1969). In this context Cohen's (1987) work on the Shetland island community of Whalsay is particularly interesting since Cohen is also author of *The Symbolic Construction of Community* (1985) and editor of a volume of studies of rural communities entitled *Belonging* (1982). Cohen's argument is that communities are best understood as communities of meaning in which 'community' plays a crucial symbolic role in generating and sustaining people's sense of belonging. For Cohen, 'the reality of community lies in its members' perception of the vitality of its culture. People construct community symbolically, making it a resource and a repository of meaning, and a referent of their identity' (1985, p. 118). Crucial to this process of constructing communities is the definition of the boundaries which serve to 'discriminate the community from other places and groups' (1987, p. 14), that is, to draw a line between a community's members and non-members. The boundaries of communities help people to identify those with whom similarities are shared and those who are different: ' "Community" suggests that its putative members have something in common with each other which distinguishes them in a significant manner from the members of other groups' (1987, p. 14). In short, communities are defined not only by relations between members, among whom there is similarity, but also by the relations between these 'insiders' and 'outsiders', who are distinguished by their difference and consequent exclusion.

### INCLUSION AND EXCLUSION

The tradition of social anthropological thought which Cohen represents emphasises the symbolic and ritual nature of the processes through which the boundaries between a community's insiders and outsiders are marked. Cohen claims that in industrialised, mass societies the symbolic boundaries of communities become more rather than less important since what he calls communities' 'structural boundaries' have been 'transformed or undermined by social change' (1986, p. 7). The physical isolation of communities has been breached:

The interrelated processes of industrialization and urbanization, the dominance of the cash economy and mass production, the centralization of markets, the spread of the mass media and of centrally disseminated information, and the growth of transportation infrastructure and increased mobility all undermine the bases of community boundaries. (1985, p. 44)

In reaction to these processes pushing towards uniformity, communities 'reassert their boundaries symbolically' (1985, p. 44) in order to sustain the distinction between members and non-members, although the basis of this distinction has, Cohen claims, become cultural rather than structural. Cohen's work focuses

particular attention on the way in which people experience
community through shared rituals, such as the annual Notting Hill
carnival (1985, pp. 54–5). This approach to community carries
echoes of Thompson's (1968) celebrated view of class being not a
'thing' but a 'happening'.

Several aspects of the boundaries of communities in contemporary societies deserve to be noted. To begin with, consciousness of
community membership changes but does not disappear in the
modern world, and may even (paradoxically) be promoted by the
forces of globalisation (Robins, 1990). If Cohen's work contests
the naturalness of community in relatively remote settings such as
the Shetland Islands, other studies challenge the reverse side of the
'decline of community' thesis by showing the continuing vitality of
community identity in urban contexts. Wallman's research into an
inner-city area of London, for example, found that 'Battersea has
"always" considered outsider status to be more a matter of newness than of colour or foreign origin, and it has "always" made the
local area a prime focus of identity and loyalty' (1984, p. 7); this is
the essence of 'the Battersea style'.

In contrast, Cornwell's study of Bethnal Green presents this area
of London as one in which ethnic origin has considerable
importance attached to it in determining insider and outsider
status, so giving a more ominous ring to her observation that
'where there is belonging, there is also not belonging, and where
there is in-clusion, there is also ex-clusion' (Cornwell, 1984, p.
53). Gilroy's work, focusing more explicitly on race, acknowledges
the influence of Cohen's ideas and comes likewise to sober
conclusions:

Community is as much about difference as it is about similarity and
identity. It is a relational idea which suggests, for British blacks at least,
the idea of antagonism – domination and subordination between one
community and another. The word directs analysis to the boundary
between these groups. (1987, p. 235)

It will be argued in chapter 5 that insider/outsider distinctions
along ethnic lines may be emerging as more rather than less
prominent in modern British society, although (as Wallman's
research indicates) this is not necessarily a uniform trend.

The second point about the boundaries of community is that
they are not fixed, but fluid. Geographical mobility inevitably

entails a reworking of the insider/outsider distinction, and chapter 4 is devoted to exploring the ways in which length of residence and other aspects of patterns of migration affect who can consider themselves members of a community. Wallman's Battersea research threw up the case of 'a Newcastle man, three years' resident, with a wife from the other side of London, [who] is called a "foreigner" by a Jamaican woman of ten years' standing who clearly is not' (1984, p. 8). In the very different context of rural Wales in the 1940s, Rees (1951) found that an individual was treated as a 'stranger' until his or her family had been in the locality for at least two generations, while Day and Murdoch in their more recent research in the same part of the country were not surprised to find an incomer 'who had been living in the valley for fifteen years and still felt excluded' (1993, p. 103). Other processes besides geographical mobility also influence the strength of the boundaries of community. For example, Waddington *et al.*'s (1991) research into the 1984–5 coal dispute suggests that the degree of social solidarity of mining communities changed significantly during the course of the strike and its aftermath.

The third point relating to the boundaries of community is that they are not freely chosen or voluntary, but are, rather, influenced by a number of social structural processes. Wallman has pointed out that 'There is no one measure that defines "us" – the people entitled to share the resources we call "ours" – but the continual shifting of the boundary of us is not random' (1984, p. 6), thus emphasising the importance of material factors such as opportunities in local housing and labour markets. 'Community' for Wallman is concerned not only with symbols but also with 'necessary resources' (1982, p. 5), and it is the nature of the social networks through which access to such resources is gained (or denied) which explains why Battersea is a relatively open community to newcomers: 'housing, jobs and people are mixed and there are so many separate "gates" into local resources that no single group, institution or ideology can claim a controlling share' (1984, p. 6). In the case of Battersea, the boundaries between 'locals' and 'outsiders' are relatively permeable, partly because of the local tradition of openness, and partly because local resources allow this tradition to be continued. This case conforms to Wallman's (1977) more general suggestion that boundaries have more of the properties of tea-bags than of balloons.

Other communities are less open than Wallman's Battersea. One classic study of exclusion of newcomers is Elias and Scotson's (1965) *The Established and the Outsiders*, where tensions between old and new residents had lasted for decades. The non-integration of the newcomers into the established community may, Elias and Scotson speculate, have had some roots in their being seen by the 'old' residents as potential competitors in the labour market, but their exclusion persisted because of the threat to the 'civilised' order of the community which they were perceived as posing. According to Elias and Scotson, the newcomers 'were felt as a threat to this order, not because of any intention they had of upsetting it, but because their behaviour made the old residents feel that any close contact with them would lower their own standing, that it would drag them down to a lower status level' (1965, p. 149). Elias and Scotson relate the 'status order' of the community to distinctions such as those between different types of housing, with terraced accommodation lacking a hall ranked at the bottom and 'houses fully detached on both sides' (1965, p. 149) at the top. Chapter 6 will explore the way in which social divisions relating to housing status now attach greater importance to tenure categories, with the owner–occupier/tenant distinction having particular prominence, but the general point remains valid, namely that communities gain much of their coherence by being exclusive. This exclusivity is frequently encountered as residential segregation, but it is not necessarily so, as Harris's (1972) study of the Ulster border community of Ballybeg demonstrates by tracing how Catholics and Protestants can be simultaneously 'neighbours' and 'strangers'.

The extent to which communities are exclusive is variable, and chapter 4 will examine the major reasons behind this in relation to geographical mobility. Alongside these processes of social closure which work to exclude outsiders, communities also operate mechanisms to sustain the involvement of their members. Keeping insiders in is as important to the integration of communities as keeping outsiders out. Communities are not voluntary associations. Heller refers to communities as groups whose members belong to them as a matter of necessity: 'A community is a structuralized or organized group ... in which a relatively homogeneous system of values obtains, and to which the person necessarily belongs' (1984, p. 34). In similar vein Greer has claimed that interdependence generates constraint, which he regards as 'the key to community' (1991, p. 309). This sense of constraint is also captured in Morris and Mogey's (1965) characterisation of community as 'common bonds', and in Calhoun's description of 'communal bonds' as loaded with the expectations of other community members, and experienced by individuals as 'Moral obligations' (1983, p. 92). It would be wrong to presume that the 'social support' which communities provide for their members comes cost-free (Oakley, 1992).

Numerous instances of the restrictive, bonding character of local social life could be cited. In traditional working-class communities, described by Damer as 'effectively prisons for their inhabitants' (1990, p. 89) because of the difficulty of effecting an escape, sanctions against deviance from local social norms included the powerful forces of gossip and shunning: 'the disgust and punishment of the community against those who offended against its moral sensibility usually manifested itself in ostracisation or in talk' (Chinn, 1988, p. 42). Newby *et al.*'s (1978) research found East Anglian villages of the past possessing many of the characteristics of what Coser (1974) called 'greedy institutions', although the all-embracing nature of local community life has for some decades been subject to erosion by ex-urban in-migration. Wallace and Pahl's study of the Isle of Sheppey speaks of unemployed people experiencing community as 'a prison of jealous eyes' (1986, p. 118), and being very much constrained as a result. Robinson's investigation into the lives of Asians in Blackburn found the 'desire to maintain boundaries' (1986, p. 176) among South Asians reinforced by residential and employment segregation, making possible 'meaningful social sanctions against those deviants who show a desire to transgress behavioural norms' (1986, p. 77). Anwar (1985) uncovered similar 'incapsulation' among Pakistanis in Rochdale. In all such instances, social networks are dense enough and the consequent 'chains of interdependencies' (Elias, 1974, p. xix) of community members strong enough to discourage individual action which goes against local traditions.

A final characteristic of the boundaries of communities to note here is that they may be more visible to insiders than they are to outsiders. As an insider of the Welsh town of Blaenau Ffestiniog, Emmett (1982) enjoyed access to local social networks and knowledge that enabled her not only to avoid being excluded herself but also to pick up on instances of the exclusion of others where those involved were ignorant of their situation. Most researchers do not have such 'home advantage', coming to communities as highly visible outsiders facing the problem of gaining access to social networks the shape and form of which is likely to be at best hazy. Frankenberg's (1957) access to the social life of the Welsh border village of Llansaintffraid Glynceiriog (given by him the pseudonym 'Pentrediwaith') was eventually effected through his involvement in local sporting activities, but not before he had been made very conscious of his exclusion as he gazed down on the houses of the self-contained, close-knit community, wondering what was going on inside them. Similarly, Gilligan's report of his entry into the local social life of the small Cornish town of Padstow stresses his awareness of the need to avoid being identified as one of the 'strangers', 'furriners' or 'emmets' who collectively make up outsiders to local Padstonians (Gilligan, 1990; Gilligan and Harris, 1989). Gilligan's account, in which he recognises that 'during the initial stages of his fieldwork he was *being* observed as much as doing the observing' (Gilligan and Harris, 1989, p. 26; emphasis in original), highlights one of many methodological challenges which face researchers in this field.

The pragmatic advantages for researchers which come from having inside knowledge of a community may present other difficulties. Finnegan's concern that studying her own community of Milton Keynes would suffer from her being '*too* much of an insider' (1989, p. 343; emphasis in original) illustrates that the reverse situation to that of the researcher as outsider is at least a potential problem. In between these two extremes is the case of the sociologist returning to a former home location to study it. Giarchi had lived in Dunoon as a child but was still left needing 'almost nineteen months to become reasonably acquainted with local residents' (1984, p. xiii) after a period of living away. One solution to the problematic issue of the researcher's status is to have a team of investigators made up of both insiders and outsiders, as happened in the case of the Banbury research undertaken by Stacey and her colleagues (Stacey, 1960; Stacey *et al.*, 1975), although such research teams do not necessarily generate a consensus view of the community being studied (Bell, 1977).

## FROM COMMUNITY STUDIES TO STUDIES OF COMMUNITIES
### AND LOCALITIES

Community research in Britain has had a chequered history over recent decades, with three broad phases being identifiable in the period since the Second World War. In the first of these phases, the field was dominated by researchers employing the community studies approach in which they conducted investigations by immersing themselves in the local social life of the particular communities under investigation, following up leads that appeared promising. The 1950s and 1960s witnessed a flood of such studies, but also a growing disquiet about their underlying theoretical and methodological assumptions. By the 1970s this critique of community studies had made empirical research in the field of community a rarity, ushering in a second phase in which 'The fashion of the times was for higher-level theorizing' (Pahl, 1984, p. 3). Subsequently, the 1980s and 1990s have seen something of a revival of interest in empirical studies of localities and community life, although there is now a much greater awareness of the pitfalls which threaten the researcher in this area. This third phase is far from being a backward-looking revival of the first.

Research monographs in what might be called (borrowing and extending Platt's (1971) term) 'the old tradition' of community studies, published during the 1950s and 1960s, were frequently characterised by a descriptive style which masked their authors' implicit theoretical leanings rooted in functionalist anthropology. The desire to produce an account of everyday community life saw a typical community study devote most of its pages to describing family and kinship networks, local work patterns, political and religious attachments and voluntary associations, to the neglect of explicit discussions of the methodological and theoretical implications of these findings. Despite the rawness of the data which they contain, these community studies of the old tradition provide a wealth of information about ordinary people's everyday lives (in particular in working-class urban districts and some of the more remote rural communities) in the two decades following the Second World War. The findings of these studies have been collated in various overviews (Allan, 1979; Bell and Newby, 1971; Critcher, 1979; Crow *et al.*, 1990; Delamont, 1980; Eldridge,

1980; Frankenberg, 1969; Klein, 1965; Macfarlane, 1977; Wild, 1981), some of which are more critical than others.

The old tradition of community studies can tell us a good deal about the ways things were in 'traditional' working-class and rural communities, provided that the circumstances in which they were produced are borne in mind (although it has to be acknowledged that this is no small proviso). Methodologically, the studies have been criticised for the impressionistic nature of their data and the absence of any basis on which their findings could be generalised. As a result, 'these studies were non-comparable and non-cumulative as far as empirical sociology was concerned' (Kent, 1981, p. 137). Put another way, 'The problem with old-fashioned community studies was that they lacked any systematic procedure for linking ethnographic observation with accounts of society as a whole' (Byrne, 1989, p. 28). Theoretically, the community studies of the old tradition embodied assumptions drawn from function-alism about the normality of social integration. These assumptions tended to direct attention away from conflict and schism, although certain researchers (Littlejohn, 1963; Rex and Moore, 1967; Stacey, 1960) stand out as exceptions on this point for their findings that the local 'community' was marked by serious class divisions and antagonisms. The old tradition was also open to criticism for taking as a starting point the notion that modern societies are characterised by a 'loss of community'. Again Rex and Moore's study was instrumental in questioning the old tradition of research and pointing out its susceptibility to 'the myth of the golden past' (1967, p. 213). By the end of the 1960s the old tradition had more or less run its course, and the research agenda in the sociology of community entered a new phase.

If one thing sums up the weaknesses of the old tradition of community studies it is that there was a fundamental mismatch between the researchers' theoretical expectations and the findings which their investigations produced. Elias hinted at this problem when he wrote that 'the theoretical aspects of community studies are less advanced than the empirical work in that field' (1974, p. ix). Abrams identified the problem more explicitly: 'the paradox of community is the coexistence of a body of theory which constantly predicts the collapse of community and a body of empirical studies which finds community alive and well' (1978, p. 12). For all their merits, classical theoretical works like Tönnies's *Community and*

*Association* (1955) (first published in 1887) posed great difficulties when it came to operationalising concepts such as *Gemeinschaft* in the context of modern societies. In this climate, Stacey's view that 'as a concept "community" is not useful for serious sociological analysis' (1969, p. 134) proved an influential one. The sociology of community stood accused of being at best insufficiently rigorous and at worst outmoded; either way, it was clear that a cavalier attitude to questions of theory and method was no longer acceptable.

The decade of the 1970s stands as a distinct phase in which little empirical community research was undertaken as community studies became 'something of a lost art' (Eldridge, 1984, p. xi). Willmott looked back on this period with regret when he noted that 'since about the mid-1960s there have been hardly any British [community] studies giving a sense of people's daily lives and aspirations' (1985, p. 140). The community studies genre had gone out of fashion (Eldridge, 1980), but the concept of community continued to receive a good deal of critical attention. The Community Development Projects (which will be discussed in chapter 7) were at this time actively engaged in community politics, discovering the salience of class inequalities, and rapidly coming to the conclusion that analysis in terms of 'community' served to obscure these inequalities. It was for this reason that Cockburn (1977, p. 159) argued ' "Community" belongs to capital', and that employing the word was best avoided. Others came to similar conclusions: 'to use terms like *Gemeinschaft*, community, or mutual loyalty in the context of the modern nation state is simply ideological and mystifying' (Ferris, 1985, p. 58). From this point of view, 'community' implies the management, control and manipulation of local people by higher-level state bodies, and in the light of its political connotations Dalley concluded that 'The continued use of the word "community" simply obfuscates matters' (1988, p. 49).

A further line of attack on the old tradition of community studies concerned their neglect of issues relating to gender inequalities. The reports contained 'malestream' biases in their terminology (Frankenberg, 1976) and in their focus on the public sphere at the expense of the private sphere in which women's lives were anchored, features which were characteristic of the discipline at the time more generally (Stacey, 1981). The feminist critique highlighted the community studies' tendency to portray women's lives in a patronising manner, or to make them invisible: 'women are described as "gossiping" but men as "discussing" in the accounts, and women's economic roles are frequently neglected' (Delamont, 1980, p. 129). The monographs were, by later standards at least, 'outrageously sexist' (Damer, 1989, p. 18); at worst they embodied 'sexist nonsense' (Whitehead, 1976, p. 200). The grand-scale theories of capitalism and of patriarchy which came to dominate much of sociology in the 1970s had little room for conceptualisations of 'community' that lost sight of class and gender inequalities in a sea of 'uniform blandness' (Riley, 1983, p. 187).

Facing mounting criticism, the concept of community was, Abrams perceived, 'slowly being evicted from British sociology' (1978, p. 13). Subsequent events have not borne out this prediction. Various authors have made out cases for retaining 'community' in the vocabulary of social science. McDowell, for example, notes that alongside idealised conceptions framed in terms of social balance,

another interpretation of 'community' is possible. The notion is not solely a bourgeois or patriarchal invention. It has a long history as an authentic working-class counterpart, as a defensive weapon in the class struggle, and also as a vehicle for neighbouring solidarity and self-help. (1983, p. 151)

The case for 'community' could thus be made by feminist writers mindful of the importance of women for community and vice versa. In an earlier period Elias and Scotson had made the intriguing observation that 'It is difficult to imagine communities without women and children, though one can imagine communities almost without men' (1965, pp. 146–7). Now the point could be made more positively: 'women are amongst the foremost members of community and voluntary organizations' (Deem, 1986, p. 58). Researchers were also uncovering the long history of women's centrality to community life. In the working-class neighbourhoods of the past 'it was the women who put the "community" together' (Damer, 1989, p. 18), and this theme will be explored further in chapter 2.

By the 1980s the case for empirical research into local social life was being made by sociologists with an interest in ordinary people's everyday activities who were increasingly frustrated by the dearth of up-to-date studies. In some instances the argument was framed explicitly in terms of reviving community studies, with Bulmer (1985) and Willmott (1985) both stressing the practical, policy-relevant nature of this type of investigation. Others were more careful to distance themselves from the community studies tradition, and several impressive studies have been published building on Cooke's argument that what is being investigated in this field is captured better by the concept of 'locality' than that of 'community'. For Cooke, 'community' is not necessarily restricted to 'the sphere of social activity that is focused upon place', and it tends to suggest social relations that are 'only reactive or inward-looking' in which 'stability and continuity' prevail; it is, he says, 'too broad in its spatial reach and too narrow in its social connotations' (1989, p. 10). Such an interpretation is contestable, of course, but what matters more is that the empirical investigation of local social life has been put back on the research agenda, producing a wealth of 'locality studies' which have recorded the local impact of and responses to economic restructuring (see, for example, Bagguley *et al.*, 1990; Cooke, 1989; Dickens, 1988; Harloe *et al.*, 1990).

The findings of the various locality studies are discussed in greater depth in later chapters, but it is worth stating at this point that the conceptualisation of 'community' on which they are based is questionable. Cooke has described community somewhat dismissively as 'the social residue of modernity' (1990, ch. 2), noting correctly that the old tradition of community studies tended to focus on '*residual* cultural forms' (1990, p. 36, emphasis in original) in marginal rural and declining industrial settings, but drawing the more contentious conclusion that modernity works only to corrode community traditions. There is no sense here that modern times may generate new community traditions. Cooke's argument is surprising given that 'community' is far from being absent in the reports of locality studies, including (for example) Meegan's (1989) account of Merseyside's (post-war) outer estates. 'Community' is still very much part of contemporary expression, including the way in which the respondents of locality studies express themselves, and in this light the summary dismissal of community studies looks ill-judged (Day and Murdoch, 1993; Dickens, 1990). A parallel may be drawn here with the word 'family' which some writers have suggested ought to be abandoned because of its imprecision and ideological connotations. Against such purist strictures Finch has argued that 'the term "family" is used in the private and the public world and people accord it social meaning', and that its use can be justified provided that it is recognised 'that it cannot be a simple descriptive word, but has many shifting meanings'. As with Finch's discussion of 'family' so too in the discussion of 'community' which follows, 'readers who feel uncomfortable about this [are invited] to place mental quotation marks around it whenever they see it' (1989, p. 4).

### PERSONAL TROUBLES, PUBLIC ISSUES AND COMMUNITY CHANGE

In *The Sociological Imagination* (1959) C. Wright Mills argued that sociology's task is to highlight the connections between the 'personal troubles' of people's private lives and the wider 'public issues' of the day. Mills took as an example of sociology's promise in this context the case of unemployment, something which is experienced as a personal trouble but which, when sufficient numbers of individuals are unemployed, becomes also a public issue. The revival of interest in locality and community research in the 1980s took place against the background of recession, restructuring and mass unemployment, a situation which made it 'imperative to examine how individuals and communities interpret current economic changes' (Roberts *et al.*, 1985, p. 2). The 'intermediary structures' of community life noted earlier are essential to the understanding of what unemployment means, and chapter 3 will draw on the great number of locality studies and other studies of community life in which researchers have set out to explore this issue.

  Two of these studies are worth singling out here for their more general relevance to the discussion of the role of the researcher in linking personal troubles and public issues. The first is Pahl's (1984) *Divisions of Labour* which was undertaken with the explicit aim of investigating 'how people without jobs in the formal sense were getting by' (1984, p. 9) since there was a widespread impression, but little supporting evidence, that unemployed people could find alternative sources of income in the 'informal economy'. Pahl's research into this question on the Isle of Sheppey in Kent threw up findings which cast doubt on such consoling beliefs, suggesting instead the more uncomfortable conclusion that the trajectories of employed and unemployed households were diverging as part of a process of social polarisation. Pahl's findings confirmed that unemployment remains a very real personal trouble and a pressing public issue. In addition, the research led Pahl on to wider theoretical questions about the nature of 'work' and the realisation of the importance of the structure of household relations for understanding work in all its forms. Pahl's study thus had not only much immediate policy relevance, but also significant implications for wider debates about the changing nature of contemporary society more generally.

The second study of unemployment which has a bearing on the question of the purpose and practice of research is also one which explored sociological as well as social problems. The effects of economic restructuring have been particularly marked in areas of traditional heavy industries, and Harris's (1987) *Redundancy and Recession* was undertaken in one such location, South Wales. The research began with the intention of investigating the impact of large-scale redundancies among steelworkers in Port Talbot, working on the assumption that out-migration from the locality would be prominent. Setting out with the aim of exploring 'the way in which family and community ties assisted and impeded migration in search of work' (1987, p. 16), the unexpected finding that people did not respond to redundancy by out-migration led to the research focusing instead on individuals' labour market careers. Access to labour market opportunities was found to be structured around 'networks' rather than the conventional ties of traditional working-class communities, a change accounted for by reference to several factors: 'geographical mobility, public housing, and urban planning and redevelopment, together with the influence of the media have . . . destroyed the traditional pattern of social life focused on local communal institutions: club/pub, church/chapel and various forms of associational life' (1987, p. 217). This change is not a straightforward 'loss of community', since public institutions remain important in local social life, especially in some commuter villages. Rather it is that these institutions 'have ceased . . . to be *common* features of the networks of individuals' (1987, p. 217; emphasis in original), with unemployed people being particularly vulnerable to social isolation through non-participation in wider networks.

A third example of recent research which has generated both policy-relevant findings and broader theoretical insights can be mentioned as further evidence of the revival of interest in studying community life. Cornwell's (1984) investigation of health and illness in Bethnal Green in East London, *Hard-Earned Lives*, has brought out the importance of the community context for aspects of ordinary people's everyday lives other than work. Cornwell observes that there is often a contradiction between her respondents' public and private accounts of community life, and that previous sociologists' portrayals which have drawn only on the public accounts of community (with Young and Willmott (1957) most prominent among them) are 'partial and one-sided'. She goes on to argue that this is not a reason 'for dismissing the notion of "community", but for re-examining its significance' (1984, p. 24). Uncritical acceptance of people's public accounts as literal truths leads inevitably to romanticism about the past, and frequently this is linked to some form of 'loss of community' perspective.

What Cornwell offers is not just another critique – it is, she says, 'not novel to criticize Young and Willmott for romanticizing Bethnal Green' (1984, p. 44) – but an explanation of why community life's lost golden age is such an enduring theme. Private accounts of community differ from public accounts, and reveal a darker side, including 'the turning of the blind eye to other people's troubles; as well as the open doors and the familiarity with others, it included the arguments, fights and brawls, particularly over children, and the petty snobberies that kept people apart from each other' (1984, p. 47). These things are ignored in public accounts because, Cornwell suggests, people have a need for a more positive image of community than the reality which surrounds them warrants, and she raises the question, 'is the romanticization of "community" by the inhabitants of the community a way of making the reality tolerable?' (1984, p. 40). Her awareness of the hard facts of inner-city life lead her to conclude that 'the real ideological significance of the idea of community in present-day East London lies in its opposition to everything that is new and different and to the possibility of change' (1984, p. 53). The idea of community is, in other words, an ideological one around which social forces may be mobilised with great effect, not least because it makes a link, however distorted, between personal troubles and public issues.

Other researchers have also found community to be a potent idea in the context of inner-city politics. Parry *et al.*'s (1987) comparison of inner areas of Manchester, Sheffield and Oldham concluded that community allegiances are an effective base for collective action. Community identity is important because 'it provides an additional political resource in the struggle to promote or to defend interests. A sense of community can help to support political activity' (1987, p. 229). Parry *et al.*'s observation that this mobilisation is often a defensive response to change supports Cornwell's argument above, and is also consistent with Marris's (1987) study of community action in the redevelopment of London's Docklands. Redevelopment can be a threatening experience for inner-city residents, and in this context appeals to a 'community of mutual aid' or a 'community of mutual protection' (1987, p. 158) are perfectly understandable, however much the resulting community movements may fail to live up to these ideals. Chapter 7 will be concerned to explore the potential, and also the limitations, of community action to have an impact on local politics.

The lesson that not all neighbourhoods or localities have the potential to sustain supportive community networks is of direct significance to policy-makers charged with tackling public issues. Willmott (1989) has argued that the concept of community has had a major effect on public policy thinking in recent decades, although it is not clear what the practical implications of this development are. Advocates of the community principle see it as 'marking a genuine change in ways of organising our collective life', while critics perceive only 'a rhetorical exploitation of high-minded ambiguity' (1989, p. 1). Willmott suggests that recent years have witnessed the emergence of 'a new kind of interest community ... the self-help or mutual aid group' (1989, p. 2), whose members are linked by a common bond through shared experiences, and it is these groups which have been of particular interest to modern policy analysts concerned with the shifting relationship between the welfare institutions of the state and the private, informal, voluntary sphere of community or 'civil society'.

There are numerous areas of social policy to which the issue of the changing relation of the state and community has relevance, and these will be examined in greater depth in chapter 8. To date, most discussion has centred on the policy of community care, where researchers have raised many awkward questions. Bulmer, for example, suggests that

in significant respects, 'community care' policies rest upon fallacious common-sense assumptions . . . . As a result there is a vacuum at the heart of care policy which is likely to lead to ineffective or deteriorating provision of services, to the extent that care is transferred to 'the community'. (1987, p. ix)

Bulmer points out that uncritical conceptions of community postulate 'a range of supportive ties which may not actually exist in practice' (1987, pp. xi–xii). Contrary to the comfortable assumptions of common sense about the ability of 'the community' to care, research findings highlight the extent to which the caring capacities of family (Qureshi and Walker, 1989), kin (Finch, 1989), neighbours (Bulmer, 1986), friends (Allan, 1989) and voluntary bodies (St Leger and Gillespie, 1991) are necessarily limited.

It has been noted already that our perceptions of contemporary community life are frequently distorted by misperceptions of the patterns of social relationships that made up community life in the past. The most obvious point of comparison with the present is what has been called 'the traditional working-class community', or 'the traditional working-class neighbourhood', although there are several grounds for caution in making such comparisons. First, it is important to note that the notion of a traditional working-class community is a model, an ideal type, which has the potential to obscure from view the diversity of the ways things were in traditional working-class communities. Secondly, it needs to be recognised that such communities were products of their time, arising out of specific conditions which no longer hold, a change which rules out the possibility that they could ever be re-created. Thirdly, it should be stated that our knowledge of these communities is not fixed, but constantly being revised in the light of new thinking and research. These are in an important sense 'remembered communities' (Bornat, 1993, p. 23), and it needs to be borne in mind that memories can be highly selective. Of particular significance here is the reconsideration that has taken place in recent years as a result of new material generated by feminist oral historians, whose work is considered in more detail in the next chapter. With these qualifications in mind, attention is now turned to the ways things were.

# 2

## THE WAYS THINGS WERE: COMMUNITY LIFE IN PAST GENERATIONS

The images which we hold of community life in times past have been influenced to a disproportionate extent by a small number of studies of working-class neighbourhoods conducted in the 1950s. Pre-eminent among these studies is Young and Willmott's *Family and Kinship in East London* (1957), described by Sanders as 'the most widely read work of sociology in Britain' (1992, p. 15) on the basis that over half a million copies of the book have been sold. A myth has grown up around this and other studies of Bethnal Green carried out by researchers from the Institute of Community Studies, in which the traditional working-class community is represented as 'a place of huge families centred around Mum, of cobbled streets and terraced cottages, open doors, children's street games, open-air markets, and always, and everlastingly, cups of tea and women gossiping together on the doorstep' (Cornwell, 1984, p. 24). In this mythical representation, community relations are built on 'the warmth, charm and humanity of working-class family life' (Wilson, 1980, p. 64). The material hardship of these neighbourhoods is not so much denied as lost sight of through the selective concentration of such studies on sentiment.

Accounts of traditional working-class life may be an exception to the rule that a book should not be judged by its cover. The Penguin edition of Young and Willmott (1957) is illustrated with a photograph of a group of five women (two holding babies) and one man in a doorway. While the women talk together the man, who is physically marginal to the group, tries to catch the eyes of one of the babies. Two of the women are in slippers, confirming the 'street-centred' character of local social relations. In similar vein, details from Lowry paintings decorate the fronts of Hoggart (1958), Forman (1979) and Seabrook (1979), while Jackson's (1968) *Working Class Community* has a picture of a brass band on its cover, and a whole chapter devoted to brass bands inside. Another recurrent theme in pictorial representations of traditional working-class communities is that of coal mining, which has had more attention paid to it than any of the other heavy industries on which Britain's turn of the century supremacy was founded. Pithead winding gear dominates the cover of Dennis *et al.*'s (1969) *Coal is our Life* in the same way it dominated the local landscape, while Bulmer's (1978b) miners' gala, Williamson's (1982) miner's family and Gilbert's (1992) scene from the strike of 1926 draw on other equally powerful images from the history of coal communities.

The study of the Yorkshire mining town of 'Ashton' by Dennis and his colleagues was undertaken at the same time as Young and Willmott's Bethnal Green research, although the findings of the two investigations are not entirely consistent with each other. The 'Ashton' study presented 'a much grimmer account of working-class life' (Wilson, 1980, p. 65), focusing primarily on the men of the community rather than the women or children, and drawing more explicitly on Marxist concepts such as class consciousness. The Bethnal Green monograph in contrast embodied a more 'affirmative view of the community' (Eldridge, 1980, p. 149). Even so, there are several similarities between the two studies, not least in that they represented traditional working-class communities as relatively homogeneous, with members linked together by a strong sense of tradition of mutual support in adverse circumstances. In their discussion of the coal industry's record of industrial disputes Dennis *et al.* argue that 'Common memories of past struggle have undoubtedly helped to bind a community such as Ashton' (1969, p. 14). Young and Willmott's study focuses more on the mutal aid effected through women's kinship networks, but the sense of cohesion arising out of shared adversity is comparable nevertheless. More negatively, both communities were held together by the application of social sanctions against those who flouted the norms of local social life, whether these were the Bethnal Green girls who went to grammar schools in the face of being 'made to feel their peculiarity' (Young and Willmott, 1957, p. 146) or the Ashton women bold enough to venture into male preserves such as betting shops. Both studies emphasise the segregation that exists between women and men, with women in particular constrained by customary notions of 'the behaviour thought correct for a wife' (Dennis *et al.*, 1969, p. 207).

These images need to be treated with a great deal of caution. Stereotypes of the Bethnal Green Mum at the centre of an extended kin network or the 'Ashton' miner and his downtrodden wife fit the historical realities of life in traditional working-class communities at best only approximately. At worst, their exaggerated features are wilful in their neglect of dimensions of local social relationships which do not conform to the idealised versions of community norms which respectively Young and Willmott (1957) and Dennis *et al.* (1969) promulgate. To speak in abstract terms of *the* traditional working-class community (as, for example, Roberts (1978) does), constructing a composite picture out of the findings of the various community studies of the 1950s, loses sight of the diversity of these communities with regard to the industries on which they were based, regional variations, differences in the degree to which women were employed, and more generally the evolving variations of their 'traditions' (Crow, 1993). In Young and Willmott's study some Bethnal Greeners regarded the neighbouring district of Bow as 'another world' (1957, p. 88), while Dennis *et al.* (1969) note that a full account of life in 'Ashton' would have to acknowledge the importance of specific factors which made the town (in some senses at least) unique. Consciousness of and pride in distinguishing local peculiarities were prominent features of traditional working-class life, however quaint such distinctions might seem to outside observers. This chapter focuses on 'traditional' occupational communities, looking at the different accounts generated about these communities, the social divisions which arose within them, and at recent reinterpretations of them.

## OCCUPATIONAL COMMUNITIES

Traditional working-class community life did not conform to a single, uniform pattern. The broad spectrum of working-class communities found in the past indicates that they were the active creation of their members as well as the product of social

structural characteristics such as their isolation or their development on the basis of particular industries. Bulmer has suggested
that the concept of 'occupational communities' offers an opportunity to incorporate both 'structurally-distinctive features of work
and community' and 'patterns of shared meaning among those
who work together in the same occupation' (1975, p. 78) in an
account of the development of mining communities, and there is
no reason why his general argument cannot be extended to other
communities besides. Bulmer's ideal-typical traditional mining
community is physically isolated, has mining as the main source
of employment, with working practices which promote social
solidarity among miners. There is little geographical or social
mobility in the community, and the great majority of the
population are working-class. Workmates spend much of their
leisure time together, while miners' wives lead a quite separate,
home-centred existence in which relations with female kin figure
prominently. Consciousness of class divisions between workers
and employers generates social solidarity, expressed through such
institutions as trade unions. In sum, Bulmer says:

The social ties of work, leisure, neighbourhood and friendship overlap to
form close-knit and interlocking locally based collectivities of actors. The
solidarity of the community is strengthened ... by a shared history
of living and working in one place over a long period of time. (1975,
pp. 87–8)

Such communities are inward-looking, and individual members
have little contact with outsiders.

Bulmer's model of the traditional mining community clearly
owes much to Dennis *et al.*'s (1969) classic study of 'Ashton' and
to Lockwood's (1975) reworking of this material, but its emphasis
on mining communities' dense pattern of social networks and
embedded traditions of class consciousness and solidarity finds
support in other social histories of coal mining. Williamson's study
of Throckley in Northumberland found 'Tight bonds of kinship,
the clear separation of the roles of men and women, and
occupational homogeneity' (1982, p. 6), while the various contri-
butions to Bulmer (1978b) also follow the broad approach. It
should be noted, however, that Bulmer's argument in his original
article was that much could be learned from instances where
mining communities did not conform to the ideal type of a solidary

occupational community, since such cases would help to identify more precisely the specific conditions which generated this pattern of social relationships.

Certainly there were important regional variations between mining communities. Moore's (1974, 1975) study of Durham mining villages in the late nineteenth and early twentieth centuries found a number of differences between these miners and those of Yorkshire's 'Ashton', not least of which was the strength of Methodism in the north-east, as well as very different trade-union traditions. Moore objects to the suggestion that mining communities produced only traditional proletarians (in Lockwood's terminology), since 'not all miners are beer-drinking gamblers' (1974, p. 15). Moore's County Durham miners 'were traditionally conservative and resisted traditional proletarian social imagery. . . . The miners had a strong sense of occupational community, but class consciousness did not develop from this in any mechanical way' (1974, p. 17). Small, relatively isolated mining villages could thus in one geographical and historical context throw up a pervasive ideology of 'us' and 'them' framed in class terms, while in a different cultural context a substantial section of miners strove to become 'amongst the most "respectable" part of the working class' (1975, p. 36), distancing themselves from others for whom the vices of 'drunkenness, gambling and violence' (1975, p. 44) held more appeal.

The significance of regional variations between coalfields is a central concern of Gilbert's (1992) comparison of the histories of Ynysybwl in South Wales and Hucknall in Nottinghamshire. Arguing that there is a 'need to provide an analysis of the complexities of particular places in particular regional contexts' (1992, p. 47), Gilbert suggests that the stereotypical mining village fitted most closely the coalfields of South Wales and North-East England, while other coalfields saw mining communities develop in different ways, due to the mining companies playing a much more active role in local life there, or simply because of the greater size and heterogeneity of their populations. Hucknall, for example, was never solely a mining town, and in Nottinghamshire more generally miners lived in a range of social situations, 'from deferential company villages through complicated and fractured local societies like Hucknall, to towns like Mansfield and the suburbs of metropolitan Nottingham' (1992, p. 247). In contrast, the mining communities of South Wales stood out because of their 'striking social homogeneity' (1992, p. 246). Gilbert concludes that the development of mining communities can be understood only as the result of 'peculiarly local responses to wider national and regional developments, and of changing local ideas of the nature of community' (1992, p. 47). Strikes, for example, played a large part in what Gilbert refers to as 'the creation of community' (1992, p. 100), although precisely how this happened varied from village to village. Very much the same point has been made about the 1984–5 coal dispute as the strikes of sixty years earlier (Waddington *et al.*, 1991).

This sense of the active participation of miners and their families in the positive creation of community life runs through Williamson's account of Throckley as a *'constructed community'* (1982, p. 6; emphasis in original). The community was understood and experienced by its members as more than a collection of institutions such as the churches, the school, the co-operative store and various clubs and events since 'these institutions were woven into the daily patterns of their everyday lives' (1982, p. 77). The extent of these institutions was taken to mark 'the symbolic boundaries of Throckley as a community', boundaries which were defined not geographically but 'by the shared system of meaning and values which people from Throckley could draw upon to give a coherent account of their social life' (1982, p. 77). The daily routines of its population reproduced Throckley as a community, although this was always a developing rather than a static entity. Additionally, and in contrast to Gilbert's (1992) case of miners in South Wales struggling to rid themselves of a 'definition of community' imposed by members of the local middle class in favour of a more authentic working-class version, Williamson found it impossible 'to disentangle cleanly that which reflected the action of the coal company and that which evolved from the men' (1982, p. 62). The paternalism of the local employer was expressed in many ways, for example subsidising the pit brass band, achieving the company's principal objective, 'to attract, support and control a mining labour force' (1982, p. 56). The mining company sought 'the creation not just of labour camps, but of communities' (1982, p. 6). In the longer term, however, experiences such as those of the 1926 strike and the long years of economic depression eroded this paternalistic element in local community life and pushed Throckley closer to the pattern of social relations depicted in the 'Ashton' study.

Mining communities were characterised not only by regional diversity but also by constant pressures to change. In inter-war St Helens, for example, the coal industry was already in decline, with only twelve pits remaining in the 1920s compared to thirty-six in the 1850s. Coal mining generated more than twice the employment of any other local industry, but still accounted for only 27 per cent of the adult male population (Forman, 1979), and as such St Helens did not constitute an 'occupational community'. Although some of its smaller districts such as Sutton Manor would have conformed to a greater extent to the pattern of 'closely knit cliques of friends, workmates, neighbours and relatives' described by Lockwood as 'the hallmark of the traditional working-class community' (1975, p. 17), the case of St Helens illustrates the more general point that the physical isolation of the ideal typical mining community was by no means always found in practice. The same point applies to other groups cited by Lockwood as examples of workers likely to form occupational communities, such as shipbuilders (Cousins and Brown, 1975) and dockers (Hill, 1976).

Hill's study of dockers in London in the period around 1970 gave only qualified support to Lockwood's thesis. He argued that 'People in Thurrock and the East End are obviously more involved in occupational communities than those who live elsewhere, though the coherence and exclusiveness of such communities must not be exaggerated' (1976, p. 167). Hill suggests that links with the workplace may be regarded as 'incidental' in cases where a worker's workmates are also known as members of the same neighbourhood; where friends are drawn from neighbours, former schoolmates, friends of friends or kin, 'it is not work but the local community which is important' (1976, p. 164). Most friendships originated through community ties rather than through work connections, although work was seen as 'influential in determining which acquaintances become close friends' (1976, p. 168). Hill was, of course, mindful of the disruptive effects on local communities which geographical mobility could have, and concluded that recent population movements were at least partly responsible for the finding that 'stable working-class communities, let alone stable occupational communities, are not as common as might have been anticipated in dockland' (1976, p. 171). It should be borne in mind here that Hill's analysis is not principally concerned with patterns of social relations among past generations of dockers, so making it difficult on his evidence to draw firm conclusions about patterns of change that have occurred.

The argument that the geographical and work dimensions of occupational communities need to be treated separately has been taken further by Salaman, who distinguishes between what he calls 'quasi' and 'true' occupational communities. According to Salaman, 'communities that are the result of a geographically isolated or spatially segregated area or work place, dominated by a single firm or industry' should be considered 'quasi' occupational communities, since such conditions necessarily generate *community-like* patterns of group life' (1974, p. 20; emphasis in original). Salaman's definition of a 'true' occupational community requires that it is the common work experiences which are crucial in determining a sense of group membership and identity, and that although certain occupational communities 'such as those of fishermen or coalminers – sometimes also tend to involve geographical or spatial separation . . . they would occur without this' (1974, p. 21). Such a definition may be unduly restrictive, as Bulmer (1975) has argued, but Salaman's focus on work-based identities sheds light on an important aspect of occupational communities. Salaman's later work follows Cohen (1985) in presenting his account of how joining an occupational community involves 'becoming an insider to the highly restricted cultural code which is incomprehensible to the outsider, and which is not open to entry until the newcomer has demonstrated his/her willingness to accept the authority of the community' (Salaman, 1986, p. 75). The restricted nature of these cultural codes means that member-ship of occupational communities can be tightly controlled, and Salaman stresses that it is by no means certain that the boundaries of 'us' and 'them' will coincide with class boundaries. Occupational communities are not necessarily groups of equals, although they may present an egalitarian facade.

The hierarchical element of occupational communities was not the immediate object of concern for researchers starting out with Lockwood's assumption that the ' "traditional" type of working-class district' derived its character from 'the relative stability and the social homogeneity of its population'. In this account, 'the strong sense of communal solidarity and the various forms of mutual help and collective action reflect the absence of any wide economic, cultural or status differences' (Goldthorpe *et al.*, 1969, p. 86). Various empirical investigations into occupational communities have thrown up findings at odds with this picture: for example, Newby's (1977) historical research found an occupational community where Lockwood did not predict one, among farmworkers, and uncovered in addition marked inequalities in status linked to skill at work among this group who to outside observers were simply 'labourers'. Newby also found the conception of farmworkers as 'deferential' oversimple, not least because of their ability to sustain both deferential demeanour with their employers and 'alternative definitions and interpretations' (1977, p. 47) of their social situation among their fellow workers. In turn, studies of groups identified by Lockwood as traditional proletarians indicated that such communities 'can just as easily provide the context for an identity and solidarity ... which are fundamentally conservative' (Davis, 1979, p. 25).

## THE SOCIAL HIERARCHY OF 'TRADITIONAL' WORKING-CLASS COMMUNITIES

Lockwood's distinction between the two types of traditional worker, 'proletarian' and 'deferential', suggested that the former would be conscious of class inequalities while the latter's 'perception of social inequality will be one of status hierarchy' (1975, p. 17). It has been noted above that empirical research into miners as an example of proletarians and farmworkers as an example of deferential workers does not unambiguously bear out Lockwood's thesis, and case studies in other industrial settings provide further grounds for caution in this respect. Just as the conclusions of Dennis *et al.*'s (1969) classic study of coal miners have been qualified by more recent researchers, so it is too with research into another stereotypical proletarian occupation, that of fishing. In Allcorn and Marsh's (1975) view, coal mining and trawl-fishing are the two industries most likely to generate occupational communities, while Mars cites miners and longshoremen as examples of 'traditional' working-class groups which 'come to possess considerable control over the resources of their individual members, both material and otherwise, and this includes claims on their time as well as their loyalties' (1982, p. 32). From this perspective the teamwork of the workplace is presumed to carry over into shared leisure activities.

The classic study of fishing is Tunstall's (1962) research based in Hull, *The Fishermen.* Like Dennis *et al.*'s *Coal is our Life,* Tunstall's study concentrates very much on the men of the community and the solidarity amongst them that comes from working in an occupation involving heavy physical labour. There are, however, elements of Tunstall's account which indicate differences between the two occupations beyond the fact that coal miners 'are regarded by fishermen as being pampered' (1962, pp. 170–1). To begin with, Tunstall notes the hierarchical nature of relations between trawler crew members, with differences in rank reflected in rates of pay and conditions of work as well as more general social behaviour both on board ship and ashore. Tunstall identifies a fatalistic outlook in the face of this 'changeless hierarchy' (1962, p. 134), and, in trade union affairs, ambivalence and 'little general sense of unity' (1962, p. 244). Ashore, there is a recognisable working-class district in which many of the fishing families live, but by no means all of them do so. Most skippers mark their upward social mobility by moving out to owner-occupied housing, but there was also a division between those lower down the hierarchy:

'Fishermen living on housing estates seemed mainly to be social aspirants. Few of them were heavy drinkers and they appeared to spend their time at home. In contrast, fishermen living near the fish-dock, often in very crowded houses, were much more likely to go to clubs and pubs.' (1962, p. 160)

Even within the dock-side streets there is considerable variation between one terrace and another. What Tunstall is touching on here is the general distinction between the 'rough' and the 'respectable' sections of the working class. The former are seen by the latter as having dubious morality and no sense of the value of privacy while the latter are accused by the former of being unsociable and 'stuck-up'.

The division between the rough and respectable sections of the working class is a well-established theme in the literature on traditional working-class communities. Damer has highlighted the uniformity with which the old tradition of community studies 'reported the existence of a "rough–respectable" split within the working class', and notes that within this genre of writing it is among the 'roughs' that 'the old patterns of neighbouring, the giving and receiving of small services, and the like' (1989, p. 17) persist. In contrast, greater affluence and relocation to new housing were interpreted as changes which promote the pursuit of 'respectability' among the better-off members of the working class, trends which point to the demise of traditional community norms. There is an element of truth in this account, in that traditional working-class communities were held together to no small degree by their poverty, and that rising living standards might reasonably be expected to weaken these bonds. Gittins has rightly observed that 'Generally speaking, the more economically insecure the household, the greater will be its reliance on community and kin' (1986, p. 251), but it does not follow from this that the patterns of behaviour among the 'rough' section of the working class reported in the community studies of the 1950s were necessarily more widespread in earlier periods. Traditions of respectability played an equally important if not greater part in traditional working-class community life, not least by defining standards by which community members could be judged.

Concern with respectability in traditional working-class community life took many forms. The significance attached to abstention from alcoholic drink and to the observation of religious codes more generally has already been noted as a feature of the Durham pit villages studied by Moore (1974), and this finding is echoed in other studies. For example, Thompson *et al.*'s account of the Lancashire fishing village of Marshside describes Primitive Methodism as 'one of the roots of the community's independence and self-sufficiency' (1983, p. 84), promoting as it did systems of mutual aid and also a strong sense of community identity. Meacham has recorded how attendance at church was a mark of respectability, but so too was the way in which those attending church were dressed, and this meant that respectability correlated to a degree with income levels: 'Public worship . . . might afford the chance to establish oneself in the sight of one's neighbours. Yet church for most was unthinkable without Sunday clothes, one fact why so few among the poor were seen in church on Sundays' (1977, p. 26). In this context the codes of respectability dictated that on Sundays it was preferable to remain indoors than to be seen venturing out in work clothes.

Poverty restricted far more than the way people dressed, of course. Housing standards were a vital element in determining respectability, with families attaching great importance to their 'type of accommodation ... [and] its degree of cleanliness and maintenance' (Gittins, 1985, p. 121). In traditional working-class communities the majority of households rented their properties privately, but there was also an aspiration to owner-occupation. This aspiration was achieved to a significant extent in certain localities such as the South Wales coalfield, where in the early twentieth century owner-occupation ranged from 15 to 60 per cent (Daunton, 1987). Among such groups the respectability of owner-occupation was

associated with independence from the state and from middle-class philanthropy and patronage. Middle-class notions of respectability insisted upon self-help in an individualistic sense, whereas amongst the working class it was expressed through collective institutions such as friendly societies which brought the members together against other groups. (Daunton, 1987, p. 73)

Where workers typically leased housing from their employers, the attraction of owner-occupation was particularly strong: 'A miner in south Wales before the First World War was likely to argue that ownership of his own house gave him independence to oppose his employer, whereas his counterpart in a rented house was in danger of eviction' (Daunton, 1987, p. 73). Achievement of owner-occupation did not necessarily symbolise the cutting of links with other members of the wider occupational community.

Concern with respectability figured even more prominently in the lives of women in traditional working-class communities. It was women who were seen as responsible for the appearance of the home, for the diet of the household, for money management and the avoidance of debt, and for a host of other standards by which respectability was judged (E. Roberts, 1984, 1986). Thus Chinn has observed that 'The cleanliness of a family and its home was to be worn like a badge of honour; its dirtiness as a symbol of its shame and particularly that of its wife' (1988, p. 129). For men and women, but especially for women, being 'respectable' meant paying 'attention to a strict but uncomplicated list of "don'ts":

swearing, except at work; drinking, in excess of an occasional weekend pint or two; gambling; persistent rowing; sexual promiscuity on the part of mother or daughters' (Meacham, 1977, p. 27). Klein implies that the distinction between the two poles of the working class is primarily a question of attitude when she argues that 'In sum, what distinguishes the respectable working-class group from the rough is the effort they make to maintain standards, and not to let things slide' (1965, p. 199). She goes on to suggest that it is among women that the 'preference for a respectable, predictable, well-regulated existence' (1965, p. 198) is strongest.

It is difficult to sustain such a simple 'rough'/'respectable' distinction. To begin with, Klein's account offers what is essentially a psychological explanation, as Damer (1989) has noted, and is thus open to the criticism of giving insufficient weight to material factors. Sarsby cites numerous examples of the simple truth that how well a woman coped with her responsibilities depended on 'material circumstances' as well as on 'individual character' (1988, p. 39). Stated bluntly, 'it was harder to stay respectable on twenty shillings a week than on thirty-five or forty' (Meacham, 1977, p. 26). It was also harder for households to sustain the status of respectability when they lived in particular neighbourhoods which had a stigma attached to them, whatever their individual characteristics. As Meacham observes, 'If an area was "rough", everyone there was assumed to be rough as well' (1977, p. 27). White's (1986) study of Campbell Bunk, labelled 'the worst street in North London', furnishes an excellent example of this phenomenon. Acquiring its notorious reputation in the late nineteenth century, Campbell Road 'became a focal point of middle-class concern' (1986, p. 25), the street and those living there being seen collectively as 'a disgrace to civilization', and shunned accordingly. This situation prevailed despite the fact that by no means all of the street's inhabitants could be considered members of the 'lumpenproletariat'. Certainly the majority were located 'towards the "rougher" end of Campbell Road's class spectrum' (1986, p. 28), but the street also included 'a small number' of property owners such as shopkeepers and 'a thin layer' (1986, p. 30) of working-class households which enjoyed secure incomes. The street also had a recognisable division between its 'top end' and 'bottom end' (1986, p. 79).

The population of traditional working-class communities did not fall neatly either side of any dichotomy, cultural or material, but formed instead a rather more subtle hierarchy with finer gradations. In the Salford community of Roberts' Edwardian childhood, social distinctions were made between neighbouring streets and even within streets:

> one side or one end of that street might be classed higher than another. ... Every family, too, had a tacit ranking, and even individual members within it; neighbours would consider a daughter in one household as 'dead common' while registering her sister as 'refined'. (1973, p. 17)

According to Gittins, among the poorest sectors of the working class 'status and respectability were defined by whether or not a house had curtains, whether the doorstep was cleaned every day, and whether or not children wore shoes' (1985, p. 122). In general, 'roughs' had a similar status within their communities to that of the outsiders discussed in chapter 1, and households and areas to which this label was attached were excluded from much of mainstream community life. The dividing line was not fixed, however, as Chinn (1988) notes of the distinction between 'dirty' and 'clean' districts and families. Since cleanliness was the 'hallmark' of all things respectable, it is not surprising to find the concept of respectability more generally being described as 'imprecise' (Davidoff, 1976, p. 129) and 'subjective' (Davies, 1992, p. 61). Intense status anxieties flowed from the blurred nature of the boundary between the rough and the respectable working class, anxieties which had a particular impact on women's lives. The recent research undertaken by oral historians has focused on the details of women's lives in traditional working-class communities which earlier generations of research less sensitive to women's accounts had (with a handful of notable exceptions) glossed over.

REDISCOVERED DIMENSIONS OF PAST COMMUNITY LIFE

It has been pointed out already that the discussion of occupational communities has been conducted with a focus on men and male-dominated occupations, with the lives of other members of these communities at best treated as secondary, at worst ignored altogether. Researchers in this field have tended not to follow the principle of 'women and children first' when identifying topics for investigation. Against this, the recent revival of interest in the sociology of community which was discussed in chapter 1 has included a number of remarkable studies which have gone a long way to making good the previous neglect of dimensions of traditional working-class communities such as women's work and the place of children. Whether or not Chinn's term 'the hidden matriarchy of the urban poor' (1988, p. 11) adequately captures the spirit of the work of other oral historians, it does highlight two important points. First, oral historians have seen it as crucial to record aspects of life previously not written down, such as the everyday routines of working-class women. For example, Pennington and Westover's (1989) study of women homeworkers has shown how they constituted (and continue to constitute) a 'hidden workforce', Ayres' (1990) research discovered women's centrality to 'the hidden economy of dockland families' in 1930s Liverpool, while in the pottery industry Sarsby (1988) has reclaimed the history of 'the forgotten missuses'. Secondly, these researchers have unearthed evidence which challenges the inherited stereotype of working-class wives as 'downtrodden, bullied and dependent' (E. Roberts, 1984, p. 124), stressing instead their power and capacity to exercise control over their lives within the economic and social constraints of their situation. Women could also act as a focal point for broader community action, as was the case during the famous 1915 Glasgow rent strike which was 'dominated by the women of the various working-class communities of the city' (Middleton, 1987, p. 25) but which also drew support from male workers and their trade unions.

The inherited stereotype of working-class women has them very firmly located within the home, responsible for the management of domestic matters and at the hub of family relations. In the study of the mining community, Dennis and his colleagues report that ' "Woman's place is in the home" is a very definite and firm principle of thought and action in Ashton' (1969, p. 174), a finding widely reported in other studies also (Crow, 1993). This situation can be attributed in part to the very low levels of women's employment in areas dependent on male-dominated industries such as coal mining, but it is important to note that many working-class women in employment 'also shared the male-breadwinner family model as an ideal to aim for' (Roberts, 1986, p. 226). Whether or not women were in employment had a great bearing on their households' status: 'Whilst there was no shame in working, other non-working women feeling pity rather than contempt for those who *had* to work, it remained the ambition of the great majority of working women to give up paid work as soon as it was possible' (Roberts, 1986, p. 230; emphasis in original). Wives who did not need to undertake paid work added to their households' respectability, and their husbands were particularly conscious of this. Skilled working-class men earning a family wage 'took great pride and accrued great status by keeping their wives and children at home as their dependants. They sought more "respectable" neighbourhoods in which to live, and attributed great importance to more spacious accommodation maintained in pristine order by their wives' (Gittins, 1985, p. 122). The views of wives and husbands thus coincided with regard to the desirability of the Victorian ideal of women's domesticity, although some writers, mindful that women's work could bring with it a degree of job satisfaction, have questioned how far this generalisation actually held (Gordon and Breitenbach, 1990).

In practice the ideal of a woman's place being in the home proved unattainable for many poorer households (Davidoff and Westover, 1986), and where economic necessity dictated that women earned an income the type of employment which they undertook was influenced in part by varying notions of respectability. In the Stoke-on-Trent potteries Sarsby found pervasive the ideas 'that women are suited to the decorating end of the pottery industry . . . [and] that they are somehow less suited to the mucky, clay end, the preserve of men' (1988, p. 12). Nevertheless, many women were employed in the heavier, noisier, and more messy clay end and responded to the decorators' view of them as 'coarse' and 'common' by regarding the decorators' claims to superiority as marks of a pretentious, 'toffee-nosed' attitude. Alongside the potteries, textile towns were also places in which relatively high levels of employment among women were found (E. Roberts, 1984), but in other parts of the country women's chances of earning an income were more restricted, with 'casual, ill-paid jobs like cleaning, taking in lodgers, childminding and homework'

(Davidoff and Westover, 1986, p. 3) prominent among the opportunities that were available. There was less of a contradiction between such work and the ideology of domesticity than there was in the case of factory work, and Davidoff and Westover (1986) point to this factor to explain why parents preferred to steer daughters towards domestic service rather than factory employment. Gittins suggests the reverse, that 'factory work tended to be regarded as more respectable/desirable than service' (1982, p. 70) when parents were placing their daughters in work, although she notes in addition that shop assisting and clerical work carried more status than either. Similar observations have been made by Lummis (1985) about the different types of female waged labour in fishing communities.

Whether or not the women of traditional working-class communities were in paid employment, they were primarily responsible for domestic arrangements, and the successful achievement of these duties in the context of general poverty necessarily drew them into networks of mutual support with other female kin and neighbours. Lummis has argued that while the occupational experiences of men in traditional working-class communities may have provided some basis for the emergence of a shared identity and patterns of mutual support,

the greater part of what is subsumed under the heading of 'community' is simply the class experience of women: it is the sum of reciprocal acts and obligations necessary to ensure their own and their family's survival given the degree of direct exploitation experienced by the main wage-earner. (1985, p. 76)

Harris suggests that the extent of the interaction that took place between working-class women produced 'what might be termed an occupational community', with 'the exchange of kinship information and domestic services' (1983, p. xvi) to the fore in these relationships. Faced with low and erratic incomes and a more general climate of economic insecurity in the period before the modern welfare state, 'Women were proud of having a surplus to lend and not so proud of needing to borrow, but all valued a system of neighbourhood support' (Roberts, 1986, p. 242).

E. Roberts argues that this was particularly the case in poorer neighbourhoods, although a 'neighbourhood' could be understood in a restricted sense geographically, and often meant 'no more than three streets' (1984, p. 184). The logic of such arrangements was simple and compelling, as Bulmer has noted:

self-help networks at the local level were a realistic response to low incomes, economic adversity and unpredictable domestic crisis. In the absence of state support for the relief in the home of illness, old age or unemployment, the 'safety net' for most families was the neighbourhood itself. (1986, p. 92)

Stated bluntly, working-class women living in areas such as Glasgow's tenements '*had* to learn to co-operate' (Damer, 1990, p. 88; emphasis in original) since they had no other options.

The finding that female solidarity was greater in poorer neighbourhoods is echoed in other studies. White argues that neighbourhood support made compelling sense in the context of the 'desperate poverty' of Campbell Bunk: 'Its machinery of mutual aid was fashioned out of sympathy for the plight of others; and from the rational assumption that all might sooner or later need assistance themselves' (1986, p. 72). This machinery of mutual aid was 'created and sustained by women', and was characterised by a sophisticated division of labour: 'Besides neighbourly help given at and after confinements, individual women specialised in housework, shopping, fixing meals for the family, all for a small payment. The street's money lenders were probably all women' (1986, p. 73). The precise nature of money-lending between women was shrouded in secrecy, as Tebbutt's (1983) study of pawnbroking and other forms of credit in Manchester and Salford notes. Female neighbours were also important in the matter of child-care (Whipp, 1990), acting formally or informally as 'auxiliary parents' (Ross, 1983, p. 12) when needed. The often precarious economic situation of working-class families meant that the mutual assistance practised by the women of a neighbourhood frequently constituted 'survival networks' (Ross, 1983) in a quite literal sense. Within these support networks individual women attained particular promi-nence, and according to Chinn such 'matriarchs were a familiar and ever-present sight' (1988, p. 29) in most lower-working-class streets.

While the material support of neighbours was an important aspect of life in traditional working-class communities, the assistance which came through kin networks stands out more prominently still. Roberts found that, compared to neighbourhood support, 'Help from relations was of a different kind. . . . Helping was part of the family's duty as understood in working-class mores and an enormous amount was given and received almost as a matter of course' (1986, p. 242). In Campbell Bunk kinship networks provided the 'basis for special obligations between families' (White, 1986, p. 73), and kin ties could be vital in securing access to housing or employment opportunities as well as providing more everyday assistance. In the Morriston area of Swansea studied by Rosser and Harris kinship ties had been at the core of the old pattern of community life: 'there was a local cluster of kin linked by continuous interaction and multiple social relationships from home to home, in the chapel, at work, in common adversity, at play' (1983, p. 12). In short, much of what went on in traditional working-class communities revolved around kinship. The distinction between neighbours and kin should not be drawn too sharply, however, since dense kin networks living in close proximity were a feature of such communities (Gittins, 1985).

The 'rediscovery' by researchers of the significance of women's lives in shaping traditional working-class communities has prompted a corresponding interest in the significance of childhood during this period (Bornat, 1993). Humphries argues that children made an important contribution to 'family survival', engaging in activities which (mindful of the poverty of working-class families) he identifies as 'social crime'. Thus he notes that, for example, 'The "picking" of coal from pit heads and slag heaps was a habit so deeply ingrained in mining communities that it formed part of the daily domestic routine for many children' (1981, p. 157). More generally Humphries suggests that working-class children's actions do not conform to the stereotype of the 'hooligan' any more than the lives of working-class women in the past are adequately captured in the stereotype of the downtrodden wife criticised earlier by Roberts. In both cases, the concern is to assert the power rather than the powerlessness of the people whose lives are being reported. This line of argument has been taken further by Chinn in his thesis that lower-working-class mothers 'succeeded, usually in a hidden way, in becoming arbiters of their own and their families' lives, as well as emerging as dominant influences within their communities', managing to 'defy society as a whole and assert their importance' (1988, p. 13), albeit in a fashion of which outsiders may well have been unaware.

Other commentators offer a less sanguine interpretation of the evidence which oral history researchers have generated. Lewis, for example, has questioned how far it is correct to see women's support networks as 'expressions of solidarity and empowerment' noting the pressure on women to conform to 'the conservative moral values of the community' (1986, p. 19). Similarly, Sarsby suggests that 'competition between women and the attainment of high status within a community' (1988, p. 43) may have made the domestic duties of a working-class wife more onerous than they need have been. She also asks whether women whose husbands did conform to 'the hard-drinking, tight-fisted stereotype' and who thrust upon their wives 'their ideal of womanhood, as sexual object, child-bearer and servant' (1988, pp. 106–7) could in practice do very much about this situation. It is one thing to argue, as Lummis rightly does, that working-class women 'were not passively shaped by the pressures of their menfolk's work but were active in creating their own social relationships' (1985, p. 167); it is quite another to interpret this creativity as power.

There is thus no contradiction between Williamson's rejection of the idea that his grandmother was 'a passive victim of circumstance' (1982, p. 120) and his portrayal of the psychology of miners' wives like his grandmother as containing a strong element of 'fatalism' (1982, p. 131), their lives locked into inevitable domestic routines from which there was little opportunity of escape. He argues that although his grandmother 'did little else but work', it was through the performance of work that women in communities like Throckley achieved both 'self-respect and the recognition of others' (1982, p. 125). In addition, the pressure to conform to community standards operated to discourage not only the traits of the rough working class, but also behaviour that might be considered excessively respectable: 'Any outward sign of a claim to be different, particularly a claim to be in any way superior, was looked down upon and would invite adverse comment' (1982, p. 125). The common bonds of such communities thus acted as a powerful barrier to change.

Where change did occur in traditional working-class communities, it occurred most often as the evolution of tradition rather than in more dramatic fashion. Drinking habits offer one example of the way in which norms shifted gradually. E. Roberts has recorded how from the late nineteenth century onwards, 'but especially during and after the [first world] war, it became more and more socially acceptable for "respectable" women to go into pubs with their husbands' (1984, p. 122). More generally, the traditions around which traditional working-class communities were constructed proved to be considerably malleable but at the same time surprisingly persistent in the face of the major social changes which Britain has undergone in the twentieth century. These changes include the processes of economic restructuring which have led to the old occupational communities discussed in this chapter being eroded, and the constant geographical mobility of the population which has made possible the creation of new communities. It is these two themes which are the subjects of chapters 3 and 4 respectively.

# 3

## THE RESTRUCTURING
## OF COMMUNITIES:
## THE IMPACT OF ECONOMIC CHANGE

The stereotypes of traditional working-class communities with which we are all familiar have a superficial attraction but are open to the criticism of being based on a one-sided, highly selective process of recall. Rosser and Harris warn of the risk of deriving somewhat 'exaggerated' perceptions through conversations with old residents whose memories tend to exclude the less sentimental characteristics and events of the past. From such sources, a picture of the Morriston district of Swansea at the turn of the century emerges as 'small in scale, limited and narrow in its social horizons, homogeneous in social composition, familiar and familistic, with a strong community consciousness generated by common residence and common necessity. It was clearly much more than a community of residence'. The roots of this pervasive community consciousness lay in the community of work 'with the men engaged in identical or similar occupations, a community of worship in the chapels, a community of basic cultural uniformities in language, in housing and material possessions, and in moral values' (1983, p. 12). Rosser and Harris are aware of the tendency of those remembering to omit 'the conflicts and internal tensions' of the community but suggest that, provided this qualification is borne in mind, the comparison of such accounts with subsequent patterns of kinship and community solidarity can tell us a good deal about the scale of the changes that have taken place.

This chapter will focus on the changes in community life that have come about through economic restructuring, concentrating particularly on unemployment, social polarisation, and the impact of restructuring on women's lives. If the writers on 'occupational communities' considered in the last chapter are correct in their

45

assumption that work was the great mainstay of such communities, then it is reasonable to infer that unemployment will have a major negative impact on community life. This has certainly been the starting point for a number of research projects in recent years, including Harris's study of the 'profound economic and social transition' (1987, p. 227) which redundancy and recession entail in areas of old, heavy industry such as South Wales. In the light of the expectation that unemployment will lead to the erosion of traditional working-class communities, it is somewhat surprising to find the evidence gathered in Port Talbot underlining 'how slow the response, at the cultural level, has been to economic change' (1987, p. 227). Harris stresses that although redundancy poses a very real threat to personal identity, it does not necessarily lead to dramatic shifts in the local social structure. Other studies (including several studies of the related but distinct problem of youth unemployment) confirm that there are strong elements of continuity as well as change in communities created around the traditional heavy industries which have seen rapid contraction of their workforces in recent years.

Economic restructuring brings with it not only redundancy and unemployment but also change in the occupational structure more generally, and the growth of new patterns of employment would also be expected to influence the development of community life in fundamental ways. Here the predominant sociological interest has been in the emergence of new occupations, treated as heralding broader social change because of their greater reliance on the workforce's skills rather than physical strength, and because of their relatively high rates of pay. The lifestyles of these 'affluent workers' have been contrasted by Lockwood (1975) and Goldthorpe *et al.* (1969) with those of the 'traditional' workers discussed in the previous chapter, with claims about the 'privatised' nature of these lifestyles to the fore in their accounts. Much of the subsequent debate has centred on the contentious concept of 'privatisation' which they employ and on the question of whether developments in towns like Luton will be reproduced in other areas of the country which have very different industrial traditions.

Other research has investigated the ways in which economic changes affect men and women differently, and the implications which these differences have for local social life. Bagguley *et al.*'s study of Lancaster, for example, demonstrates 'the centrality of gender relations for the analysis of restructuring' (1990, p. 10).

Similarly, Warwick and Littlejohn's account of mining communities in West Yorkshire found women 'much more obviously part of the labour market than they were in the 1920s' (1992, p. 103), but still far from being men's equal in occupational terms. Hebron and Wykes (1991) reported a similar situation of persistent gender inequalities in neighbouring coalfields, while Rees and Thomas (1991) suggest that restructuring has had a more profound effect in the South Wales coalfield where the changing gender balance of employment has been a key contributory factor to differentiation within working-class communities.

Economic restructuring is thus associated with both change and continuity in a variety of ways. Contemporary theories of employment may stress women workers' 'flexibility' but this is by no means a new phenomenon, as Stubbs and Wheelock note by observing that 'Women (and men) on Wearside have juggled jobs and family life for decades' (1990 p. 23). More generally, traditional working-class communities never conformed to a single, fixed pattern but were, on the contrary, strikingly diverse and shifting entities, influenced by unfolding industrial, geographical, political and historical forces. Gray has rightly questioned the way in which 'Commentators, in harking back to a golden past, usually seem to have in mind just one of a range of different working-class localities.' He goes on to argue that closer inspection of the evidence reveals a quite different picture: 'Supposedly "traditional" communities . . . often appear surprisingly modern and in a constant state of flux. Industrial communities were moveable feasts, developing, evolving and sometimes withering according to the dictates of industrial change' (1989, p. 451). If there is a difference between the present situation and the past it is not that stability has been replaced by change, since change was ever-present; what is new, arguably, is that in the context of 'globalisation' the scope of this change is wider than ever before and its pace is accelerating.

UNEMPLOYMENT, SOCIAL ISOLATION AND THE PERSISTENCE
OF TRADITIONS

One of the more surprising findings thrown up by recent research into economic restructuring is the discovery that the rapid decline of employment in traditional industries has not been accompanied by wholesale change in the communities which grew up around the mines, factories and other workplaces of Britain's industrial areas. Gallie has reasoned cogently that if 'unemployment leads households to withdraw from active participation in the community, then presumably high levels of unemployment could lead, by a chain effect, to an undercutting of activities and facilities that would affect the wider quality of life in the community' (1985, p. 528), but the empirical evidence available is at best ambiguous on this matter. Harris's study of Port Talbot confirmed that redundancy resulted in 'the segregation of the unemployed from the social life of their own locality', there being 'a sense in which the unemployed have "fallen" *out* of the local social structure' (1987, p. 226; emphasis in original). It does not follow from this, however, that the local social structure is undermined by redundancy. Harris found it impossible to draw a simple distinction between employed and unemployed groups, discovering instead the presence of an intermediate category of individuals whose 'chequered' labour market careers (in which employment is sporadic and frequently informal) attest to their determination to remain part of the existing social networks of working-class life. While the long-term unemployed responded to two-and-a-half years without paid work by 'beginning . . . to renegotiate their marital relationships and their whole attitude to life as they come to realize that the supports of the old way of life have gone' (1987, p. 227), this was interpreted negatively, as an adjustment to failure, and as such represented a very strong incentive to sustain involvement in existing patterns of social relationships for as long as possible.

Harris's investigations suggest that redundancy may have the effect of heightening the significance of local social networks as individuals and households struggle to escape the social isolation which long-term unemployment threatens to bring. The restricted social life of the long-term unemployed leads to their failure 'to reproduce their identity', and avoiding this outcome requires active 'network maintenance and participation' (1987, p. 217). Other studies support this general conclusion. Research undertaken by Turner, Bostyn and Wight in 'Cauldmoss', a former coal-mining village in central Scotland, describes the community as 'very conservative' (Bostyn and Wight, 1987, p. 139) despite male unemployment rates of over 30 per cent. What is striking about 'Cauldmoss' is the persistence of traditions rooted in the bygone era when coal mining dominated the local economy and provided the main source of male employment. These traditions include a strong commitment to the work ethic and a 'moral obligation to maintain a respectable standard of living' (1987, p. 140). Maintaining 'respectable' levels of consumption (whether in terms of food, alcohol, fuel, or things for the children) was highly prized, while less materialistic attitudes were seen to involve condoning idleness.

The contradiction between the 'consistent informal pressure, through gossip and public opinion, to conform to the norms of "full employment" ' (1987, p. 139) and the material reality of unemployed people's inadequate resources was managed by a variety of coping strategies. Stretching limited budgets to cover socially approved levels of expenditure necessarily involved households in patterns of reciprocal exchange and loans in which kin ties were prominent, perhaps unsurprisingly given that some 60 per cent of the population had kinship links with others in the area (Turner *et al.*, 1985). Despite the presence of such support, however, in the long run unemployment pushed individuals into a marginal, isolated and excluded position peripheral to mainstream community life. Turner and his colleagues found a strong sense of shame about unemployment, and they argue that attachment to 'strikingly conservative' values was general among 'Cauldmoss' folk, employed and unemployed alike. This conformity to norms more fitting to a past period than to the present is explained by unemployed people not being in a position to change things: 'In a conservative community like Cauldmoss, it is hard enough for those who *can* satisfy society's requirements to be innovative, let alone for those who lack the legitimation and self-respect gained from employment' (Bostyn and Wight, 1987, p. 151; emphasis in original). In 'Cauldmoss' as in Port Talbot, cultural change occurs much more slowly than economic change.

Resistance to the idea of long-term unemployment was also discovered in the working-class district of Eastlough in Protestant East Belfast. What Howe found here was that, despite an unemployment rate of 26 per cent, for unemployed men 'the dole still constitutes an *interruption* of work. Legitimate employment is

still overwhelmingly that which is sought and desired and which is
strongly supported by long-standing attitudes and values' (1990, p.
55; emphasis in original). At over 50 per cent, unemployment rates
in the Mallon Park district of Catholic West Belfast were double
those of Eastlough, and in this context the view of unemployment
as an interruption of a normal working life was harder to sustain:
'it is beginning to be seen as a permanent condition imposed
externally by a permanently depressed economy' (1990, p. 66).
Howe argues that some Mallon Park residents have evolved 'new
notions of how to get by whilst unemployed', including a more
tolerant attitude towards 'doing the double', that is, 'using welfare
benefits as a base on which to build by taking, whenever possible,
jobs in the black economy' (1990, p. 66). This practice has
'attained a fairly high degree of moral acceptance' (1990, p. 68) in
the wake of the virtual disappearance of legitimate job opportunities.

Even here, however, 'traditional' ideas about the propriety of
working for one's income remained powerful. Among Catholics as
well as Protestants and among unemployed as well as employed
individuals the distinction between the 'deserving' and 'undeserving' poor was a pervasive one. The 'undeserving' category was
seen to be made up of people who 'don't want to work' (1990, p.
2), and fear of the stigma of being labelled undeserving 'induces in
many unemployed strong feelings of private shame, and an almost
crippling degree of anxiety concerning which category others are
thought to assign to them' (1990, p. 3). As a result, unemployed
people may become involved not in supportive social networks
with fellow jobless individuals but in 'the denigration of others'
(1990, p. 189). In consequence, their lives become further
impoverished by 'social isolation, fragmentation and distrust'
(1990, p. 3). Evason's study of men who had experienced long-
term unemployment in another part of Northern Ireland, Derry,
echoed Howe's findings, arguing that 'these men have not, in
general, evolved a more collective, outgoing life-style. The picture
that emerges is one of men isolated at home – the problem is a
private one' (1985, p. 59). In addition, Evason detected 'some
support for negative attitudes towards the rest of the unemployed'
(1985, p. 59), and even though these were minority opinions, there
are still obvious parallels between this situation and the division
between the 'respectable' and 'rough' categories of traditional
working-class life discussed in the previous chapter.

In periods of high youth unemployment it might be reasonable to suppose that distinctions between deserving and undeserving groups will become weaker among younger people, but the available evidence suggests that such ideas continue to be reproduced across the generations. Jenkins's study of Ballyhightown, a housing estate on the outskirts of Belfast, records the reproduction among its youth of familiar divisions within the working class. Jenkins argues that the rough/respectable distinction is reproduced in the division among young men between 'lads' and 'citizens', with a third group, 'ordinary kids', occupying an intermediate position. Occupational aspirations were higher among the 'citizens' than among the 'lads', but it remained the case that among the latter group unemployment 'is seen as the result of personal failure, even though the lads know that there are not enough jobs to go round' (1983, p. 45). The social isolation of the long-term unemployed in the adult population also had its counterpart among the youth, since it could be observed that 'those lads who are unemployed for long periods form a distinct group' (1983, p. 45). Unable to afford to participate fully in the reciprocal networks of employed friends who disapprove of 'scrounging', these 'brue-men' 'spend much of their time together in the evenings and at weekends'. They even 'appear to regard unemployment as a virtue, in contrast to "working like a mug" ' (1983, p. 45), although Jenkins points out that such ideas reflected the lads' 'ad hoc response to the problems of long-term unemployment' (1983, p. 47) and were not evidence of the abandonment of the 'protestant ethic'.

The pressures on the lads to find work of some sort were not only economic and official ones, but involved also the complex relationships between the sexes in Ballyhightown. Jenkins is mindful of the fact that there was 'no female life-style equivalent to the lads' (1983, p. 44), and suggests that the development of a 'rough' female lifestyle was inhibited by a variety of factors, including the way in which the ideology of 'respectability' is more constraining for young women than it is for young men. During courtship, young women play an important role 'in "settling down" the lads or the "rougher" members of the ordinary kids network' (1983, p. 133), and this process is deepened when couples set up independent households and women take on the role of homemakers. Women are socialised into being more conscious of the need to maintain ' "respectable" standards in the eyes of the local world' at both of these stages of the life-course, and it is on this basis that Jenkins argues that 'the habituation of male labour is at least partly achieved through the pressures of female "respectability" ' (1983, p. 133). In a culture where teenage marriage was common and where 'boys have to have a wage before they can really compete for girls', young people's social networks continued to be structured by what Jenkins calls 'the economics of courtship' (1983, p. 80) to a significant degree.

It is interesting to note that Jenkins' findings tally with those which Gillespie *et al.* (1992) derived from the older established areas of West Belfast. In both the Protestant Shankill and the Catholic Upper Springfield areas, the brunt of the rise in unemployment which accompanied industrial decline has been borne by young people, with fewer than one in five finding jobs within two years of leaving school, but again the response to this was not collective opposition. What Gillespie and his colleagues found was that despite the air of social disintegration there was a surprising degree of social continuity, with perpetuation among young people of divisions between the sexes and distinctions between members of the working class according to whether they were 'rough' or 'respectable', 'non-conformist' or 'conformist' (1992, p. 124). Even in districts which have been comprehensively redeveloped in recent decades the researchers discovered that 'many old customs have survived' and that 'the disrupted communities have to an extent reconstituted themselves in the new housing developments' (1992, p. 18).

The north-east of England is another economically depressed area in which research has been conducted into young people's transition to adulthood against the background of widespread unemployment. Coffield *et al.*'s study of young people growing up at the margins of the labour market in the three contrasting localities given the pseudonyms 'Shipton', 'Milton' and 'Hillsborough' found employment patterns not dissimilar to those among adults which Harris referred to as 'chequered'. Roughly half of the fifty or so young women and men in their sample had moved between low-paid work, training schemes and unemployment or, as they themselves put it, 'in and out of shit jobs, on and off govvies and on the dole' (1986, p. 84), and in this context the fourteen who 'were kept on after their government training schemes ended and were in full-time employment for the period of the study' (1986, p. 6) were an advantaged minority. In contrast to Ballyhightown's marked 'lack of communal identity' (Jenkins, 1983, p. 25), Coffield and his colleagues found among the Geordies 'rich networks of mutual support which have been built up over generations by families, neighbours and friends, self-sufficient and resourceful communities, which have not lost hope for themselves and their children and which give security and warmth to those members who are unemployed' (1986, p. 11). At the same time there were pressures towards fragmentation in working-class communities, as the processes of economic restructuring continued to unfold, giving a contradictory appearance to the overall picture.

The social networks of the young people were far from uniform, and the researchers discovered 'a wide range of experiences from hectic social lives to loneliness and isolation' (1986, p. 13). In the difficult circumstances of economic marginality it was necessary to devise means for coping, and Coffield *et al.*'s findings confirm Bagguley's (1991) suggestion that 'community' can be drawn upon as a 'cultural resource' by unemployed people. Of particular relevance here is 'the ethos of the locality, which prides itself on mutual support, co-operation and friendliness' (1986, p. 143) and in which there is a 'heightened sense of solidarity' (1986, p. 142). Feelings of inclusion in this community life buttressed individual identity, and also brought direct material benefits such as access to 'family and neighbourhood networks for hearing about jobs' (1986, p. 141). The young women and men were very much the product of the 'traditions of the neighbourhood to which they belonged ... traditions which persist over and above the individuals involved' (1986, p. 130). Membership of the community required conformity to its traditions, as patterns of alcohol consumption showed: 'The strongest tradition followed by the young adults we knew was drinking alcohol. The culture of drink was all around them and hard to avoid even if they wanted to' (1986, p. 132). Pride in such traditions, which were understood as specific to the region, produced a culture in which 'localism' was prominent.

Coffield and his colleagues are sceptical of the conventional wisdom 'that there has been a gradual decline in the spirit of such communities since the nineteenth century' (1986, p. 140). There were 'discontinuities with earlier cultural forms' (1986, p. 141), but there were also continuities, and these made the simple decline of community thesis questionable. Community life was characterised by a number of divisions, some of which were peculiar to the 1980s, others of which had deep-seated antecedents. Deep divisions 'between those who supported the [1984–5 miners'] strike and those who did not . . . between the employed and the jobless; between those who "shop" their neighbours to the DHSS and those who do not . . . between those who can afford to buy their council houses and those who cannot' (1986, p. 142) were as much suggestive of continuity as they were of change. Another, 'less serious' division, that 'between "outsiders" from southern England and "insiders"' (1986, p. 143) parallels Williamson's (1982) account of his great-grandparents' arrival in the north-east from Norfolk. The decline of community thesis makes sense only if the socially cohesive and harmonious character of the past are exaggerated. It would be more accurate to point to the persistence of old divisions, such as that between the 'rough' and the 'respectable', which were found to be present. The identification of 'certain housing estates and even particular streets that had been stigmatized . . . a clear hierarchy in housing with fine gradations within any one estate' (1986, p. 143) echoes White's (1986) research on Campbell Bunk which was discussed in the previous chapter.

One of the most striking things about the account of community life which Coffield *et al.* present is the centrality of family and kinship relations. The interconnections of family and neighbourhood are illustrated by one nineteen-year-old respondent, Reg, who described the following network:

There's me mam. There's her brother . . . with two kids, they live next door. Me mam's other brother lives further down the street and he's got – one, two, three, four, five, six kids. And, er, two brothers are married to two sisters, and their mother lives in the middle of the street. (1986, p. 117)

Living 'surrounded by relatives' had the effect of reinforcing the young people's ties to the neighbourhood and their commitment to established values. This finding coincides with the argument put forward by Allatt and Yeandle that young people's labour market careers are influenced to a significant degree by the actions of relatives, 'how families deploy their resources' (1992, p. 20). What Allatt and Yeandle found in the working-class area of Newcastle upon Tyne in which their research was conducted was that families offered help to and put pressure on young people to find employment partly out of a sense of duty and familial solidarity and partly because of a commitment to 'the moral community' (1992, ch.5) which they perceived to be threatened by unemployment. This 'moral community' endorsed the work ethic, frowned on 'fiddle jobs' (1992, p. 57) and generally embodied a 'traditional sense of what was proper' (1992, p. 126), with the result that many families 'tried to maintain the status quo' (1992, p. 140) despite the greatly changed circumstances ushered in by economic restructuring. Morris and Irwin's (1992) research in nearby Hartlepool reports similar patterns of kinship support for unemployed adults, and it is notable that these networks are particularly strong among women.

## SOCIAL POLARISATION, PRIVATISATION AND BEYOND

Economic change brings with it many other social consequences besides unemployment, of course, and it would be misleading to discuss the people most disadvantaged by recent shifts in the labour market without also mentioning the beneficiaries of this restructuring. It has been the theme of much recent research that a profound social change is in train, with a widening gap emerging between the majority of the population (whose circumstances are more or less comfortable) and a disadvantaged minority excluded from all but the most marginal labour market opportunities. Pahl has referred to this as a process of polarisation, 'with households busily engaged in all forms of work at one pole and households unable to do a wide range of work at the other' (1984, p. 313), and his research work on the Isle of Sheppey in Kent has played an important part in the development of the social polarisation thesis. Located in the prosperous south-east of Britain rather than in the depressed regions in which many other studies of the relationship between economic and social change have been conducted, Sheppey's position is nevertheless somewhat isolated and marginal. Aware of the fact that 'Sheppey is a distinct milieu with its own distinctive traditions, experiences, possibilities and constraints'

(1984, p. 155), Pahl set out in his study to gain an insight into ordinary people's everyday lives in a situation where unemployment was present alongside more widespread affluence and upward social mobility.

Pahl describes Sheppey as a small, relatively self-contained island community in the Thames estuary with a long history of its people being employed in dockyards and other traditional working-class industries; its more recent experience has been of redundancy and de-industrialisation. In the context of economic recession and rising unemployment rates, Pahl was struck by the deep historical roots of people's responses to 'the basic problems of getting by', problems which 'have remained remarkably similar for centuries' (1984, p. 152). Working-class culture is taken by Pahl to involve 'an intensely conservative and traditional set of household practices for grappling with difficult material circumstances' (1984, p. 155), and he argues that the household type which such circumstances have promoted is 'the privatized, home-centred domestic unit based on the nuclear family' (1984, p. 321). He suggests that 'the reorientation of working-class life to being more home-centred' (1984, p. 108) can be traced back at least as far as the mid-nineteenth century and argues that there is nothing particularly new about home-centredness or privatisation as such, an argument which can call on a good deal of evidence in its favour (Crow and Allan, 1990; Pahl and Wallace, 1988).

What is different about the current situation, Pahl claims, is that the fortunes of members of the old working class have diverged, with a substantial number rising into the 'middle mass' while those on the other side of the 'new line of class cleavage' (1984, p. 324) have been downwardly mobile into the 'underclass'. The households of the former group, 'more privatized, inward-looking, home-centred and autonomous, are consumption-oriented and consider that they can achieve their individual goals more readily through private plans than through collective action' (1984, pp. 319–20). What Pahl highlights in particular in this regard is the growth of owner-occupation which he says indicates disillusion with 'working-class solidarity' and 'collectivism' on instrumental grounds, since this collectivism has delivered soulless council estates 'which do not seem self-evidently good things' (1984, p. 323). Against this background, owner-occupation represents the realisation of widely held aspirations to upward mobility in housing, aspirations based in part on the assumption that owner-occupation allows a higher degree of control over the activities of everyday life than that enjoyed by tenants. Owner-occupation thus offers to some the prospect of greater self-sufficiency, but as those households with advantaged work positions 'retreat within themselves' (1984, p. 197), so the options of lower-income households become more restricted and their 'survival strategies' more precarious. They find themselves 'increasingly isolated, politically impotent and socially invisible', caught in 'a downward spiral of economic and social detachment' (Pahl and Wallace, 1985, pp. 221, 224). Pahl's initial hypothesis that community networks might provide a cushion against unemployment had to be abandoned in the light of mounting evidence that unemployed people have few chances to engage in informal economic activity where more affluent households monopolise work opportunities.

The process of polarisation described by Pahl as 'developing among ordinary working people' (1984, p. 310) had a geographical expression which could be expected to deepen as localities, like households, 'come to look more within themselves' (1984, p. 197). This 'localism' had fewer of the connotations of 'community' than that identified in the north-east by Coffield *et al.*, and the ubiquitous distinction between rough and respectable areas was expressed somewhat differently too, having 'strong moral connotations: those who were able to demonstrate their respectability through having comfortable, affluent life-styles also thought of themselves as morally superior to the less fortunate. Thus, they were unlikely to form alliances with those whom they perceived to be the "undeserving poor" ' (Pahl and Wallace, 1988, p. 139). These distinctions were based in part on tenure patterns, with some areas being almost exclusively owner-occupied while others were more mixed, not least because polarisation was also taking place within estates, where some 'houses look smart, with new front doors and obvious double glazing, indicating clearly that they have been bought from the council; others have the characteristic scuffed door and concrete path, with a scattering of broken toys and odd bits of wood that may or may not be rubbish' (Pahl, 1984, p. 153). Polarisation was working to divide neighbours as well as areas on the island.

Wallace's linked study of young people on Sheppey growing up in and out of work also found evidence of social polarisation, with those in work tending to see their future 'in terms of the acquisition of a house, a family, and various consumer goods' while in contrast 'the long-term unemployed tended to see themselves as helpless flotsam and jetsam washed around by the receding economic tide' (Wallace, 1987, p. 221). These young people were conscious of the 'cultural divisions between "rough" and "respectable" households based upon the ownership and physical maintenance of property' (1987, p. 14), and in consequence 'argued that they would postpone getting married until they had saved up the money for a house, a proper wedding and the material goods for the matrimonial home' (Pahl and Wallace, 1988, p. 140). This said, it is worth noting that the situation among Sheppey's young people was not a mirror-image of that of their parents' generation, and Wallace did not find a strong link between unemployment and social isolation. Unemployed teenagers on Sheppey 'did not depend solely upon the workplace for their sources of social contact. In a small community, with large numbers of people being unemployed for at least some period in their teenage years, there was no shortage of social contacts' (1987, p. 74). Any connection between unemployment and social isolation was mediated by other factors:

> Those who did complain of isolation were young people who had lost contact with their friends from school, who were kept at home deliberately by parents for fear of them drifting into bad ways, who lived in isolated locations, or whose friends were all working full-time. (1987, p. 75)

What Wallace refers to as 'the long-term cumulative experience of unemployment' (1987, p. 222) had not had time to assert itself fully among teenagers.

There is an obvious danger in generalising on the basis of Pahl and Wallace's Sheppey research, as Pahl himself admits in noting that the island cannot be said to be straightforwardly 'typical', but the findings do nevertheless relate to changes which have a wider significance. *Divisions of Labour* is acknowledged even by critics as an 'important locality study in a rather unusual place' (Byrne, 1989, p. 24), not least because of Pahl's argument about there being no inevitability of working-class life throwing up 'affective solidarity' (Pahl, 1984, p. 323) and his observations concerning the deep-seated nature of working-class privatism. Allowing for the fact that Sheppey has (by national standards) 'an unusually high proportion of home owners' (1984, p. 175), including among working-class households, and that the island's culture is highly individualistic, it can nevertheless still be said that certain areas 'do typify in many respects urban working-class industrial communities' (1984, p. 182). It is not only on Sheppey that owner-occupation has shown a dramatic rise in recent decades, reflecting rising living standards among the majority of the population, while a disadvantaged minority are excluded from the benefits of this affluence.

Like Goldthorpe and Lockwood before him, Pahl argues that the growth of affluence among sections of the working class does not herald 'embourgeoisement', that is, the adoption of middle-class lifestyles. Pahl and Wallace find greater utility in Goldthorpe *et al.*'s (1969) concept of 'privatisation' in which home-centredness and family-centredness come more to the fore in people's everyday lives at the expense of 'traditional' patterns of community sociability, but they are aware that home-centredness is by no means a straightforward phenomenon and that privatised lifestyles may in practice be made up of several discrete elements which it would be better to analyse separately (Pahl and Wallace, 1988). The distinction between 'voluntary and obligatory privatization' (Pahl and Wallace, 1988, p. 127) serves to draw attention to the fact that poorer households may be 'involuntarily home-centred' (1985, p. 224) rather than choosing to withdraw from wider social networks, a point which squares with Binns and Mars' description of daily life as 'grimly "home centred" ' (1984, p. 674) in the context of long-term unemployment. Harris, too, suggests that the growth of home-centredness may have more than one source, as 'poverty, unemployment and geographical stability push in the same direction as affluence and mobility insofar as they both increase the tendency to the isolation of the nuclear family and the child-centredness it already exhibits' (1987, p. 226). The consequences in each case are quite different, however, with 'the decline of communal sociability and reciprocal flows of aid which were once the very essence of working-class culture and solidarity' (1987, p. 225) being a much more serious loss for the long-term unemployed than they are for the upwardly mobile.

Various terms have been used to describe the impact of privatisation on community life in the context of economic restructuring and unemployment. Binns and Mars' study of 'The Heights', a post-war council estate in south Glasgow, predicted that unemployed families faced 'deepening *atomisation*' (1984, p. 689; emphasis in original), while Beynon *et al.* speak of Teesside experiencing 'polarization and fragmentation' (1989, p. 293). Likewise the account of south-west Birmingham as 'One locality, several "communities" ' (D. Smith, 1989, p. 235) suggests that polarisation has increased local divisions, with those in employment enmeshed in 'networks based on home and kin' (1989, p. 264) and also workplace, the Longbridge and Bournville works providing for their workers and families 'a framework of social relationships extending beyond the factory gates' (1989, p. 256) from which unemployed people are excluded. Restructuring has thus produced a situation in which there is, in Dickens's term, ' "Community" for Some' (1988, p. 131). For those excluded from the vestiges of industrial Britain's occupational communities, the term privatisation has a somewhat sanitised ring to it.

Dissatisfaction with the term privatisation has also been voiced in relation to its ability to capture the realities of life away from areas in which unemployment is concentrated. Procter's research in 'Ivybridge', a typical post-war suburb of Coventry, found communal sociability not absent but 'alive and well' (1990, p. 161). Contrary to the expected privatised lifestyles, Procter discovered people with

an attachment to the local area, in regular and frequent contact with relatives, knowing a large number of their neighbours, having local relatives and friends to help with problems, joining in organisational activity and spending some leisure time outside the home with associates from outside the household. (1990, p. 171)

He goes on to criticise the 'periodisation of working-class life in which communal sociability and privatisation are regarded as essential features of different stages', proposing instead that both should 'be regarded as recurring features of working-class life' (1990, p. 175). What Procter is suggesting is that, given time, communal sociability may evolve even in those conditions of geographical mobility and relative affluence previously taken to be most conducive to privatised lifestyles.

Devine's re-study of Luton, the location of the original *Affluent Worker* research, did not come across the same degree of communal sociability which Procter discovered in Coventry, but her findings do still raise doubts about the link between affluence and privatised lifestyles posited by Goldthorpe *et al.* (1969). She argues that while 'men and women do lead home- and family-centred lifestyles' (1989, p. 99), this can be attributed to a considerable extent to the limitations placed on their involvement in wider social networks by the demands of the busy daily routine. Rather than highlighting attachment to the values of privatism, Devine stresses the limited amount of time available for sociability, having found 'little evidence to suggest that people positively desire to exclude others from their lives and to live a home- and family-centred existence' (1989, p. 99). One of the major changes in her respondents' lives in recent years noted by Devine was the increase in employment among married women, a development which limited women's opportunities to engage in the types of sociability characteristic of the 'traditional' working-class communities discussed in chapter 2. This was true not only for those women who were in paid work, but also for those caring for children full-time. These mothers' home-centred lives involved 'a greater degree of isolation than in the past' (1989, p. 93) because, with the growth of women's employment, there were relatively few others in the neighbourhood during the day with whom they could develop anything more than casual social contacts. It is thus apparent that economic change has had a quite different impact on women and men, and that the gender biases of the theory of privatisation which come from its treatment of men's experiences as typical (Allan and Crow 1989; 1991) are a serious handicap to the understanding of the full implications of economic re-structuring.

## THE ECONOMIC SIGNIFICANCE OF WOMEN'S SOCIAL NETWORKS

The concentration on men's experiences in conventional accounts of the structure of occupational communities, the growth of home-centredness and the impact of unemployment produced a corresponding invisibility in relation to women's experiences. It was noted in the previous chapter that recent research into women's roles has led to a re-evaluation of the nature of life in 'traditional' working-class communities, and very much the same point can be made about community life in the contexts of privatisation and economic restructuring. Consideration of some of this literature will be deferred until the discussion in chapter 6 of women's experiences of the growth of owner-occupation, while this section focuses more specifically on the economic significance of women's social networks. It will look first at women's responses to unemployment and then go on to consider the impact of the growth of employment among women.

A repeated finding of researchers investigating the social consequences of unemployment among men has been that much of the burden is passed on to women (Morris, 1990a). In their study of the families of unemployed men in Kidderminster, McKee and Bell (1986) observe that in addition to continuing to carry out conventional domestic tasks wives were expected to perform minor miracles of household money management in the context of reduced incomes. They argue too that the social isolation of wives was more acute than it was for their husbands, a situation which has been noted elsewhere (Glyptis, 1989). The social contacts that were maintained by women often served practical purposes, as when they contributed to their spouses' job searches, 'asking friends, mobilising family resources, and maintaining morale' (McKee and Bell, 1986, p. 145). Unemployed families were also involved in patterns of reciprocity with neighbours, and 'Women's networks were often the key to these exchanges' (McKee, 1987, p. 113). Overall, McKee and Bell (1986) describe the situation within the household as one of 'his unemployment, her problem', while in the wider community 'unemployment does not automatically guarantee or enlist a favourable, or any, response' (McKee, 1987, pp. 104–5). Support has to be actively recruited, and in this women's role is vital.

A related finding is that the burdens of youth unemployment also fall disproportionately upon women as mothers. Hutson and Jenkins' study of youth unemployment in South Wales found that the problems of 'family management' fell mainly on mothers, who had a central role in their households as 'the source of care and emotional support' (1989, p. 59). Mothers were expected to be capable of 'taking the strain' in such circumstances, and so the 'problem of the son or daughter's unemployment . . . in all of its aspects – emotional, financial or whatever – is one with which "mam" copes' (1989, p. 59). Hutson and Jenkins describe mothers as 'the managers, mediators and negotiators at the heart of the symbolic economy of family relationships' (1989, p. 153), not least because of their role in defusing conflict between family members. Mothers, along with fathers, perform the further service to their children of providing information about job opportunities (Allatt and Yeandle, 1992; Coffield *et al.*, 1986; Morris, 1990b), and in this context it is significant that in White and McRae's sample of young adults who had been unemployed for longer than six months 'more than one in six were from single-parent family backgrounds' (1989, p. iii).

Women's access to informal networks of information about opportunities for paid work is also important in explaining their own patterns of employment. In South Wales it was found that women's employment frequently arose through informal channels: 'A network of friends, relatives and acquaintances relayed information which enabled women to identify and gain access to "suitable" employment' (Harris and Morris, 1986, p. 91). Similarly in Hartlepool Morris found 'a long-established tradition of informal recruitment' (1990b, p. 91), and she goes on to observe how such networks have the effect of channelling women into part-time work. Thus 'there are many married women who need a supplement to the income their husband's wage provides, but who cannot accommodate their domestic and child-care obligations if they enter full-time employment. They accordingly use friendship links to seek out part-time work' (1990b, p. 93). To employers, informal networks have the advantage of being a relatively low-cost method of recruitment.

The attractiveness to employers of the 'flexibility' which women workers offer has been widely noted (Bagguley *et al.*, 1990; Stubbs and Wheelock, 1990), and against this background Wheelock (1990) argues that unemployed men on Wearside whose partners are in work are taking on a greater share of domestic tasks. She argues further that attention should be concentrated less on local culture and more on 'the role of the state in perpetuating traditional ideologies' (1990, p. 144). Wheelock accepts that the traditional ideologies of men as breadwinners and women as home-makers are challenged successfully in only a minority of instances, but her case study nevertheless indicates the need for caution when generalising about the impact of economic change on women's lives. A similar point about the significance of household diversity is made by Bagguley *et al.* who found that this led to 'varied experiences for women in the service class' (1990, p. 104) in their study of economic restructuring in Lancaster. At the same time it remains the case that 'pre-existing sets of gender relations in particular places are an important consideration in understanding how places change' (Bagguley *et al.*, 1990, pp. 26–7), and that economic restructuring does not lead in the direction of a single, homogeneous pattern of gendered employment.

A good example of the continuing influence of traditions of gender divisions inherited from past generations is provided by Warwick and Littlejohn's analysis of mining communities in West Yorkshire. The communities studied by Warwick and Littlejohn include 'Ashton', the site of Dennis *et al.*'s classic community study of the 1950s, and this allows comparison to be made on a number of points. While the proportion of women with jobs in the locality had risen by 1987 to 58 per cent, it is noted immediately that 'of those almost half are part-time' (1992, p. 103), carrying the implication that the economic dependence which was a marked feature of 'Ashton' is still very much a reality. Indeed, these figures may be considered high for mining communities more generally, since another recent study of pit villages in Yorkshire, Derbyshire and Nottinghamshire found the considerably lower figure of 29 per cent for 1988 (Waddington *et al.*, 1991). In West Yorkshire, Warwick and Littlejohn detected 'a domestic division of labour which carries memories of the old male dominance, and changes still have not led very far down the road of gender equality in the home or in paid employment' (1992, p. 131). The observation that 'There is no strict segregation of roles in such households, but male dominance still exists, even if it is not accompanied by the necessity for women to be completely imprisoned in the household' (1992, p. 130) captures neatly the degree of change that has occurred.

Warwick and Littlejohn are conscious that several forces, including the decline of employment in the coal industry and the in-migration of non-mining households as well as the growth of women's employment, have eroded the bases of local occupational communities, but they are aware too of the ways in which the coal industry continues to cast 'a long shadow over the localities'. In particular, what they identify as 'local cultural capital' is, they suggest, embodied in 'traditional social institutions' such as household and kinship networks, and it is these networks that carry 'echoes' from the past: 'Traditional social networks linking households with kin, friends and neighbours provide resources and constraints in a manner not unlike those of earlier communities, and a basis around which community identity is still maintained' (1992, pp. 15, 103, 131). They also serve a very real material purpose in the present, since 'women, particularly working-class women, regarded the task of maintaining the kinship network as important to the security of their household' (1992, p. 124). Restricted economic opportunities and cultural inheritances thus both operate to limit 'the potential for women to escape the demands and expectations of pit village life' (Waddington *et al.*, 1991, p. 91). To the extent that change in these networks is occurring, it is doing so through a process of social polarisation in which two distinct and geographically discrete social worlds can be identified, 'one for the securely employed and one for the not securely employed and those without employment' (Warwick and Littlejohn, 1992, p. 131). This change bears more than a passing resemblance to Pahl and Wallace's description of developments on Sheppey.

It is, of course, difficult to determine precisely how far such a situation can be attributed to the impact of economic restructuring and how far other influences (such as patterns of in-migration) may be seen as contributory factors. Like unemployment, geographical mobility does not necessarily have the effect of undermining local social structures and may even work to reinforce them. In Pahl's Sheppey study 61 per cent of respondents had been born elsewhere, but at least some had come 'because they had relatives already living on the Island' (1984, p. 212), and these kinship links help to explain the persistence of what Pahl calls 'the *traditions* of the Island' (1984, p. 193; emphasis in original) among what is by conventional standards a mobile population. Other writers have arrived at similar conclusions. Migrants to Coventry were also likely to reproduce the association of skill with a male workforce, the town being one in which 'old ideas die hard. The fabric of the community remains infused with its identity as a place of craftsmanship; the craftswoman is an oddity, a contradiction in terms' (Grant, 1990, p. 243). Grieco's study of the role of kin networks in securing employment opportunities for migrants found a very strong connection, and one, moreover, in which women played a pivotal role. Her account stresses 'the complexity of the community of kin that can be constructed through the female link' (1987a, p. 36), not least where migration over long distances is involved, as in the case of workers recruited to Corby from Scotland. Women's role as 'broker or recruitment agent for the male employment net' (1987a, p. 36) plays an important part in the re-creation of community in such circumstances. How typical this situation is of the impact on community life of geographical mobility is the subject of the next chapter.

# 4

## MOVING IN AND MOVING ON: THE SIGNIFICANCE OF GEOGRAPHICAL MOBILITY

The exclusive nature of many local social networks has already been noted in chapter 1, where it was observed that researchers face a number of problems in gaining entry into a community. These problems of access and acceptance face all strangers who have not had time to build up relations of trust and reciprocity in their new neighbourhood, but they are likely to be amplified for newcomers to an area who are seeking permanent rather than temporary involvement in local social life. Moving to a new locality by no means guarantees that opportunities to participate in community life will be forthcoming, and it is frequently the case that newcomers become conscious of and involved in local social networks only gradually. Their covert nature makes it difficult to gain access to what Finnegan calls 'pathways in urban living' (1989, ch. 21), as her own research on the 'hidden musicians' of Milton Keynes amply demonstrates. This chapter examines the impact of geographical mobility on social cohesion, looking specifically at processes of social acceptance, conflicts over resources and the selective character of migration.

The sociology of community furnishes numerous instances of the systematic and deliberate exclusion of in-migrants by established local groups, and while such practices might be expected to break down over time, the process of accommodation can be a lengthy one. This was the situation in the midlands suburb of 'Winston Parva' studied by Elias and Scotson (1965), in which the 'established' members of the community continued to stigmatise the most recent in-migrants as 'outsiders' and 'foreigners', notwithstanding their residence in the locality for a period of some twenty years. The study describes the resulting community structure as a 'blend of interdependence and antagonism' (1965, p. 20), and argues that the status distinctions between the 'civilised' established group and the so-called 'problem' families who made up the outsiders were all set to be reproduced into the next generation. In this case, at least, the passage of time was not sufficient to offset the mechanisms operating to exclude people who had settled in a new area and brought with them distinct cultural mores.

In other places barriers to the acceptance and integration of newcomers into local community life have been less enduring, although the patterns whereby new populations are accommodated are rarely straightforward. The diversity of the social consequences of geographical mobility reflect the greatly varying contexts in which migration takes place. The second study of Banbury carried out by Stacey and her colleagues concluded that 'no simple and close association could be assumed between social and geographic mobility and particular sets of attitudes and behaviour' (1975, p. 27), contrary to the popular expectation that migrants would be less 'locality-oriented' than native Banburians were. Distinctions between geographically mobile 'cosmopolitans' and locally born 'traditionalists' had been an oversimplification of the situation even during earlier periods of the town's history. Such lines of cleavage were subject to further erosion as time passed and Banbury society's 'many cross-cutting ties' (1975, p. 3) generated new identities and alliances alongside the old ones that persisted, confirming the finding of Stacey's first Banbury study that any tensions between newcomers and those born and brought up in the town were modified by the 'many and complicated ties of opposition and co-operation that run through Banbury society' (1960, p. 176). Banbury's relatively fluid social structure and the sustained economic expansion of the town made it a generally favourable setting in which immigrants could adjust to their new surroundings.

Geographical mobility is often associated with upward social mobility as people relocate in order to take up better-paid employment, and it is interesting to note that Lockwood pointed to residential mobility as one of the characteristics which distinguished affluent privatised workers from traditional workers. In his account privatised workers were likely to live on housing estates which 'bring together a population of strangers' (1975, p.

22) who have little in common except their experience of migration. He argues that such communities contrast sharply with occupational communities, and that in the absence of communal sociability 'workers on the estates tend to live a socially isolated, home-centred existence' (1975, p. 22). Subsequent research has shown this picture to be overdrawn. In Banbury by no means all of the immigrants were strangers to each other, many having moved there with their relocating employers (Mann, 1973; Stacey *et al.*, 1975). In addition, consciousness of the problems faced by outsiders of integrating into community life has made migrants mindful of the advantages of moving to a locality in which they already have contacts. Grieco's (1987a; 1987b) work on the role of kinship networks in directing geographical mobility is a good example of this process in action, demonstrating how the recruitment of workers to Corby from Scotland 'generated a distinct ethnic community' (1987b, p. 37) in the town. Friends may also play the role of sponsoring migration and introducing newcomers to an area's social networks, and Devine's (1992) study of Luton shows how both kin and friends can 'regroup' following long-distance geographical mobility. The Trinidadian expatriate community in Aberdeen, attracted to the city by work in the industries associated with North Sea oil, is another example of how cultural bonds can be reproduced in new settings (Clark and Taylor, 1988).

Much less is known about the situation in which communities lose numbers through out-migration, although the studies that have been conducted of the processes involved also tend to confound common-sense expectations. It has been argued that loss of population in certain circumstances leads to the strengthening of local community ties, a conclusion which appears less paradoxical when it is borne in mind that out-migrants may well be those least integrated into community life and who in consequence have least to lose by moving on. In the mining communities of West Durham, for example, it was found that migration 'tends to remove the dissenting members from the community, and this increases the social cohesiveness of those who remain' (Bulmer, 1978a, p. 36). Cohen, too, has observed that 'The strength of local culture . . . does not necessarily diminish as the locality becomes increasingly precarious' (1982, p. 7). Of course in the longer term out-migration is likely to make it difficult to sustain community traditions, as Brody (1973) found in rural Ireland. In the context of Teesside's declining heavy industrial base, 'Migration out of the area to seek work down south or abroad has further undermined community and cultural ties' (Allen, 1990, p. 195). In extreme cases economic decline runs parallel with a process of what Porteus calls 'community winding down' (1989, p. 228), eventually reaching the point at which it is possible to speak of 'the deaths of communities' (1989, p. 229). Even here, however, what is striking is the strength of people's ties to particular localities and their reluctance to follow what may appear to disinterested observers as the rational course of moving out. As was found in the study of redundant steelworkers in South Wales, the strength of 'locality attachment' (Harris, 1987, p. 101) should not be underestimated.

THE PROBLEMATIC PROCESS OF BECOMING ACCEPTED AS
A 'LOCAL'

The central theme of Elias and Scotson's classic study *The Established and the Outsiders* (1965) is not, the authors admit, what they originally set out to investigate. One of three areas in the community of Winston Parva had the reputation locally 'as a neighbourhood where delinquency was rampant' (1965, p. ix), and although its distinctiveness in terms of rates of offending was declining, its negative image proved more resilient. Elias and Scotson begin by noting that the community was divided into one middle-class and two working-class zones, but then observe that there was little solidarity between the inhabitants of the working-class zones: 'the social barriers dividing the two working-class neighbourhoods from each other were at least as great, if not greater than the barriers to social relations and communications between working-class neighbourhoods and the middle-class neighbourhood' (1965, p. 2). More puzzling still was the way in which the residents of the area stigmatised as populated by 'notorious' and 'problem' families acquiesced to this situation, seeming 'to accept the status inferiority locally accorded to their own neighbourhood' (1965, p. 2). The key to understanding the local system of ranking in which social class divisions were overridden appeared to lie in the different groups' relative length of residence.

The crucial factors distinguishing the population of the established working-class neighbourhood from that of the newer housing estate were the former's greater claim on the locality as a symbolic resource and their control over local networks of communication. The contrast was between on the one hand those inhabitants who were 'members of families who had lived in that neighbourhood for a fairly long time, who were established there as old residents, who felt that they belonged there and that the place belonged to them' (1965, p. 2) and on the other those relative newcomers who remained 'outsiders'. Within the established group certain families were particularly influential in shaping opinions, and once the positive image of 'the village' community had been set against the negative image of 'the Estate', the idea of the relationship between the two being one of opposition quickly became entrenched. The status distinctions were 'spread and maintained by a constant stream of gossip which fastened on any event in the "village" that could help to enhance the "village" community and on any event among the Estate people that could reinforce the negative picture of the Estate' (1965, pp. 18–19). The established group also denied the newcomers opportunities to defend themselves against the stereotyping to which they were subject. Feeling their status and identity to be under threat, the established group 'closed their ranks against the newcomers. They cold-shouldered them. They excluded them from all posts of social power whether in local politics, in voluntary associations or in any other local organisation where their own influence dominated' (1965, p. 18). In short, they practised social closure to consign the newcomers to a permanently inferior position.

The case of Winston Parva is not typical of all situations in which established and immigrant populations develop relations, but nor is it unique, and it is possible to identify in it certain common processes. To begin with, Elias and Scotson observe that there was among the old residents the expectation that newcomers should conform to local norms and beliefs. Had they done so, the established group might have accepted the newcomers as people in need of help if they had submitted to their patronage, had been content with taking in their status hierarchy the lower position usually allotted to newcomers at least for a probationary period by already established, more closely knit and status conscious communities. (1965, p. 17)

Given the expectation on the part of the old residents that they would 'show their willingness to "fit in" ' (1965, p. 17), the newcomers' continued attachment to patterns of behaviour regarded as normal and acceptable in their communities of origin but disapproved of by the old residents made it unlikely that tension between the two groups would be avoided. They came into conflict less in the workplace than in their leisure time, where both groups sought 'relaxation in the company and in the manner which they liked and to which they were used' (1965, p. 17). The 'noisy enjoyment' (1965, p. 18) which characterised the new-comers' pub-going habits was looked down upon by the old residents, who regarded such behaviour as the antithesis of respectability. A similar set of assumptions underlay the negative reactions of residents of seaside resorts to the arrival of 'the young migrant unemployed seeking cheap seaside accommodation and casual employment, who were seen as the harbingers of a Costa del Dole' (Buck *et al.*, 1989, p. 167). In the case of the Thanet resorts where such a link was made between social problems and 'outsiders' there was more than a little irony that 'A large part of the local population, particularly among the retired and older workers, are themselves migrants from elsewhere' (Buck *et al.*, 1989, p. 167).

The conflict between the old residents and the newcomers in Winston Parva did not prevent the development of some social ties between individual members of the two groups, but these were always within limits, and were hampered by the stereotypes which emerged, typified by the designation of the estate's population as 'foreigners'. Elias and Scotson argue that the old residents, as a relatively close-knit and coherent group in a powerful situation, established an image of themselves which idealised them favourably, being 'modelled on the "minority of the best" ' among them. In contrast, the image of the newcomers as outsiders tended 'to be modelled on the "minority of the worst" ' (1965, p. 7), inclining (as in other cases) towards denigration. Thus the estate's population was known collectively as 'Londoners' or, more derisively, 'the cockney colony', even though many of their number had originated from Durham, Lancashire, Wales and Ireland, those from London's East End simply being the most obvious and identifiable group. Similar processes were found in Banbury by Stacey and her colleagues (1975), with negative images attached both to groups of in-migrants (such as the 'Banbury Irish') and to their areas of settlement (such as 'The Aviary', a part of the town so called because it housed many workers who had moved to Banbury with their employer, Birds). Some earlier immigrants had managed to break into 'the traditional Banbury society ... based on a long-standing network of relationships between families and friends, for whom conformity, stability, conservation of established institutions were keynotes' (1975, p. 2), with marriage between the children of the two groups being an important mechanism for cementing these ties. Such assimilation was far from automatic, however, and newcomers inhabiting areas with the reputation for being 'rough' found themselves all tarred with the same brush. Elias and Scotson suggest that such tensions may be 'the normal concomitants of a process in the course of which two formerly independent groups became interdependent' (1965, p. 17), and thus indicative of the social consequences of in-migration more generally.

This view would be supported by Cohen's observation that outsiders encountering a community about which they know little 'are bound to perceive it and make sense of it in general, perhaps stereotypical, terms' (1987, p. 14). It is only with increasing knowledge of a community that its internal variations can be discerned and more subtle discriminations made, and it is not always the case that outsiders are willing to gain sufficient familiarity to do this. Nor are they necessarily capable of doing so, Cohen suggests, since much of what is symbolically significant to the members of a community may be invisible to an outsider's untutored eye. The process of stereotyping can be found to work both ways in the relationship between old residents and in-migrants, with each group lumping together all members of the other as homogeneous masses of (respectively) 'outsiders' and 'locals' while at the same time being conscious of their own group's differentiation and heterogeneity. The situation is more complex still where in-migration occurs in several stages over a lengthy period of time rather than in one rapid episode, for this adds the complication of intermediate groups whose status is ambiguous. Such a situation was found by Gilligan in his research into the social and economic life of the Cornish town of Padstow.

The tensions commonly found between insiders and outsiders were complicated in Padstow's case by the complex patterns of in-migration and out-migration which mark the town's history. A significant number of Padstow's population had moved there from elsewhere, many of them being long resident in the town, but residence in Padstow was not a sufficient condition for being considered a 'local' person. Such individuals remained 'outsiders', that is, 'persons resident in Padstow who are not classified by native Padstonians as "Padsta people" ' (Gilligan, 1987, p. 66), a distinction echoing those between 'Pentre people' and 'outsiders' (Frankenberg, 1957), 'Gosfer folk' and 'offcomers' (Williams, 1956) and 'countryfolk' and 'strangers' (Williams, 1963) which earlier generations of researchers found. Thus a woman who had lived in the town since infancy (a period of over sixty years) was conscious of being treated as an 'outsider' because she had not been born there, observing that 'When people say they are Padstonian, it means their parents and grandparents came from here – it's a matter of families' (Gilligan, 1987, p. 77). Another in-migrant with an even longer period of residence was aware that he was 'not a Padstonian by birth', although he went on to describe himself as having been 'naturalised'. At the other end of the spectrum of non-Padstonians were holiday-makers and tourists, termed 'visitors', who in some ways represented the continuation of the town's tradition of providing hospitality to temporary residents which was formerly associated with the visits of seasonal fishing fleets (Gilligan, 1984). In between these two extremes were groups of more transient residents, such as the constantly shifting populations of elderly retired migrants (seen as 'coming here to die' (Gilligan, 1987, p. 77) ) and personnel at the local Royal Air Force station, whose ambivalent position was reflected in the possibility of their being classified as either 'visitors' or 'outsiders'.

Among Padstonians, Gilligan found the greatest hostility reserved for those in-migrants whose economic activities connected with tourism were felt to be transforming the town and threatening its very identity. Unlike the outsiders who came to settle in Padstow and sought to become assimilated into local community life as far as they were allowed to by native-born

Padstonians, the 'tourism entrepreneurs from "up-country" ' (1987, p. 77) were resented for having bought up property in the town in order to cater for expanding numbers of tourists. The relatively powerful economic position of this group made them somewhat immune to the conventional mechanisms employed by Padstonians to control newcomers. Gilligan argues that traditionally Padstonians have sought to preserve local culture by setting the standards to which in-migrants are expected to adjust and conform. By 'employing a double mechanism of inclusion and exclusion, of incorporation and resistance, to deal with all non-Padstonians' they are able to allow a proportion of outsiders to become 'more or less "accepted" within certain bounded criteria' (1987, pp. 76, 79). Such sanctions are effective only against those newcomers who are concerned about being accepted and are conscious of the status which is bestowed upon those who achieve acceptance. Others less sensitive to the censure of having 'come in and taken over' have not been inhibited from speeding the commercialisation of the town, a transformation which has left Padstonians with a 'sense of dispossession and impotence' (1987, pp. 79, 80), as the town's openness to 'strangers', retired 'furriners' and tourist 'emmets' (literally 'ants') has increased.

The complex nature of local/newcomer relations in Padstow is illustrated by the fineness of the distinctions made between the various categories of outsiders. What Gilligan calls 'a sliding scale of exclusiveness' (1987, p. 80) can be seen to be in operation, ranging from the long-standing resident who had been 'naturalised' to the unwelcome 'up-country people' and 'emmets'. In addition, 'on an individual level, not all outsiders experience the overt hostility of Padstonians toward the general category of which they are members.' No single, hard-and-fast distinction between local 'Padsta people' and non-Padstonian 'outsiders' exists since a great deal depends on the context in which Padstow is being conceptualised as a community: 'different definitions and boundaries of localism operate in different contexts' (1987, pp. 79, 76). The definition of what constitutes being a Padstonian is at its most exclusive on May Day during the town's Obby Oss (hobby horse) festivities, when 'the fierce loyalty of Padstonians to "Padsta" ' (Gilligan and Harris, 1989, p. 22) is very much in evidence. Even here, however, it is possible to find degrees of insider/outsider distinctions rather than a single, sharp dividing line, since there are two hobby horses which parade on May Day, one older than the other, the newer dating back only as far as 1919. Two extended kin networks made up the core of the Old Oss supporters, and their exclusivity led to their being known locally as 'the "Closed Society" ' or 'the "Padsta Mafia" ', their meetings being 'shrouded in mystique and secrecy'. Gilligan refers to the Old Oss Party as 'this inner sanctum of Padstonian exclusiveness', constituting 'the essence of traditional Padstonian society' (1989, pp. 27, 28). By contrast, the newer Blue Ribbon Oss signified the recognition that Padstow could not survive unchanged, and its supporters had correspondingly less claim on local tradition despite also being 'Padsta born and bred' (Gilligan, 1987, p. 76).

Gilligan links the distinction between the two sets of hobby horse supporters to Padstow's economic history in which, for the town to survive, new industries like tourism have had to be nurtured in the wake of the decline of old ones such as fishing and the consequent out-migration. Thus, he argues, Padstow's development embodies the contradiction that the maintenance of tradition requires acceptance of change: 'Both the old and the new have their Osses, and both are genuinely Padsta, but the conflict between them symbolizes the contradiction between "maintenance" and "adaptation", between "tradition" and "change" ' (1990, p. 183). Any original conflicts of interest or social, religious or moral differences which may have underlain the division between the two followings in the past have less significance today, Gilligan suggests, than the dilemma which new industries like tourism present to the town's inhabitants. Tourism is associated in the minds of many Padstonians with the loss of a 'traditional way of life', and it has most certainly had very real effects. At the same time many Padstonians are dependent upon the ' "up-country" owners of capital whose shops, businesses and guest houses cater for tourists and provide the locals with employment' (Gilligan and Harris, 1989, p. 23). In this context even the most excluded in-migrants can be seen to have some claim on a place in Padstow's economic life, however much they may be denied opportunities to participate as 'locals' in the town's social and cultural networks.

Gilligan's research illustrates the general point that becoming accepted as a member of local society can be an uneven, protracted and ultimately unfinished process for in-migrants. The case of

Padstow also demonstrates that the arrival of newcomers may serve to tighten bonds between old residents, heightening their 'sense of Padstonian communal solidarity' (Gilligan, 1984, p. 108). The common bonds which are stressed in such contexts are cultural ones, invoking attachment to local heritage and traditions, but it would be an error to presume that material factors are not also germane in explaining friction between insiders and outsiders. In Padstow the resentment against 'up-country' in-migrants was due at least in part to the changes which they had wrought in the local retail and housing markets:

Local service shops have been bought up and replaced by 'tripper-trapper' shops, and such dispossession is compounded in residential terms with the displacement of Padstonians from 'downtown' to the outlying council housing estates, as outsiders have gentrified the older unmodernised slate and stone cottages. (1987, p. 78)

The presentation of a cultural critique of the newcomers by the old residents was thus interconnected with conflicts of material interests between the two groups, and this is a situation which other researchers into the impact of in-migration have also highlighted.

### GEOGRAPHICAL MOBILITY AND CONFLICTS OVER RESOURCES

Conflict over material resources between old residents and new-comers was one of Moore's principal expectations at the outset of his research into the local impact of migrant labour working in the oil industry of North-East Scotland. Moore's study focused on Peterhead, a town at the other end of Britain from Padstow, and equally remote, described as 'a very small speck on the map' with 'a tiny population' (Moore, 1982, p. 7). In other respects Peterhead was quite different, being an industrial rather than a tourist centre and one which 'receives no casual visitors' (Moore, 1982, p. 2). Moore observes that Peterhead appeared at first sight to be 'a true "community" of seafaring folk', an idea that 'is locally cultivated by Peterheadians' (1982, p. 78). The town's inhabitants conveyed a sense of belonging to an integrated community 'by reference to a common history and to a recent past when the fortunes of everyone depended upon the fishing industry'. These common bonds were reinforced by the facts that the 'majority of Peterheadians speak a common dialect, a few surnames appear again and again in the town and like any small isolated population it is heavily intermarried' (1982, p. 78). Peterhead thus exhibited many of the hallmarks of a traditional occupational community.

Moore warns that the appearance of social homogeneity in the town was deceptive, however, since there existed important divisions along lines of religious affiliation, and also familiar residential inequalities: 'There are posh and down-at-heel areas within Peterhead and posh and down-at-heel people living in them' (1982, p. 79). Distinctions between the town's 'fishing people and the remainder' and between the traditional elite and newly powerful groups indicated further lines of fragmentation, and the inescapable conclusion was that 'there is no single homogeneous Peterhead community' (1982, p. 80). The divisions within the town's population predated the area's oil-related development, and Moore argues that oil served only to make more salient these 'inter- and intra-class conflicts' (1982, p. 183). Support for or opposition to oil-related development was an important issue of local politics, with supporters arguing that such development would bring benefits to the local economy in the form of new jobs and more trade for local businesses while opponents predicted adverse effects on the local housing situation and the growth of social problems more generally as in-migration proceeded at a pace faster than that which could be managed. There were elements of truth in both arguments, although in each case Moore found that the changes that did take place (notably the growth in the employment of women in the service sector and house price inflation) reflected national trends as much as they did the local impact of oil.

Contact between local people and the in-migrant workers was in practice restricted by the latter being housed in temporary accommodation camps which 'had little effect on the local community' (1982, p. 148), but antipathy towards them remained, with one site acquiring a particularly notorious reputation. This may be explained in part by deflected hostility towards the speculators who were responsible for the presence of the workers and who were more unambiguously 'outsiders'. Also relevant in explaining the negative attitudes towards in-migrants was the fact that the development which they represented had exposed divisions in the local community and its powerlessness. Moore suggests that 'antipathies within the community' prevented the emergence of a unanimous voice, but that anyway Peterhead's experience indicated that key decisions were taken elsewhere, thus 'calling into question the whole notion of the town as an autonomous "community" which might have controlled the impact of North Sea developments' (1982, pp. 48, 8). Critics of the expansion of oil-based activities could censure particular local individuals for ' "going over" to the oil interest', but the power of such individuals was exaggerated, as was the power of local people to oppose change: 'The most significant fact about the proponents and opponents of oil related developments was that the former had little to offer incomers, beyond professional services, and the latter could do little to prevent developments' (1982, pp. 91–2).

Moore concludes that one of the most important effects of the economic changes was to demonstrate the impotence of local people in the context of decisions made by nation states and multi-national companies: 'Peterhead was being acted upon and had no part in the decisions that most closely affected its future. None of the oil-related economic growth was autonomously controlled from Peterhead nor in the interests of the town alone' (1982, pp. 167–8). Although local political debates about the desirability of attracting outsiders to Peterhead to promote oil-related develop-ment highlighted deep differences of attitudes between various sections of the town's population, in practice they had little effect on the outcome, and in this context Moore is critical of the 'sentimental rejection of oil as something threatening a way of life' (1982, p. 75). It is a romantic myth to regard Peterhead as a small fishing community which was threatened with change from outside, since the local fishing industry was already experiencing a marked shift in its fortunes, and the central question facing the townspeople was how best to respond to these changes. The situation was 'explicable more in terms of interest than sentiment' (1982, p. 75), however much people employed the familiar theme of the loss of community when discussing it. Moore rejects the view that the social impact of oil and its associated in-migration had made Peterhead ' "worse" than in the 1960s' since this was a period not of communal stability and integration but a time 'when young people left in large numbers to work in Corby, when fishing profits slumped and employment alternatives seemed remote' (1982, p. 168). A far longer period than a decade had elapsed since Peterhead bore even a remote resemblance to the 'self-contained almost self-sufficient community' (1982, p. 80) of local mythology.

There are strong parallels between Moore's Peterhead study and Giarchi's (1984) research into the impact of industrial and military development on the town of Dunoon on the west coast of Scotland. The construction of oil platforms for the North Sea oil industry and the siting of a United States nuclear submarine base in the locality both brought considerable numbers of mainly male migrants to the vicinity, and relations between these incomers and the area's established residents were characterised by a good deal of friction and on occasion active hostility. As in Peterhead, perceptions of the impact of the incomers did not always square with the reality. Giarchi found that of the local residents whom he interviewed only 8 per cent did not criticise the incomers at any time, and the list of complaints among the majority was a long one, relating to competition for scarce local resources and also to more general cultural differences.

The image of an invasion of the locality by incomers who were responsible for the decline of the local way of life contrasted with the reality of their segregation from the established residents most of the time. The industrial workers and the navy personnel lived in social worlds of their own which in practice meant that they had few points of contact with local people, and could even be said to have consciously 'shunned local involvement' (1984, p. 224). The conflicts which arose were most acute when the incomers' leisure-time activities were perceived as a 'quest for "wine, women and song" ' (1984, p. 223). Agreement about the precise impact of the incomers was impossible in the absence of any consensus about the situation before their arrival. Some local people, particularly older ones who had themselves moved to the area because of its attractive location, 'painted the past in glowing colours', but such images were not available to many of the younger generation who were more conscious of 'the ugly reality of the present' (1984, p. 114) and of the dangers of attempting to escape from this by living in the past.

Belief in the idea of a lost golden age of communal solidarity can be found in a number of different settings, but it has a particular force in rural society, where it has a long history. It is not surprising to find continuing attachment to the idea of a loss of community in contemporary villages in the wake of sustained in-migration by an urban, middle-class population of commuters and retired people. Newby *et al.*'s research in East Anglia revealed that farmers and farmworkers have been brought closer together by the changing social composition of the village as their growing consciousness of their shared distance from the newcomers worked to generate 'a common identity as "locals" ' (1978, p. 194). Originating from towns where many of them continue to work, the newcomers constitute a group of 'immigrants' who 'have brought with them an urban, middle-class lifestyle which is largely alien to the remaining local agricultural population' (Newby, 1980, p. 165). In turn, the farming population feels misunderstood, threatened and overrun by outsiders, and their ensuing 'community of feeling' or 'communion' overrides the divisions between them and 'helps what is actually a very diverse group with conflicting interests to unite and speak with one voice' (Newby *et al.*, 1978, p. 195). In this respect they were unlike the locals of Peterhead who found such unity difficult to achieve, although it should also be noted that this solidarity and the consequent representation of political issues as 'conflicts between "locals" and "interfering outsiders" ' (Newby *et al.*, 1978, p. 273) has the effect of perpetuating established power relations within the agricultural population.

Housing is one of the commonest issues over which the agricultural population and newcomers to the countryside come into conflict. In-migration by middle-class commuters has produced a situation in which newcomers 'compete with the locals, contributing to the higher demand for rural housing which, together with the restricted supply, has led to extensive changes in the nature of the rural housing market' (Newby, 1980, p. 167). Farm workers' low incomes make it difficult for them to gain access to accommodation on the open market in the face of competition from affluent newcomers, and in consequence they have become increasingly dependent on local authority housing or on tied accommodation provided by their employers. One effect of this is the creation in some villages of an 'encapsulated' community which 'consists of the rump of the former occupational community who now become a self-contained and tightly-knit group of locals, often physically encapsulated from the rest of the village in a council house estate', forming 'a community within a community' (Newby *et al.*, 1978, p. 194) or 'a village within the village' (Newby, 1980, p. 166). In other instances change in the countryside has led to still more marked segregation through the creation of 'the farm-centred community' in which the provision for workers of tied accommodation on farms pushes them into an even closer relationship with their employers.

The retreat by the remaining agricultural population into what Newby *et al.* call the ideology of 'localism', which 'lines up farmers and workers *on the same side*' (1978, p. 195; emphasis in original) against what were perceived to be threatening outside forces, was the product not only of workplace contact but also of social networks more broadly. In particular the social world of farm-workers was 'remarkably self-contained', since their 'networks of friends and kin consisted primarily of agricultural workers or workers employed in industries with somewhat similar work conditions' (Newby, 1977, pp. 361, 359). The limited nature of the contact between the agricultural population and the new-comers reflected the latter's greater independence as a group. A newcomer 'does not enter the village as a lone individual who has to win social recognition locally in order to make life tolerable', it being rather the case that newcomers can disregard 'the mores of the village; if necessary, social contacts can be established among fellow-newcomers or even outside the village altogether' (1977, pp. 329–30). Economic factors were also at work in restricting local/newcomer interaction, as the 'gulf between the resident poor and immigrant rich in the encapsulated community means that there is often little contact between the two sides' (1977, p. 330).

Pahl's (1975) study of commuter villages in Hertfordshire found similar processes of polarisation between middle-class newcomers and working-class locals, and he adds the observation that the women among the newcomers were far more active than the men in establishing and maintaining social networks. These findings were also confirmed in Connell's (1978) study of central Surrey, and Strathern's (1981) anthropological analysis of the Essex village of Elmdon, where the subtle distinction between those residents who were 'real Elmdon' (that is, genuine villagers) and those who were not pervaded every aspect of local life. Day and Murdoch's research in the more remote rural location of the Upper

Ithon valley in Powys suggests that incomers there are relatively less self-contained than comparable groups in commuter areas. New residents are under greater pressure to 'enter social life on terms set by the existing population' who enjoy the advantage of 'a well-integrated local network' (1993, p. 108) in which traditional, farm-orientated culture continues to predominate. In the context of developments in the housing market, however, there was a perception that 'English people are coming in and taking over the area' (1993, p. 107), and this issue was a source of considerable local friction.

In general, newcomers to the countryside are socially and economically self-reliant to a degree which is unusual among migrants, but in other respects their impact on local social life has parallels elsewhere. In-migration has undoubtedly been a major factor in the transformation of rural society, but it is more appropriate to see the newcomers' arrival as coincidental with the demise of the traditional occupational community of farmworkers rather than as a cause of it. Migration from the countryside predates the arrival of the newcomers and reflects the long-term decline in job opportunities in agriculture, and it is this process that has allowed them 'to be replaced in many areas by commuters, retired couples and weekend-cottagers' (Newby, 1977, p. 329). However much the residual agricultural population may direct its hostility towards these strangers, identified variously as 'newcomers/outsiders/aliens' (Newby *et al.*, 1978, p. 194), their presence is merely a symptom of the deeper restructuring of the rural economy akin to those changes responsible for the erosion of the 'traditional' working-class communities of urban Britain outlined in earlier chapters. Indeed, there are striking similarities to the situation found in towns such as Swindon, where 'The influx of migrants is associated with a (romanticized) loss of community' (Bassett *et al.*, 1989, p. 77). Swindon's past is often remembered as the occupational community of a railway town, but in-migration is merely one aspect of the more general processes of economic restructuring in which 'Working class solidarity, collectivism and community ties have given way to home-centred individualism and social fragmentation' (1989, p. 83). Put another way, it is not only geographical mobility which promotes the adoption of 'privatised' lifestyles.

There is an assumption underlying much of the literature on
migration and community that the integration of newcomers into
local social networks is a norm towards which developments will
tend over the longer term, even though the evidence on this point
is far from conclusive. Indeed, the lesson to be drawn from several
of the studies discussed above seems to be that the arrival of in-
migrants frequently creates or reshapes local patterns of spatial
and social segregation rather than eliminating them, although the
precise course of events will depend on factors such as their
numbers and resources relative to those of the established local
population. Other things being equal, in-migrants will be in a
stronger position where they already have contacts in their new
locality, as occurs, for example, with chain migration. Similarly,
the established local population will generally be less able to
practise social closure against newcomers where their own
numbers have been denuded by out-migration. In such situations
the people remaining are often those with fewest resources.
Certainly it is true that migration is a selective process. In inner-
city areas, for example, it is 'the younger men or couples, with
more skill, more confidence and higher incomes, who are most
likely to move out' (Archbishop of Canterbury's Commission on
Urban Priority Areas, 1985, p. 14). In contrast, and unsurprisingly, it is among 'the old and the poor, the unskilled, the single-
parent families, the sick, and the unemployed' (1985, p. 14) that
the lowest rates of migration are recorded.

   The selective character of migration is also demonstrated by
research which has shown very definite patterns relating to
migrants' destinations. R.G.A. Williams has pointed out that it is
possible to preserve ties of kinship even when the migration
involved is on a large scale as it was in the case of London, arguing
that 'local kinship is continuously re-created through a variety of
migration strategies' (1983, p. 386). The reproduction in a new
locality of social networks among kin and friends is something of
an 'art' (Williams, 1981), and the 'conservative migration' which
produces it is far from accidental, even if it is not planned in a
formal sense. There is, for example, a greater propensity to
migrate and regroup at certain points in the life course, including
its later stages, when parents commonly move to be closer to their

(adult) children. Wenger notes that 'Proximity to children increases with age and widowhood' (1984, p. 73), the younger generation thus acting as pioneers in a new locality. Regrouping may even occur in opposition to formal planning, as it did, for example, in the chain migration which occurred in the movement from inner-London to the New Towns (Deakin and Ungerson, 1977). It has occurred also among refugees from Vietnam, who have responded to Home Office plans to disperse them by moving from their first areas of settlement in order 'to be closer to relatives and friends' (Dalglish, 1989, p. 128).

Patterns of migration are also commonly found to be structured around kinship ties where migrants are able to secure access to work opportunities for their relatives. Family networks were at the heart of the chain migration discovered by Grieco, who describes how

Migrants who have been successful in obtaining employment transfer resources and information on employment opportunities back to their families in their area of origin. ... These 'spearhead' migrants are important in inducing further migration from the home area. ... Eventually a clustering of family members in the new location occurs. (1987a, p. 51)

Grieco argues that such migration is more usual among working-class families than middle-class ones, and that employers may collaborate in this process of keeping employment 'in the family'. Employers adopting these 'bulk recruitment practices' (1987a, p. 85) included the steel industry in the midlands New Town of Corby which recruited workers from other parts of Britain, notably Scotland. During the period 1956–60, for example, over 400 workers left for Corby from the town of Peterhead, where declining job opportunities following the contraction of the fishing industry made out-migration an attractive option.

Grieco's work confirms the hypothesis developed first by sociologists of the Chicago School that kinship networks operate to promote chain migration by channelling information about job vacancies and by providing residential aid to new migrants. In the context of limited opportunities for private renting which was characteristic of New Towns like Corby, 'relatives and friends take on additional importance as major suppliers of accommodation' (1987a, p. 106). Grieco goes on to argue that in terms of their restricted housing options and their subjection to stigmatisation as newcomers to the locality, the experience of the Scottish migrants to Corby 'closely parallels that of ethnic entry to the inner city' (1987a, p. 106). Identifiable as a distinct group by their accent, the newcomers to Corby remained a separate community who were 'on the whole, *socially unconnected* to the indigenous population' (1987a, p. 103; emphasis in original). Grieco is also keen to stress women's importance in maintaining kinship networks across geographical distance, since 'wives may play a major part in servicing and managing the links between their husband and his kin' (1987a, p. 36). Alongside these kinship links, friendship ties also operated to secure the regrouping of communities following migration, although kinship was without question the stronger of the two.

It is interesting to note that a significant proportion of the workers who migrated from Peterhead to Corby in the wake of the fishing industry's decline were later to move back to North-East Scotland in response to the boom associated with North Sea oil. In part this reflected the contraction of the steel industry in Corby in the 1970s, but it indicated too Grieco's more general point about the advantages which migrants enjoy when they already have contacts in an area. Not least among these advantages was access to accommodation, and Grieco notes that 'All of the return migrants in the study received residential aid from kin' (1987a, p. 162). Other researchers have also found evidence of return migration and the importance of maintained kinship networks in facilitating this. Taylor (1979), working on coal miners returning to County Durham from the midlands, notes that it is difficult to determine precisely what motivates people to retrace their steps, since their justifications are prompted in part by fear of being seen to have 'failed'. Unfavourable comparison of the midlands mining areas to the Durham villages was framed in terms of the merits of 'the old and tried ways of the Durham mining community' (1979, p. 486), even though there were signs all around that the village institutions were subject to

long-term and deep-rooted processes of decay. The overgrown gardens and allotments, the unpainted and flaking exteriors, the unkempt war memorial, the Welfare Hall still advertising Bingo games which were played three years ago, were all due, in part, to migration. (1979, p. 487)

Cohen has observed that remote communities in general 'face a perennial threat of depopulation' (1987, p. 17), and meet it by nurturing a sense of collective identity to which individuals are committed. Economic pressures to leave thus need to be set against social and emotional attachments to the area which operate as pressures to stay or to return, although Townsend *et al.*'s account of the mining villages of County Durham sees disappearing job opportunities leading to 'the young being forced to move away', despite the 'close-knit character and deep sense of identity' (1988, p. 90) found in their communities.

It is necessary to take into account the costs of migration in terms of the loss of everyday contact with kin and friends if phenomena such as return migration to areas of high unemployment are to be understood. Such community ties also help to explain the durability of people's attachments to localities, both in former times and more recently. Jordan *et al.*'s research on a deprived council housing estate in Exeter found such kinship and community ties to be central to the routines of everyday life and a major reason for not wanting to move. The study describes how 'men learn to be workers and providers within their networks of male relatives and friends, which in turn give them information, help with transport, and assistance with home improvements; they are socialised and sustained by kin and community.' A similar situation was found among women, whose 'employment, as much as their caregiving, is enabled by female kin and neighbours' (1992, p. 255), and in the context of such networks of interdependence it is not difficult to see why individuals would regard moving to other locations as undesirable, even though they were living in 'an area of some notoriety' (1992, p. 254). For all its problems, the community provided them with a 'culture with which they were familiar . . . where they got support and a sense of membership' (1992, p. 7), and they would give these things up only with reluctance. Harris refers to such 'network embeddedness' in his account of the limited mobility out of Port Talbot following redundancies among steelworkers, most of whom agreed with the statement that 'moving away from my family and friends would be a very great hardship' (1987, p. 101).

An important influence on people's preparedness to consider moving from an area is their perception of their place in its community structure, however much at variance with reality that perception is. Bellaby's research in Stoke-on-Trent notes that 'migration in and out of the Potteries is and has been exceptionally low', a fact which is explained locally by reference to 'the links of family and kinship between community and workplace' (1987, p. 55). As a result, 'people often say they do not want to move from the Potteries, however much better job prospects may be elsewhere, because their roots are in the area' (1987, p. 55). This 'folk model' of the community was found by Bellaby to be at variance with the evidence which he collected on kinship ties at the workplace, where fewer than half of his shop-floor sample had any such ties, thus casting doubt on the presumed presence of 'continuity between their experiences in home, community and work' (1987, p. 57). The perpetuation of the 'myth' of an occupational community Bellaby explains in terms of local power relations, since it was employed by both managers and workers 'to give a natural, unnegotiable appearance to male dominance over women in production . . . naturalising the inequalities of class, age and gender among the workforce' (1987, pp. 60, 63) and in the process legitimising the status quo.

To the extent that people's perceptions of local social relationships are at variance with reality they can be considered to be living in 'imagined communities' (Anderson, 1991). Pahl argues that the 'communities in the mind' (1975, p. 36) of middle-class newcomers to the countryside were at odds with the reality of villages whose heterogeneous populations did not constitute a 'community' as such, but rather discrete groups moving in separate worlds. A similar point has been made by Wright about the middle-class incomers to Stoke Newington whose imaginative 'appreciation of the remaining past has facilitated their settlement in the area', contributing to its gentrification since the 1960s. Other local people, in particular the area's ethnic-minority communities, are less oblivious to 'the greyness, the filth and the many evidences of grinding poverty', and hold profoundly different senses of place to those of the white middle class. In sum, 'People live in different worlds even though they share the same locality: *there is no single community*' (1989, pp. 284, 285, 290; emphasis in original). Wright suggests that 'Stoke Newington is fairly typical of many inner-city areas in which a white working class coexists with a diversity of minority groups and an incoming middle class' (1989, p. 282). The complexity of the patterns of social relationships found in such areas has been the subject of extensive research in recent years, and it is this topic to which the next chapter is devoted.

# 5

## ETHNICITY, SOLIDARITY AND EXCLUSION: RACE AND SPATIAL SOCIAL SEGREGATION

One of the principal conclusions reached in the previous chapter was that geographical mobility frequently results in social segregation, with newcomers being restricted to certain areas of a locality and developing only limited social contacts with established residents. Nowhere in Britain is this phenomenon more pronounced than in the case of minority ethnic groups, whose social segregation is so 'marked and enduring' (S. Smith, 1989a, p. 18) that geographical mobility alone is clearly insufficient to explain it. The exclusion practised against 'outsiders' has an added dimension where ideas about 'racial' differences are involved, and ethnicity continues to exert a powerful influence on where an individual lives independently of how long ago migration occurred. Not only has social segregation along ethnic lines survived when it might have been expected to diminish with the passage of time, it is also the case that in particular places physical separateness has become more prominent. In Birmingham, for example, official statistics indicate that 'urban segregation is increasing', with inner-city districts becoming predominantly black and Asian while the outer city areas remain 'as White as Torquay' (Rex, 1988, p. 31), and this type of situation can be found in many other urban areas, as well as at a regional level (S. Smith, 1989a). The adequacy of different explanations of this segregated pattern of residence may be a matter of disagreement but the reality of manifest and persistent social segregation along ethnic lines is itself beyond dispute. The first two sections of this chapter describe the patterns of segregation which have occurred and the different explanations given for it. The final section concentrates specifically on the ways in which social policies have influenced ethnic segregation.

Attempts to explain the enduring connection between social segregation and ethnicity have a long and controversial history. The writings of members of the Chicago School which date back to the earlier part of the twentieth century are of vital significance in this context since these ideas have provided a starting point for a variety of later considerations of the subject. For some researchers this examination of the writings of Robert Park and his colleagues is primarily a critical, path-clearing exercise whereby the 'myths' underpinning their work are exposed, allowing 'the debris of Chicago' (Cohen, 1985, p. 28) to be removed before going on to develop alternative theories stressing the symbolic nature of community. Other commentators have drawn more positive conclusions about the utility of the Chicago School's legacy, arguing that the 'specific, researchable questions' (D. Smith, 1988, p. 132) asked by Park and his fellow sociologists continue to have great relevance to the study of patterns of urban life. It is possible to combine elements of both positions by recognising that the empirical tradition inspired by the Chicago sociologists has produced a number of invaluable studies investigating the extent of segregation without granting sufficient recognition to the fact that 'segregation has *meaning*, in social, political and economic terms, quite irrespective of the degree of spatial separation it entails' (S. Smith, 1989a, p. 15; emphasis in original). Clearly much hangs upon not only how social segregation is to be measured but also the logically prior question of how it is to be defined.

There is, of course, no consensus about precisely what constitutes segregation, nor about the appropriateness of terms such as 'zones', 'colonies' and modern 'ghettos' in the analysis of segregation patterns. In the absence of agreement on these matters several conflicting interpretations have emerged of situations approximating to the hypothetical case where the white population is 'uniformly distributed across the whole city, but the black population ... remain concentrated in the central area' (Peach, 1981, p. 20). Cashmore and Troyna regard it as improper in such circumstances to use the term 'ghetto' since 'there is nothing approaching all black areas on a large scale in any UK city' (1983, p. 103). They do go on to doubt the voluntary nature of the segregated patterns of residence that do exist, however, stressing instead the prominence of economic constraints in the lives of migrant settlers. In contrast, Robinson suggests that residential segregation in Blackburn could be described as 'massive' and 'substantial' (1986, pp. 130, 151), but accounts for this and for the tendency of the average Asian in the city to 'become progressively more residentially isolated' (1986, p. 131) in terms of cultural as well as structural forces. An implication of this latter approach is that segregation can be regarded as positively valued and sought after by at least some minority ethnic groups.

The issue of how accurate it is to represent patterns of segregation as the outcome of choice is a complex one, not least because the presence of divisions within the ethnic minority population makes generalisation hazardous. Robinson's (1986) work indicates that different groups may be 'encapsulated' to greater or lesser degrees according to factors such as country of origin and religious affiliation, with East African Asians more assimilated than their South Asian counterparts. Within the latter group Pakistani Muslims were found to be more encapsulated than either Sikhs or Gujurati Hindus. Another study plots the positions of Pakistanis in Britain along an 'incapsulation continuum' (Anwar, 1985, p. 210) according to their occupations, with night-shift workers the most highly segregated and professionals the least. It can also be argued that the social isolation of women is greater than that of men in certain ethnic-minority communities such as the Chinese (Baxter and Raw, 1988). Werbner (1988) found a further basis of diversity among Pakistani women in Manchester whose involvement in more or less exclusive social networks varied according to their economic situation, greater 'openness' being associated with lower-income groups.

In addition, the question of the extent to which segregated patterns of social networks are chosen leads on to consideration of where in physical terms the people engaged in those networks are located. As Sarre and his colleagues have noted, it is possible to accept that 'voluntary aspects matter' in determining who lives where and at the same time to stress the vital importance of recognising that 'cultural preferences for ethnic clustering do not provide a complete explanation of a pattern in which ethnic concentrations invariably coincide with the poorest residential areas' (Sarre *et al.*, 1989, p. 37). It is reasonable to assume that people do not freely choose to live in the most disadvantaged environments when other options are available to them, and such reasoning has led Rex to the conclusion that segregation 'has been imposed upon dark-skinned immigrant communities' (1988, p. 31). Several researchers have been led to focus their attention on the ways in which what Henderson and Karn call 'racial concentrations' (1987, p. 9) are the product of racial bias and discrimination embedded in institutions such as local authority housing departments and schools. Structural explanations in terms of the operation of these institutions make up a crucial part of accounting for who lives where and how unequal residential patterns are reproduced and amplified.

ZONES, GHETTOS AND THE MEANING OF 'SEGREGATION'

The writings of the Chicago School have had an enormous influence on the development of sociology in a number of branches of the discipline (Bulmer, 1984; D. Smith, 1989), but it is in the field concerned with race relations and patterns of urban segregation that their legacy is arguably at its 'most significant and enduring' (Harvey, 1987, p. 120). Park's 'race relations cycle' portrayed successive immigrant groups as passing through various stages of adjustment to their new cultural environment and envisaged this process leading ultimately to their assimilation, but only after a period of competition with more established local groups which was likely to be resolved by the latter themselves moving to a new area. The model inspired a generation of sociologists to probe the kaleidoscope of Chicago's diverse patterns of collective existence from seemingly every angle, their reports recording the multiplicity of vibrant and contrasting ways of life found co-existing within the city. Subsequently the analysis of urban life in terms of 'human ecology' fell into disuse, having been brought into question on several grounds. Notable among the Chicago School's shortcomings were the 'uncritical and limited empiricism' (Mellor, 1977, p. 237) of many of its investigators, its 'intrinsically American hatred of deviation and radicalism' (Madge, 1970, p. 125), and its theoretical underpinning by the presumption of a long-term trend towards the re-establishment of cultural conformity (Cohen, 1985). Bell and Newby make the further suggestion that the approach declined as Chicago became 'overstudied' (1971, p. 94).

Having said this, the work of the Chicago School remains relevant to contemporary sociology since it directs attention to the dynamic nature of the relations between ethnic groups and the structural processes leading them into conflict. In addition it raises as a research issue the need to identify the reasons why ethnicity has proved such a powerful organising principle of community life within modern cities. The influence of Park and his colleagues on the research agenda in modern Britain can be seen through the terminology and analytical frameworks used in studies such as those of Patterson (1965) and Rex and Moore (1967). Patterson's study of West Indian immigrants in Brixton was framed explicitly in terms of 'zones' of settlement and the emergence of a 'ghetto', and embodied the assumption that such segregation was undesirable from the point of view of delaying absorption of new citizens into the dominant culture. Ghettos were problematic because of their tendency 'to perpetuate minority group values and traits, to limit social and cultural contacts between newcomers and local people, to reinforce local views on the alienness of the newcomers, and so to retard ultimate integration or assimilation' (1965, p. 195). Physical segregation was explained as the outcome of the cultural strangeness of the migrants' new environment:

In spite of overcrowding and physical discomfort, the incipient 'ghetto' in which most West Indians live in Brixton eases the immediate processes of adjustment and adaptation for the newcomers. It provides something of an oasis where they can relax among their own people. (1965, p. 194)

There are echoes here of the accounts of Chicago's slum areas of the 1920s in which their attraction for minority ethnic communities was attributed to the welcoming familiarity of the culture found there (Madge, 1970).

In their study of Sparkbrook in inner Birmingham, arguably 'the most widely read book on race relations within a British context' (Eldridge, 1980, p. 156), Rex and Moore took the Chicago School's notion of differentiated residential zones in cities as the explicit starting point of their investigation into the relationship between race and community life. They accepted the idea that in each zone there existed 'a relatively self-sufficient and internally integrated sub-community' (1967, p. 8), segregated from the sub-communities of the surrounding zones, and involved in a complex process of residential succession as established groups moved to the outer parts of the city. Following the migration of more affluent and 'respectable' groups from inner areas to the suburbs,

Their deserted homes then pass to a motley population consisting on the one hand of the city's social rejects and on the other of newcomers who lack the defensive communal institutions of the working class, but who defend themselves and seek security within some sort of colony structure. (1967, pp. 8–9)

Rex and Moore challenged the idea that the inhabitants of this 'zone of transition' enjoyed 'a happy segregated community life of their own', since they were likely to develop resentment against their disadvantaged position, particularly when their efforts to follow others to 'the most desired style-of-life in the suburbs' (1967, p. 9) were frustrated. Community life in such inner-city areas was understood as having a transitional character, so that 'the communal institutions which it evolves are to be regarded as a means of fighting discrimination and providing temporary security until some kind of outward move can be made' (1967, p. 9). Segregation on a more permanent basis and the denial of opportunities which this entailed carried with it the sombre prospect of intensified social conflict.

The Sparkbrook research undertaken by Rex and Moore found little evidence of immigrant groups regarding assimilation into the dominant culture as a genuine option, due either to the long-term objective of returning to their country of origin or to their experience of discrimination. Among the latter group, 'The situation of most immigrants desiring assimilation is that they do encounter discrimination and that each step which they take to claim rights in the host society, especially the right to a home, encounters opposition' (1967, p. 283). In this context it made sense for individuals to 'try to improve their living conditions in the area where they are or try to find some area less desirable than the suburbs as a secondary area of settlement' (1967, p. 283). Such areas were characterised by 'a mixed population of varying degrees of permanence and conflicting interests' (1967, p. 284), and the deep-rooted nature of the resultant friction posed serious problems for both local community organisations and wider policy-making bodies. Sparkbrook's population of almost 18,000 was notably heterogeneous, juxtaposing people of English and Irish origins, West Indians and Pakistanis, along with smaller numbers of

Indians, Cypriots, Poles and Arabs, all of whom had distinct
migration histories and social characteristics. The racial, class and
status divisions existing between and within these groups made it
nonsensical to speak of Sparkbrook as a coherent 'community'.

Having identified 'three Sparkbrooks' according to their different types of housing, Rex and Moore found 'no coloured
immigrants in Sparkbrook 3' (1967, p. 49) even though non-white
minorities made up an estimated 14 per cent or more of
Sparkbrook's population overall. This suggested 'a considerable
degree of segregation within Sparkbrook as a whole', although on
a still more local level, individual houses and streets were
frequently found to have 'markedly unsegregated populations'
(1967, p. 53), highlighting the problematic nature of the concept
of segregation. Sparkbrook in the 1960s could thus be described as
an area which was 'partially segregated' (1967, p. 41), but
becoming increasingly so due to the highly selective nature of
patterns of in-migration and out-migration. Rex and Moore
argued that local authority housing policies contributed to this
situation by being in practice discriminatory, even if this was an
unintended consequence. In the absence of positive political
interventions to prevent it, the discernible 'drift towards racial
segregation' (Rex, 1973, p. 135) in areas like Sparkbrook could be
predicted to continue.

The theme of relations between the various groups in inner-city
locations inevitably involving conflict is one that was developed in
P. Cohen's (1984) analysis of social change in London's dockland.
The East End has a history of providing 'a kind of unofficial
"reception centre" for a succession of immigrant communities'
(1984, p. 109) going back several centuries (Eade, 1989; Hobbs,
1989), and over this time a pattern of integration of new groups
emerged which was not unlike that described by the sociologists of
the Chicago School. Cohen argued that immigrants were very
definitely not assimilated, but were rather involved in a process
whereby

each new subcommunity, in turn and over time, became an accepted, but
differentiated part of the 'East End' by allying itself with the longer
established sections of the community against another, later sub-
community. The outsiders become established, become insiders, by
dissociating themselves from an even more conspicuous set of outsiders.
(1984, p. 109)

He then suggested that this pattern of integration had been sustained by the area's traditions of extensive kinship networks, the ecology of its working-class neighbourhoods and the diverse structure of the local economy, all of which had made possible the incorporation of newcomers over the longer term.

The East End's capacity to integrate new groups of immigrants within a fluid local social system was for Cohen exemplified by the Jews, whose initial 'pariah' status was overcome by first social and then geographical mobility. For many Jews, 'the distance from Bethnal Green to Golders Green was two generations', repeating the pattern of earlier immigrants in their tendency to 're-emigrate from the East End to the outer ring of middle-class suburbs' (Cohen, 1984, p. 112) once they had become established. Others who were unable to secure a foothold among the 'respectable working class' were vulnerable to social exclusion as 'outsiders' and found themselves made scapegoats as the supposed cause of the community's problems. Cohen argued that this system began to break down in the 1950s as the redevelopment of the area commenced, resulting in its social structure being profoundly altered. In particular, he identified the 'respectable working class' as 'traditionally the social cement of the community' (1984, p. 117), and claimed that the wholesale geographical relocation of large numbers of its members together with the economic marginalisation of those who remained deprived the community of effective political leadership and left neighbourhood relations in a state of crisis.

One broad conclusion which can be drawn from the work of writers such as Rex and Moore and Cohen is that little evidence exists of recent immigrant groups to Britain becoming integrated into the established social and political organisations of the white working class. In the context of limited social contact between white and minority ethnic groups in inner-city areas like the East End it is not surprising to find mutual misunderstanding and intolerance. For example, Cornwell's study of Bethnal Green reports that almost all of her (white) respondents 'expressed some degree of hostility towards the local population of Bengalis and towards West Indians and Asians more generally'. Minority groups were objected to on the grounds that they were seen as being 'more interested in maintaining a separate cultural identity than in becoming more "like us"' (1984, p. 53). The conception of 'community' which underpins such prejudice is, of course, an ideological construction, and a peculiar one at that in its expectation that newcomers with very different experiences and traditions can quickly and easily fit into the local area's pre-existing institutional arrangements. A similar naivety was found by Eade (1989) among those white Labour Party activists in the East End who attempted to incorporate the Bangladeshi population into their already formulated perceptions of politics in class terms, and who were forced to adopt a more flexible approach in order to find common ground.

Events in Spitalfields conformed to the Chicago School's model in several respects. Residential succession was clearly underway as the Bangladeshi population rose in the context of white out-migration and overall population decline in the ward: 'As in other urban areas of Britain with large concentrations of ethnic minorities Bangladeshis appeared to be taking over space that white residents did not want or wanted less keenly than space elsewhere' (Eade, 1989, p. 28). The process of chain migration produced a situation in which most of the settlers came from the Sylhet district of Bangladesh, and in consequence had religious affiliations and dialect in common. Estimates suggested that Bangladeshis constituted 13 per cent of the population of the borough of Tower Hamlets but almost half of the population of Spitalfields, and within the ward there was further segregation, since 'Bangladeshi settlers were mainly confined to council blocks from which white residents had moved or to the quickly disappearing privately rented accommodation in Central Spital-fields and the streets immediately east of Brick Lane' (1989, p. 28). This 'broad separation between whites and Bangladeshis' (1989, p. 29) was found not only in the field of housing but also in the spheres of education and employment, with the result that segregation could be understood as resulting in sharply contrasting lifestyles.

A further study of Bethnal Green found several white respondents holding racially prejudiced views, and objecting to members of minority ethnic groups on the grounds that 'They're just not like us' (Holme, 1985, p. 22). Holme argues that although such attitudes are framed in terms of skin colour and different cultural habits, their presence has to be understood in the context of the adverse material conditions within which people live, and their lack of a historical perspective: 'It is ever the case that each generation, absorbed in the impact of the current wave of immigrants, forgets how previous ones have become assimilated' (1985, p. 36). Put another way, the presence of ethnic minority groups in inner-city areas is problematic only from certain points of view, and these are contestable. This is the conclusion of Wallman's research in the Battersea area of South London, which 'does not find race or ethnic relations a central or even a consistently important issue' despite being conducted in 'a mixed inner-city area'. For Wallman, a person or a household's 'national/regional/racial origin' is only one of several characteristics that affect the way in which they 'relate to the area and people around them' (1984, p. 2), and it is by no means always prominent in her respondents' accounts of their everyday lives. The 'Battersea style' involves placing 'emphasis on local over ethnic identity, and on heterogeneous over homogeneous forms', despite the presence locally of 'plenty of scope for ethnic solidarity or discrimination (1984, p. 6). It goes without saying that these findings do not sit easily alongside 'popular expectations' (Wallman, 1982, p. 3) based on conventional wisdom.

In Wallman's account, crucial importance is attached to the distinction between ethnic categories and ethnic groups which is fundamental to the study of ethnicity (Watson, 1977). Ethnic categories are designated by outsiders who seek to sort people 'on the basis of their origins without reference to how they behave or feel. The same people do not form a *group* unless they identify together from the inside, whether for purposes of action or affect' (1984, pp. 15–16, emphasis in original). Wallman's anthropological methodology leads her to conclude that ethnic categories have only a limited bearing on the everyday existence and experiences of the population of Battersea, and highlights instead the complex way in which boundaries between groups are defined and understood. As was noted in chapter 1, Battersea has an established reputation for attaching more significance to length of residence than to ethnic origin in determining who counts as an 'insider' and who does not, with the result that 'neither colour nor language nor the presence of "blacks" or "foreigners" are central or persistent issues' (1984, p. 8). To illustrate this point, Wallman cites the example of the allocation of local authority housing where the issue was posed in terms of competition between 'locals' (that is, established residents) and 'outsiders', understood as people without 'long-standing connections or kin in the area'. In this setting, consideration of ethnic affiliation was 'beside the point' (1984, p. 9). Similarly, vulnerability to unemployment in Battersea was found to be inversely related to length of residence, but 'largely independent of birthplace or colour', adding further support to the view that 'Battersea's style is at once localist and a-ethnic' (1984, p. 7). Clark's (1987) study of responses to redundancy which was also carried out in Battersea suggested that ethnicity did have an influence, but his explanation of this finding in terms of different groups' social networks is consistent with Wallman's general theme.

The disparities between Wallman's conclusions and the findings of researchers investigating ethnicity and segregation in other localities may be accounted for in part by reference to the peculiarities of Battersea, and in particular its diversity and openness. Battersea is characterised by an 'unusually wide variety of resource stock and relatively open access to it' (1984, p. 6). In economic terms the presence of many ' "gates" of entry' (Wallman, 1985, p. 194) into work opportunities has meant that 'No incoming population category has been exclusively associated with one industry or one industrial role, and there is no evidence of ethnic niches or ethnic-specific patterns of employment' (1984, p. 7), while in the housing sphere the situation is similarly 'mixed'. In Bow, by contrast, '94% of housing is publicly owned, so residents do not have the same range of choice concerning how they will live, where they will live, whether to buy or sell, whether and when to move' (Wallman, 1986, p. 239). At the same time, the methodological and theoretical stance of Wallman's study needs to be considered as a factor contributing to the distinctiveness of her findings, since one of her principal concerns was to challenge mainstream assumptions about the equation of inner-city life with 'race' and with social problems. Wallman questioned the legitimacy of associating 'disadvantage, the inner city and minority ethnic status' (1982, p. 2) and suggested that such associations reflected the dominant research perspective: 'more attention has been paid to "vertical" relations, between ethnic communities and the majority establishment than to "horizontal" relations among the people sharing any one residential space' (1982, p. 4). A very different picture emerged from focusing attention on group membership rather than relations between categories of people, including the finding by one of Wallman's research team that out-migration was not widely sought: 'the majority of respondents have no plans to move out of the neighbourhood' (Dhooge, 1982, p. 121), fewer than 10 per cent disliking the area sufficiently to want to leave.

Battersea's non-white population can be considered more established than that of East London, for example, since 'By 1978 most of the Caribbean-born had been settled for a generation' while a further 15 per cent of the local population had been 'born in Britain with one or both parents born in the New Commonwealth' (Wallman, 1984, p. 14). The general conclusion reached is that over time ethnic origin becomes 'relatively insignificant' in people's everyday lives, having 'markedly less effect on local involvement than age, family cycle, work commitments and social class', and implying that 'incomers of any origin can "become insiders" on the basis of long residence or active participation in local activities' (Dhooge, 1982, p. 123). This pattern has been reinforced by the absence of close-knit social networks typical of 'Very homogeneous (dockland type) areas' (Wallman, 1985, p. 195), discussed in chapter 2 as 'occupational communities'. The links of Battersea's established population with kin and friends were not exclusive but 'dispersed in a way which makes the integration of newcomers feasible' (Dhooge, 1982, p. 120). Women's significance in these networks of local social contacts is reflected in their identification as 'kin keepers' (1982, p. 114) and in the recognition of their role in establishing and maintaining local ties more generally. In this environment, consciousness of segregation was notably absent, as was the feeling that Battersea was 'the kind of place in which no one with any options would choose to live' (Wallman, 1982, p. 2). Such a view is more likely to be held by those who see inner-city life in terms of ethnic categories than of those cognisant of the complexity and fluidity of ethnic-group identities.

MIGRANT NETWORKS, CULTURAL PREFERENCE AND
ENCAPSULATION

It will be apparent that the assumption of a uniform 'race relations cycle' is untenable in the light of the evidence showing the diversity

of various immigrant groups' situations and experiences. If it is
acknowledged that acceptance and assimilation are by no means
automatic outcomes, the task arises of identifying the factors
which have caused some ethnic groups to be subject to more
marked social segregation and exclusion than others. An initial
hypothesis in answer to the question of why certain minority
groups lead lives which are manifestly more self-contained or
'encapsulated' relates to their patterns of migration. It has already
been noted in chapter 4 that 'chain migration' can produce the
effective re-establishment of dense, close-knit networks of kinship
and friendship in new localities, and several studies have confirmed the occurrence of this process among South Asian immigrants to Britain (Anwar, 1985; Shaw, 1988; Werbner, 1984).
Chain migration has been defined as 'the movement in which
prospective migrants learn of opportunities, are provided with
transportation and have initial accommodation and employment
arranged by means of primary social relationships with previous
migrants', and such support networks have been identified as a
major element in the process of 'ethnic neighbourhood formation'
(Anwar, 1985, pp. 14, 19). As initial settlement patterns are
reinforced by chain migration, so 'incapsulation' may well result,
as it has done frequently among Pakistanis, who find themselves
geographically clustered and locked into 'multiplex relations and a
close-knit type of network . . . [which] makes for consistent moral
pressure on individuals and conservatism' (1985, pp. 15–16). Such
networks may be founded on a number of different bases,
including friendship and religious or political affiliations, but the
single most important basis is usually kinship.

The way in which migration occurs can thus have a powerful
bearing on not only where migrants settle but also their subsequent opportunities and obligations. Ballard has observed of South
Asians that

In the course of settlement in Britain aggregations based upon common-
alities of religion, area of origin, caste and most especially kinship have
grown up, and the greater part of most migrants' domestic and social
interactions are now conducted within arenas ordered in these terms.
(1982, p. 180)

By no means all immigrant groups will be enmeshed in such
networks, of course, but it is instructive to note that 'It is in

principle possible, by tracing chains of migrants, to account for virtually the whole Pakistani population of Oxford' (Shaw, 1988, p. 22). Shaw suggests that similar concentrations of Pakistani migrants from particular villages settled in other places such as Huddersfield, Rochdale and Glasgow, and that while these chains had small beginnings, they have led to the establishment of interconnected populations of several thousands. Shaw estimated that Oxford's Pakistani community numbered between three and four thousand, most of them concentrated in East Oxford, where they were able to maintain their distinctive cultural traditions, or at least variants of them. Anwar's study of Pakistanis in Rochdale arrives at similar conclusions, and argues that the kinship and friendship networks around which chain migration was based have contributed to 'the persistence of ethnic values and norms among the Pakistanis in Britain', not least because of the obligations which are written into the 'networks of sponsorship and patronage' (1985, p. 26) through which chain migration is effected.

The different experiences of migration reported by early migrants, the 'pioneers' (Ballard and Ballard, 1977, p. 28), and more recent settlers reflect in part the growing presence of women in minority ethnic communities. The arrival of wives and families of male migrants signalled the end of the phase of migration during which it was possible to sustain the 'myth of return' in which residence in Britain was viewed 'as a temporary, economically-motivated expedient' (Robinson, 1986, p. 75); it marked a shift for immigrant groups from the status of 'transients' to the status of 'settlers'. In addition, the arrival of wives and other relatives led to significant changes in housing arrangements among minority ethnic groups and the adoption of new lifestyles, albeit not necessarily conventional British ones (Ballard, 1982). Werbner's research among Manchester Pakistanis found that while the lifestyles of early migrants were typically 'puritanical and abstemious' (1984, p. 133) and governed by an overriding concern with saving, the subsequent phase following the arrival of dependants saw greater prominence given to the demonstration of wealth through conspicuous consumption or 'costly giving and extravagant hospitality' (1984, p. 138). Werbner argues that Pakistanis, 'like other South Asian people, are extremely conscious of status differentials and attach great importance to preserving and, if possible, advancing their status', and that in the new phase of migration this status consciousness has produced 'fierce internal competition' (1984, pp. 137, 140) within minority communities.

The social implications of this more recent phase of migration are contradictory. Keener competition for status has in one way worked to reinforce the close-knit nature of relationships among Manchester Pakistanis by leading 'to an intensification of ritual and ceremonial behaviour and thus, in effect, to a greater emphasis on culturally distinct forms of activity' (1984, p. 140). Against this it needs to be noted that a positive reputation may also be achieved through the acquisition of 'status "emblems" such as consumer goods or higher education, in a system of values shared with the host society', and to the extent that this is the case old values and customs may be 'compromised' rather than 'revived' (1984, pp. 140, 133). There is no agreement among Manchester Pakistanis over what constitutes the ideal degree of involvement in main-stream British society, and there are in consequence significant differences in their more general attitudes and lifestyles. The distinction between 'educated' Pakistanis and 'villagers' refers less to actual origins and qualifications than it does to the division between those who wear Western-style clothes, are fluent in English and have a wide circle of friends and those who prefer 'traditional' modes of behaviour. There are also important lines of cleavage between those with 'elite' status and others, and accord-ing to whether or not women are in paid work, and because all of these distinctions may be blurred and cross-cutting, the categories in which they are framed are surrounded by ambiguity and 'can only be used situationally, depending on the issue at hand' (1984, p. 146). Werbner argues that a hard-and-fast dividing line cannot be drawn between those who conform to 'traditional' conservative norms and those who are independent of their fellow Pakistanis' close-knit networks, and suggests that the situation is better conceptualised in terms of a continuum.

The absence of assimilation does not imply the presence of any single and uniform pattern of 'encapsulation' since the degree to which segregated lives are led varies enormously. Werbner's account of the Pakistani 'residential enclave' portrays it as an intensely private environment, where 'social life takes place in the seclusion of the houses, behind closed doors and closed curtains' (1988, p. 183). As a general rule the social networks of elite families are more exclusive than those of lower-income migrant families, among whom there are greater degrees of openness. In the extreme, individuals can be 'constantly caught up in rituals, ceremonials and public events', and such activities may 'generate an *increase* in network density' (Werbner, 1984, pp. 138–9; emphasis in original) and hence in encapsulation. This type of process in which actions are aimed to preserve distinct ethnic identities has been called 'self-segregation' (Aldrich *et al.*, 1981), although it has to be recognised that the 'voluntary' nature of these actions needs to be placed in the wider context of restricted opportunities and the experience of hostility and prejudice. Ballard has spoken of 'the growth of reactive ethnicity' (1979, p. 126) among second-generation South Asians to counter their subjection to racism, and Anwar (1985) also represented encapsulation as being a logical response to the experience of discrimination and exclusion, although it is unclear how far this can account for the significant variation in the extent to which groups are encapsulated or integrated.

Robinson's study of Asians in Blackburn found the South Asians of the town 'less conscious of their relative deprivation' than East African Asians living there in superior conditions, and argues that encapsulation in close-knit social networks 'shelters South Asians from the full force of hostility and inequality which exist in the wider society' (1986, pp. 176–7). By contrast East African Asians were found to have 'less restricted aspirations, a built-in drive to social and economic mobility, and a more limited desire to retain community association', with the result that their situation is better described as being one of 'marginality' (1986, p. 177). This finding confirms Bhachu's observation that the homogeneity of Asian migrants to Britain is the view of a poorly informed outsider who is insensitive to the 'clear differences among them of class, caste, experience of migration, [and] origins (from rural or urban areas)' (1985, p. 2). The experience of being 'twice migrants' for East African Asians meant that they never embraced the 'myth of return', having adopted distinctive 'attitudes and orientations towards settlement in the UK' because their 'decision to migrate permanently had already been taken before the actual event' (1985, pp. 3, 60). Robinson's Blackburn data pointed to finer internal differences within the town's Asian population, and allowed the construction of 'a notional continuum of ethnic association such that assimilated groups lie at one end and encapsulated or traditional groups lie at the other' (1986, p. 195). The two extremes are represented by East African Asians and Indian Gujurati Muslims respectively, with ten other ethno-linguistic groups located at various intermediate points on the basis of quantitative data relating to the measurement of variables such as patterns of contact and orientation towards return migration.

Robinson's 'continuum of ethnic association' is clearly far more methodologically sophisticated than either Anwar's 'incapsulation continuum' (1985, p. 210) (in which the five occupational categories of night shift, day shift, self-employed, transport and professional are listed in descending order) or Werbner's continuum with its extremes marked by 'conformity' and 'independence' (1984, p. 146), but the common thread in all of their thinking is that assimilation and encapsulation are both problematic objectives to adopt. To strive for assimilation is to risk rejection by white society and consequent marginalisation and resentment, while the opposite strategy of minimising contacts with white society through the creation of an encapsulated community carries with it a different set of drawbacks, not least the danger of reproducing the conditions of social and economic disadvantage to which most ethnic minorities are subject. The dilemmas over the nature and extent of links with mainstream white society are arguably most acute among Asians, but the issue is a more general one. Rex and Tomlinson have oversimplified the matter somewhat by suggesting that 'the West Indian retreats into a "ghetto mentality" after first striving for assimilation, the Asian immigrant never envisages anything other than maintaining his own cultural and social order in a strange land' (1979, p. 95), but the statement conveys the essence of the choice facing migrants none the less.

This is not to imply that the choice is a static one, since several factors may be seen as contributing to 'the persistent weakening of the desire for social and spatial encapsulation' (Robinson, 1981, p. 167). Werbner argued that close-knit networks are positively rejected by some immigrants who 'choose to be free to seize economic opportunities and remain highly mobile' (1984, p. 134), while Saifullah Khan has pointed to the stresses experienced by Pakistani women locked into dense networks of social relationships characterised by 'fast internal communication' and consequent 'pressure to conform' (1979a, p. 53). One result of this has been the growth of women seeking employment, both for the companionship it offers and because it represents 'a move towards greater independence' (Werbner, 1988, p. 180). In addition, children of migrants can never simply reproduce the social networks of their parents, and the resultant ambiguities create a situation of 'conflict, continuity and change' (Ballard, 1979). Further pressure for change comes from the pursuit of 'respectability', and Robinson's study of Asians found 'many of the groups have as great an interest maintaining social distance from what they consider to be less desirable Asian sub-groups as they do in maintaining distance from whites', some even valuing 'the avoidance of contact with other Asians *more* highly than they do avoiding contact with whites' (1986, p. 195; emphasis in original). Pryce (1979) found the desire of West Indians to move out of St Paul's in Bristol more due to the area's low status, but the result was the same, namely pressure for housing relocation. Against this background, the erosion or reproduction of segregation is a matter on which social policy has a direct bearing.

SOCIAL POLICY AND THE REPRODUCTION OF SEGREGATION

Of all the areas of social policy which have relevance to the issue of the social segregation of minority ethnic groups, housing is the most important. Housing policy has contributed directly to the processes whereby segregation has, if anything, increased, for despite 'evidence of some dispersal between 1971 and 1981, the 1980s began with a higher proportion of black people living in the most segregated areas than did the 1970s' (S. Smith, 1989a, p. 33). In part this situation has arisen as an effect of what has been termed 'white flight' from inner-city areas to suburbs, but this in turn raises the question of why members of Britain's black population have not followed similar migration patterns. Part of the answer to this lies in the 'racially and socially discriminatory housing allocations' (Henderson and Karn, 1987, p. 271) which have been identified for local authority properties. In Birmingham, Henderson and Karn found processes of allocating council housing 'operated to the disadvantage of racial minorities, women and less "respectable" working class people generally' (1987, p. 273), and these findings echo the results of other studies which have indicated the reworking of old and 'bureaucratically convenient' (Clapham *et al.*, 1990, p. 18) distinctions such as that between the 'deserving' and 'undeserving' poor. Flett (1979), for example, found notions of 'Englishness' crucial to the understanding of how bureaucrats responsible for the allocation of local authority properties determined the 'eligibility' of applicants.

To operate with a conception of nuclear families as a norm leads by default to other 'atypical' household types being treated by housing managers as 'somehow deviant' (Karn and Henderson, 1983, p. 71). Henderson and Karn argue that such processes were responsible for certain groups being channelled into less desirable properties and areas, and that these unequal outcomes could not be explained in terms of applicants' choices, nor were they solely the result of racial prejudice among individual housing officers. Rather, the housing allocation system itself was found to be at the heart of the matter, particularly 'its dependence upon categoris-ation of people and property as "suitable" for one another and the sources of information on which that categorisation was based' (1987, p. 277). The racial connotations of administrative categories of 'respectable' and 'disreputable' applicants, of 'problem families', of 'rough' areas and of 'suitability' led directly to the over-representation of white tenants in the more desirable suburban houses and the concentration of black tenants in the less desirable properties and areas, despite the fact that 'dispersal' of racial minorities was an official policy objective.

The unequal spatial distribution of the population along ethnic lines can be attributed to the workings of the owner-occupied sector of the housing market as well as the public rented sector. In the Saltley, Soho and Sparkhill areas of Birmingham, the 1970s saw property buyers increasingly drawn from Asian and, to a lesser extent, West Indian ethnic minorities, resulting in the areas 'becoming more homogeneous during this period in terms of the buying population' (Karn *et al.*, 1985, p. 19). In Soho (the most extreme case) white buyers had fallen to 8 per cent of the total by the late 1970s, and most of these were sitting-tenant buyers. There were also differences along ethnic lines in terms of the types of properties purchased and the means of financing these purchases, with Indian and Pakistani buyers tending 'to buy low-priced, leasehold houses with unconventional finance' (1985, p. 107). Karn *et al.*'s overall conclusion was that ethnic divisions had combined with social-class inequalities to produce a situation in which 'Buyers have been sorting themselves into the differentiated stock of dwellings according to their ethnic origins, relative socio-economic status and incomes' (1985, p. 51). Subsequent experi-ence of council property sales, which have been highest in the suburban wards and lowest in the inner-city, will have furthered the polarisation among owner–occupiers whereby 'typically Asian and West Indian households own older, smaller, low value properties with inferior amenity provision, in poor condition and in poor localities' (Forrest and Murie, 1988, p. 72).

The phenomenon of 'ethnic clustering' is by no means restricted to the large conurbations, as Sarre *et al.*'s study of Bedford shows. Sarre and his colleagues argue that 'Ethnic minority housing segregation and disadvantage is pervasive and well established throughout the UK, although it may take different forms in different places' (1989, p. 37). Residential concentration and segregation along ethnic lines can be described as 'enforced' due to the way in which various 'filtering mechanisms' (1989, p. 20) in the housing market have operated to restrict the opportunities open to ethnic-minority groups. The owner-occupied and rented sectors are organised around 'predominantly white British dominated housing institutions', and public housing authorities have a history of adopting 'direct and indirect discriminatory policies and practices' while in the private sector estate agents and lending bodies such as building societies have practised 'institu-tional exclusion' and 'institutional hostility' (1989, pp. 21, 180, 236–7). The outcome of such practices was 'the production of essentially two Bedfords: a multi-racial centre with a prosperous white suburbia', the inner area having many of the characteristics of a 'ghetto' (1989, pp. 117, 100) which stood in stark contrast to the more favoured area of the exclusive 'white highlands'.

The historical account of the emergence of segregation in Bedford given by Sarre and his colleagues suggests that policy-makers struggled to adapt to the emergence of a multi-ethnic population. The arrival from the 1940s onwards of first Italian and then West Indian and Asian minority groups challenged the town's 'sense of history and place' since prior to this immigration

'Bedford was a quiet, slumbering market town, introspective and conservative in its habits, values and outlook. One could legitimately speak of a Bedford *community*. It was a town of essentially one complexion' (1989, p. 58, emphasis in original). The newcomers were not absorbed into this community because 'It takes two to assimilate: the newcomer and the town' (1989, p. 115). In practice, ethnic-minority groups which did not conform to 'English ways and English standards' found themselves effectively excluded, and the housing allocation system was particularly important in the creation of 'ethnic villages' whereby 'ethnic minorities lived in isolation on their own "reservations" in the inner areas' (1989, pp. 115, 110). Having said this, Sarre and his colleagues are keen to avoid the suggestion that the reproduction of such structures is automatic, and they note in particular the importance of the policy changes in the housing department now that it is beginning to confront more directly multi-racial issues. Periods during which housing markets were buoyant were also characterised by ethnic minority households moving into better housing in previously non-ethnic areas, although the reverse side of this process is that 'Racial and ethnic status ... remain important categories of differentiation and come to the fore when resources are scarce' (1989, p. 296). In this context mention of the tendency for ethnic minorities to be located disproportionately amongst low-income households indicates their general economic vulnerability and serves as a reminder of the limitations within which policy-makers have to operate.

The influence of housing on the creation and reproduction of ethnic segregation is reinforced by the workings of the labour market. Anwar has noted that 'Most of the original ethnic minorities who came to Britain were economic migrants', and that their concentration in certain locations reflected their being granted access to only 'a limited range of occupations' (1986, p. 13). It is also clear that processes comparable to those discussed above which produced segregation in the housing market can operate in the employment market as well, it being well documented that 'the urban economy typically offers scope for "ethnic" economic organisation in particular niches' (Wallman, 1979, p. 1; Okely, 1983). The existence of clusters of Asian workers in west midlands foundries has been explained by Brooks and Singh in terms of 'recruitment networks and brokers' (1979, p. 95) reminiscent of the sponsorship networks of chain migration, while Ward's (1985) work suggests that 'ethnic niche' opportunities exist for shopkeepers and others to provide services within minority communities in areas of residential succession such as Bradford, Bolton and Rochdale. The reproduction of segregation may also be seen as an outcome of the labour market when considering the uneven distribution of unemployment, and in particular the high levels of joblessness among black youths (Brah, 1986; K. Roberts, 1984; Ullah, 1987).

Other aspects of social policy which have a bearing on ethnic segregation include education, where its effects are stark. For Rex, 'The segregation which has been imposed upon dark-skinned immigrant communities is reflected and amplified in the schools' (1988, p. 31). Rex has pointed out that Handsworth in Birmingham has under 10 per cent of its secondary-school population made up of whites, an institutional segregation more marked than that of the local population generally, a situation he explains in terms of the fact that 'The inhabitants of the Inner City who are not Black or Asian are nearly all either retired people whose children and grandchildren have fled to the suburbs or Irish immigrants whose children attend Catholic schools' (1988, pp. 31–2). It is a matter of controversy whether Rex is correct to maintain that such developments signal the development of ghettos and the creation of a black 'underclass', but there are strong grounds for believing that traditional boundaries between ethnic minority groups are subject to erosion by the way in which mainstream institutions do not register distinctions between Mirpuris and Sylhetis (for example), rather treating them all indiscriminately as 'Asians' (Saifullah Khan, 1979b). In similar fashion identification with a single black 'community' has emerged alongside the consciousness of the differences between West Indians arising from their particular Caribbean island origins, particularly among youths (Parry *et al.*, 1987). Gilroy has even suggested that 'the language of community has displaced both the language of class and the language of "race" in the political activity of black Britain' (1987, p. 230), although this is the language of opposed communities in conflict not co-operation. To the extent that this is the case, the challenge to social policy-makers is a profoundly disturbing one.

# 6

## HOME OWNERSHIP AND HOME LIFE: CHANGING IDEALS OF HOUSING AND DOMESTICITY

The growth in the level of owner-occupation over the course of the twentieth century in Britain has been dramatic by any standards, and the social implications of this change are correspondingly far-reaching. In the extreme it has been claimed that the emergence of 'a nation of home owners' constitutes a 'peaceful revolution' which 'has turned out to be one of the most popular revolutions in history' (Saunders, 1990, p. 13). More sceptical observers may question the appropriateness of such glowing acclamation, but they do not dispute that the growth of home ownership has had a profound impact, involving 'substantial changes in the way housing is produced and consumed; in the way it is financed, exchanged, managed and controlled; and in housing costs and patterns of wealth, inequality and saving' (Forrest *et al.*, 1990, p. 1). Further, as Pahl and Wallace have noted, 'The value of home-ownership extends beyond the financial advantages it undoubtedly confers' (1988, p. 146). They suggest that owner-occupation may be seen as having a certain status attached to it relating to established notions of 'respectability' (something found also in Luton by Devine (1992)), although they are doubtful of the proposition that owner-occupation promotes 'privatised' lifestyles which undermine community solidarity. In the context of the owner-occupied sector comprising two-thirds of all households it has become a matter of considerable importance to determine precisely what owner-occupation and tenancy have come to signify in contemporary society, and what has happened to the meanings attached to 'home life', 'domesticity' and 'community' in the process. The first section of this chapter examines the rise of home ownership and the social divisions which this has generated. The chapter then addresses questions about the impact of increased home ownership on male and female community involvement, and finally turns to the question of the changing character of 'private' and 'public' space.

The long-term rise in the level of owner-occupation which has occurred during this century can be explained in part by the economic advantages which accrue to owner–occupiers relative to tenants. Owner-occupation is a form of investment which, short-term fluctuations in house prices aside, promises to combine the benefits of an appreciating asset with attractive credit rates (subsidised through mortgage interest tax relief), offering to owner–occupiers the prospect that they 'may gain more from the housing market in a few years than would be possible in savings from a lifetime of earnings' (Pahl, 1975, p. 291). It is possible to conclude that the divergent economic interests of owner-occupiers and tenants place them in 'fundamentally different housing class positions' (Pahl *et al.*, 1983, p. 78), although discussion in these terms rarely sees owner–occupiers as members of a single, homogeneous housing class. Important lines of cleavage exist, for example, between owner–occupiers in inner-city areas and those in other localities (Karn *et al.*, 1985), between outright owners and owners with a mortgage (Forrest *et al.*, 1990) and between affluent home-owners and others (Forrest and Murie, 1987). It is necessary to recognise that there are, in Short's words, 'owner–occupiers and owner–occupiers' (1982, p. 144), and that the rented sectors of the housing market are similarly characterised by heterogeneity. Increasingly council housing has become associated with 'a new non-working class of long-term unemployed, young never-employed, working-class elderly and single parents' (Forrest and Murie, 1987, p. 332), but it is not exclusively so, and it would be mistaken to locate all local authority tenants within a uniform housing class. Comparable observations could be made about the growing diversity of tenants in the deregulated private rented sector (Morris and Winn, 1990), adding weight to the general conclusion that 'location in the same tenure category can conceal enormous differences in housing experiences' (Hudson and Williams, 1989, p. 70).

The debate on changing tenure patterns and their implications for housing classes has been concerned with inequalities between different groups of households. A separate discussion has focused on the implications of shifting housing patterns for gender inequalities. Women's disadvantaged housing position relative to men's has led some commentators to conclude that 'women experience the housing system differently from men' (Morris and Winn, 1990, p. 117) and that the operation of the housing system 'has an active role ... in exacerbating gender inequalities' (Clapham *et al.*, 1990, p. 71). Challenging an important part of this feminist perspective, Saunders has questioned the validity of the assumption that women 'experience home negatively as an oppressive and alienative environment', arguing instead that 'the association of home with images of comfort, relaxation, warmth, love and affection is no male myth, for it is shared by men and women alike' (1990, pp. 307, 308). Saunders' position on this issue is a minority one, since most studies support the general proposition that domestic experiences are not gender-neutral, but they tend to do so in a qualified fashion. The extent to which disadvantages in housing and domestic life fall disproportionately on women varies significantly according to factors such as household type, with single women being especially vulnerable in the housing system (Watson with Austerberry, 1986), and life-course stage, with the situation of women with young children being particularly constrained (Tivers, 1985). There are also suggestions that gender relations in the home may vary between owner–occupiers and tenants (Madigan *et al.*, 1990), between social classes (Hunt, 1989) and between ethnic groups (Werbner, 1988).

An additional complication to the analysis of housing inequalities, gender divisions and home life is raised by the ways in which the boundary between private and public spheres has shifted over recent decades. The expansion and then (since 1979) contraction of local authority housing marks one way in which public and private have carried with them different meanings at different times, the thrust of contemporary assessments being that 'council housing is becoming a *residual* service' providing 'welfare housing for marginal groups' (Forrest and Murie, 1988, p. 65; emphasis in original). Programmes of urban redevelopment have also embodied shifting notions of public and private space and have contributed substantially to the polarisation not only of tenure groups but also of localities and the lives of their inhabitants. In the East End of London the interplay of social and spatial polarisation is exemplified by the contrast between the situations of two young women described by Holme: 'One, with her husband, owns her attractive Woodford house. The other lives with her parents in a grim block of council flats in Bethnal Green. In their way of life there is virtually no meeting point' (1985, pp. 159–60). The divisive effects of redevelopment are at their most marked where they have resulted in the gentrification of formerly working-class areas into exclusive enclaves of middle-class households with consumption-orientated lifestyles (Byrne, 1989), but such situations merely highlight the broader trend whereby 'urban areas in general and inner cities in particular are becoming increasingly divided places' (Bondi, 1991, p. 110). Bondi's further observation that women are 'prominent on both sides of the divide' confirms the complexity of the interaction between changes in housing, households and wider community patterns.

HOUSING CLASSES AND THE RISE OF HOME OWNERSHIP

The idea that housing inequalities can be understood in terms of housing classes can be traced back to Rex and Moore's (1967) study of Sparkbrook which has already been discussed in the context of ethnic segregation in chapter 5. Rex and Moore argued that certain groups enjoyed advantaged situations in the housing market while others were disadvantaged, and that there will be 'as many potential housing classes in the city as there are kinds of access to the use of housing' (1967, p. 274). The actual classification which the study proposed has an anachronistic ring to it now, but it remains of relevance since the identification of these housing classes has shaped much of the subsequent debate. The seven housing classes in Rex and Moore's classification were outright owners of whole houses, mortgage payers buying whole houses, council tenants in houses with a long life, council tenants in houses awaiting demolition, private tenants of whole houses, owners of houses who sublet rooms to tenants in order to repay loans used to buy the property, and tenants in these properties. Rex and Moore argued that the housing classes were listed on 'a scale of desirability' (1967, p. 275), with outright owner-occupation carrying the highest prestige and legitimacy while tenancy of rooms has the lowest. They also noted that the different housing classes conform to 'a definite territorial distribution in the city' (1967, p. 274), with higher status groups likely to be found in suburban areas while more marginal groups tend to be concentrated in the inner-city 'zone of transition'.

There are several grounds on which Rex and Moore's model has been criticised, including an element of self-criticism by the authors themselves. Both Rex and Moore have suggested further groups which could be added to the list of housing classes, such as 'workers living in company hostels' (Moore, 1977, p. 106), one-parent families (Rex, 1977), or homeless people and tenants of charitable housing associations (Rex and Tomlinson, 1979). Still other groups (for example, those in residential 'homes') could be identified as housing classes, and if it is recognised that 'it is possible to divide up any given housing class into further categories' (Abercrombie *et al.*, 1988, p. 327) then 'taxonomic innovation' can create 'dozens of potential housing classes' (Saunders, 1986, p. 142). Followed to its logical conclusion, Rex and Moore's point about different degrees of access to housing means that 'the number of classes is almost limitless' (Marshall, 1990, p. 140). It is not at all clear that the original seven or the revised list of eleven (Rex and Tomlinson, 1979) housing classes are sufficient to capture the diversity of housing market positions even within Birmingham (where Rex and his co-researchers conducted their investigations), let alone the wider society, and on these grounds several commentators have come to the conclusion that 'as it stands, the Rex and Moore model simply will not do' (Elliott and McCrone, 1982, p. 113).

Further complexity is added to the picture when the question of the differential prestige attached to housing is examined more closely. Rex and Moore have been criticised for making the assumption 'that there is a common value system about the desirability of housing' (Morris and Winn, 1990, p. 214), since it is debatable whether suburban owner-occupation is a universal ideal to which everyone aspires. The attribution of high status to outright owner-occupation in suburban areas and low status to tenants in houses of multiple occupation 'reflected Rex's own values rather than any objective evidence of the existence of such a pecking order' (Saunders, 1990, p. 325), as has been confirmed by a number of subsequent studies. Instances of some people preferring private tenancy to both council tenancy and owner-occupation (Couper and Brindley, 1975), and of others continuing to let out property to tenants after the economic necessity of doing so had passed (Dahya, 1974; Davies, 1972; Davies and Taylor, 1970) indicate that there is no consensus on the relative merits of different housing-market situations. Preference for inner-city locations may be found among single women, including lone mothers, who 'do not value suburban housing so greatly' (Abercrombie *et al.*, 1988, p. 327), and among certain ethnic-minority groups, as Rex and Tomlinson (1979) came to acknowledge. This is a significant problem for the analysis of housing inequalities in terms of housing classes, since Rex's concession 'that many of those in apparently disadvantaged housing conditions do not aspire to suburban living . . . removed the grounds for arguing that the housing classes he identifies are in conflict with one another' (Saunders, 1986, p. 145). Rex and Moore's critique of the housing system as one which forced minority groups into disadvantaged situations became harder to sustain in the light of the discovery of higher than expected satisfaction levels with rented housing and inner-city locations.

Rex's response to the discovery of diverse housing aspirations was to challenge the methodology by which such findings are generated. Statements of preference for one type of housing over another are suspect according to Rex because 'we can never know what significance to attach to replies to questionnaires about housing preference' when 'certain preferences are not expressed simply because they are unrealistic' (1973, pp. 37–8). Subsequent research has confirmed the need for statements of housing aspirations to be placed in context, since individuals' housing histories inevitably influence their expectations. Watson and Austerberry's research into women and homelessness, for example, led them to conclude that 'When questioned as to their ideal accommodation, women who have been living in institutions for a long time are inclined to set their sights very low' (1986, pp. 149–50). Similarly, Holme's finding that 'tenure differences *are* reflected in housing aspirations' (1985, p. 158; emphasis in original) was accounted for in part at least by the greater range of actual choices open to home-owners. Having said this, housing aspirations have changed significantly since Rex and Moore's theory of housing classes was first formulated, superficially at least resembling more closely the celebration of the ideal of suburban owner-occupation identified by Rex and Moore as 'a built-in aspiration' (1967, p. 9). The percentage of people questioned for whom owner-occupation was their preferred tenure has risen from 66 per cent in 1967 to 81 per cent in 1989, and over the same period actual levels of owner-occupation rose from 48 per cent of households to 65 per cent (Forrest *et al.*, 1990, pp. 43, 57), but while such data appear to suggest a movement towards the shared definition of 'desirable' housing which Rex and Moore posited, there is no agreement about how these trends should be interpreted.

The boldest interpretation of the trend towards wider owner-occupation is offered by Saunders, who argues that it has to be understood in terms of 'the desire of people to own their own homes' (1990, p. 57). For Saunders the widespread preference for owner-occupation reflects a natural aspiration, and people who become home-owners do so for straightforward, sensible reasons which others would emulate given the opportunity. Owner-occupation is the tenure-type which people would ideally choose, and which almost two-thirds of households have actually chosen, since it satisfies 'the desire for security, privacy and personal identity which owners articulate when they talk about their experience of their housing' (1990, p. 118). Saunders supports his arguments not only by reference to trends in national figures but also by discussion of the findings of his research into the growth of mass home ownership in the three predominantly working-class towns of Slough, Derby and Burnley. These findings 'show that the preference for home ownership is high and is widespread' (1990, p. 63), and Saunders claims that this is because it is positively sought after due to its intrinsic advantages, as well as because of the disadvantages of renting. The desire to own was strongest among those with mortgages, but even among council tenants Saunders found between 71 per cent (in Derby) and 87 per cent (in Slough) stating a preference for owner-occupation (1990, p. 63). He suggests that owner-occupation is also 'infinitely preferable to a state-sector alternative for which they harbour no aspirations or ambitions' (1990, p. 117) among Asian households. It is on this basis that Saunders can claim that, in cultural terms if not yet so completely in practice, 'we are a nation of home owners' (1990, p. 3).

Saunders is aware, of course, that Britain is a long way from being a property-owning democracy in which owner-occupation is universal. Conscious of the processes of social polarisation which have produced 'a majority of private owners and a minority of increasingly marginal and dependent state-sector tenants' (1990 p. 370), Saunders advocates the extension of opportunities to become owner–occupiers among 'the marginalized minority', so that they too can enjoy the financial gains and the 'stronger sense of belonging and personal achievement' (1990, p. 314) which home-ownership fosters. In this discussion, Saunders recognises that the current situation is some distance from the ideal of 'a tenure-neutral system . . . in which consumers can choose whether to rent or to buy without their decisions being influenced by a confusing and often contradictory system of controls and subsidies' (1990, pp. 370–1), not least because many people's 'choice' of owner-occupation has involved 'the help of state subsidies' (1990, p. 335). Yet subsidisation of owner-occupation has tended to grow over time while subsidies to public sector housing have been squeezed (Clapham *et al.*, 1990; Forrest *et al.*, 1990), and the politically contingent conditions within which this shift has taken place raise at least some questions about the 'naturalness' of home-ownership which Saunders posits. In the context of its being 'massively subsidised by the state', Lowe has argued that owner-occupation's growth is attributable not to preferences but to 'a series of unique tax concessions and investment advantages' (1988, pp. 149, 156). Further doubts are raised about Saunders' claims that the desire for owner-occupation is 'fuelled by certain natural dispositions' by the observation that 'council housing is preferred by few' (Saunders, 1990, pp. 83, 314) since in such an account trumpeting the attractions of owner-occupation it remains problematic why anyone should prefer alternative tenure types.

Part of the answer to this question of why commitment to owner-occupation is less than universal can be found in the divergent interests of different social groups. Saunders' own data show the desire to own being lower among outright owners than it is among mortgaged owners, and while the difference is slight and the overall proportions are small, they are sufficient to prompt the observation that the group of outright owners 'tends to include elderly people (for whom upkeep and repairs are more likely to be a problem) and some of the cheapest and poorest quality housing stock' (1990, p. 62). Oldman has written in this context of the 'myth of independence' for elderly owner-occupiers in York, arguing that 'for many older people owning a home becomes a liability not an asset' (1991, p. 141). This is a conclusion reached also by other studies (Daunton, 1987; Dickens, 1988; Forrest *et al.*, 1990), suggesting that alternative tenure types may be better suited to the needs of diverse groups of people. A similar point has been made about owner-occupation in inner-city areas where ethnic minority purchasers in particular find that their expectations of capital gains on their properties are by no means always realised (Karn *et al.*, 1985). More generally, Kemeny has spoken of 'the myth of home ownership', arguing that owner-occupation fails in several ways to live up to its billing as 'the "natural" tenure which . . . everyone wants' (1981, p. 144), and that a truly tenure-neutral housing policy would introduce a more genuine freedom of choice.

Arguments about the 'natural' character of owner-occupation also have geographical and historical dimensions. Saunders describes the proportion of households in Scotland in 1981 which rented their homes from the state as 'a staggering 55 per cent', explaining this in terms of 'lower average incomes and a strong Labourist and statist tradition of working-class politics' (1990, pp. 15, 17). In contrast, rates of owner-occupation have always been relatively high in Wales, and in 1986 the figure of 67.5 per cent dwarfed the Scottish figure of 42.1 per cent (1990, p. 17). Saunders again accounts for this in terms of 'tradition', concluding that 'there are important *cultural* variations which can only be explained by analysing the distinctive histories of various places' (1990, p. 43; emphasis in original). Traditions which vary as significantly as these do not sit easily alongside theories which regard owner-occupation as a timeless 'natural' preference. The history of the ' "naturalisation" of owner-occupation' (Crow, 1989a, p. 26) is a long and complex one, and the treatment of other tenure types as somehow less natural is a relatively recent occurrence. Owner-occupation has been the norm in the statistical sense of being the majority tenure type in Great Britain only since 1970 (Forrest *et al.*, 1990, p. 57), and the 'pervasive ideology of tenures that portrays 'owning' as desirable and advantageous . . . and stigmatises renting' (Ford, 1988, p. 68) was much less widely held in earlier decades, when analyses of housing had a markedly different character. Forrest *et al.* have noted of a 1940s study, for example, that 'What is striking is how far discussion of privacy or independence and general housing quality is divorced from discussion of tenure' (1990, p. 45), and it can be observed more generally that considerations of the relative merits of different types of housing from earlier in the century did not treat individuals' attainment of home-ownership as having overriding importance.

A third dimension to the debate on the naturalness of home-ownership concerns the psychological benefits which it is alleged to confer. Saunders argues that owner-occupation 'enables a greater sense of emotional security and a stronger development of self and identity' (1990, p. 292), and that this 'ontological security' is expressed by home-owners in a number of ways. On the basis of his three towns survey Saunders claims 'that owners are much more strongly attached to their homes in emotional terms than tenants are' (1990, p. 312) and notes that these attachments cannot be attributed to length of residence, since this was if anything greater among tenants. Saunders' data also suggest 'that owners invest a different meaning in their homes than tenants, such that they tend to equate their houses with images of comfort and relaxation, whereas tenants generally find it difficult to draw such an association' (1990, p. 312). Less 'alienated' than tenants, owners not only had a stronger sense of belonging in their homes but were also more involved in social networks beyond the household: 'owner–occupiers are often *more* actively engaged in social life than are tenants . . . owner–occupiers are *more* likely than tenants to participate in clubs and organizations outside the home' (1990, p. 311; emphases in original). Such findings stand, as Saunders observes, in direct contradiction to the widely held tenet that home-ownership is associated with privatised lifestyles, and offer further confirmation to the doubts expressed in chapter 3 concerning the privatisation thesis and the impact which economic change has had on community life.

One response to Saunders' argument that owner-occupation is linked to greater ontological security has been to contest the strength of that link. In the three towns study, 64 per cent of home-owners reported a strong feeling of attachment to their homes while only 40 per cent of council tenants did so, and absence of such feelings was reported among 28 per cent of home-owners and 46 per cent of tenants. Saunders describes this situation as 'a highly significant finding' (1990, p. 294), but an alternative interpretation is to regard these figures as evidence of 'some tenants expressing more ontological security than some owners', constituting a challenge to the idea that 'certain attitudes and responses are exclusive to a tenure' (Forrest *et al.*, 1990, p. 177). Forrest and his colleagues go on to propose the abandonment of the attempt 'to demonstrate that tenure produces certain attitudes' in favour of seeing tenure 'as an achieved status reflecting housing histories, strategies, choices, opportunities and constraints' (1990, p. 178). Daunton argues a similar case in his account of the historical variability of the meanings attached to owner-occupation and renting, where he notes that 'What needs to be considered very carefully is the exact nature of the social relations emerging in each tenure at each point in time: nothing can be automatically read from tenure alone' (1987, p. 96). Daunton's conclusion that it is necessary 'to reject "housing class" as a crude and unhelpful concept' is based on his challenge to 'the assumption that tenure changes attitudes' which, he says, 'does not assist in the analysis of British society in the twentieth century' (1987, pp. 96–7).

This latter perspective shares some common ground with Saunders, who has sought in his work to go 'beyond housing classes' (Saunders, 1984) and to analyse the importance of home-owners' 'housing investment strategies' (1990, p. 202) in his explanation of housing market behaviour. Where the two approaches part company is on the issue of the overall significance of the goal of maximising property values, since Saunders regards the acquisition of capital gains as far more important as a motivation among owner–occupiers than his critics do. Housing mobility among the affluent home-owners in Bristol studied by Forrest and Murie was generally undertaken for employment reasons and was rarely 'determined by conscious housing strategies or manipulation of the housing market to maximise wealth or shelter' (1987, p. 354). Lower down the 'housing ladder' among working-class home-owners in Bristol, the reasons for moving included 'to be nearer kin or friends . . . to obtain a larger house because of children, or a better garden, or a better area' (Forrest *et al.*, 1990, p. 50), and again the acquisition of a more valuable property was not of paramount importance. Karn and her colleagues' investigation of owner-occupation among inner-city ethnic minorities found it 'clear that the housing strategies of West Indians, who have mostly been in this country for a considerable time, are significantly different from those of the most recently arrived Pakistanis' (1985, p. 61). As with Holme's study of East London, it is possible to accept that 'families take a rational approach to their housing future' (1985, p. 158) without presuming them all to be narrow economic maximisers. It can be allowed that owner-occupation is the tenure type most suited to those pursuing 'housing investment strategies' without it necessarily following that home-ownership is the most rational or valued objective for all households to pursue.

### GENDER DIFFERENCES IN THE EXPERIENCE OF HOME LIFE

The subject of housing strategies is an interesting one not only because of the range of objectives which it is possible for households to pursue but also because of what it reveals about power relations within households. Household strategies may reflect the wishes and interests of all household members, but they cannot be presumed to do so in every case (Crow, 1989b), and there are several studies which point to gender inequalities in the formulation of housing strategies. Forrest and Murie's research into affluent home-owners found their respondents' housing histories to be '*male* dominated in the important sense of determining *when* moves occurred', it being the case that 'the employment needs and possibilities of the female partner are unlikely to necessitate or justify housing moves' (1987, pp. 352–3; emphases in original). Similarly Edgell found among his sample of middle-class couples that 'Decisions concerned with moving house, for example, when and where to, were regarded by every couple as extremely important and reported by every couple as husband-dominated' (1980, p. 61), reflecting the general subordination of family life to men's work careers. In her study of East London, Holme discovered a less marked degree of gender difference in housing priorities, but still noted the finding that fathers 'set a greater premium on home-ownership compared with mothers' (1985, p. 150). Whether or not the growth of owner-occupation constitutes movement towards a 'property-owning democracy'

(Daunton, 1987), it remains doubtful that universal suffrage has been extended to relations within households.

The subordinate position of women in the formulation of households' housing strategies does not necessarily mean that they feel differently about the home, of course, and this issue needs to be treated as a separate question. In his three towns research Saunders found no evidence of an association 'between gender and positive or negative experiences of home life', and concludes that women 'see the home in the same positive light as men do' (1990, p. 312). Accepting the received sociological wisdom that 'home is more of a "workplace" for women than for men', he argues that this does not translate into consciousness of exploitation, since '*None* of the women in our sample spontaneously referred to home as a place of work or oppression' (1990, pp. 308–9; emphasis in original). Rather it was the case that 'Women are just as enthusiastic as men in volunteering images of warmth, love and comfort when asked what the home means to them' (1990, p. 309). Saunders is aware that his account of gender relations and home life is at odds with most of the other literature in the field on this issue, and that this divergence needs to be explained, although his claim that feminist writing is based substantially on assertion rather than empirical research is neither accurate nor adequate as an explanation.

To begin with, it is possible to mention numerous empirical investigations into domestic relations which have identified significant differences between women and men in the experience of home life. Saunders' finding that the meaning of home frequently has associations with family, privacy, sanctuary, comfort, independence and other valued elements of personal life squares with much other evidence (Allan and Crow, 1989; Forrest *et al*., 1990), but there are grounds for believing that women and men relate to these components of the home in quite different ways. For example, 'privacy' means something quite different for a carer than it does for other household members, and Graham has drawn on the findings of a number of studies to observe that caring 'demands the adoption of a life-style which isolates the carer (and frequently the cared for) from the outside world. Home, as the setting in which most caring is carried out, becomes not so much a haven from the rigours of the labour market, as a prison' (1983, p. 26). Subsequent research reports have supported this account.

Typical of these is Lewis and Meredith's study of daughters caring for mothers at home in which 'Very few had any privacy for entertaining guests' and, overall it appeared that, 'To an outside observer, the majority of respondents led remarkably restricted lives' (1988, p. 87). In the context of expectations that carers will be predominantly women (Finch, 1989), caring responsibilities will be one important basis for gender differences in the way 'home' is experienced.

Women with young children also experience home life in a distinct way. Tivers speaks of many such women being 'largely confined to home in the daytime by young children' and notes of her Merton study sample that 'For those without close friends and kin living locally, extreme loneliness may be the result of the gender-role constraint' (1985, p. 32). In general the 'amount of assistance with housework and child care received from husbands is small' (1985, p. 233), and domestic responsibilities led to the denial of opportunities to participate in social or recreational activities, something which was a source of dissatisfaction and low quality of life among many of these mothers. Tivers cites the national finding that only 8 per cent of husbands with children under five would change places with their wives while 'nearly one-third of non-employed wives with young children favour changing places with their husbands' (1985, p. 236) to support her argument that in the daily lives of women with young children the home is experienced very much as a sphere of constraint, whereas for their male partners it is less so. Sharpe's interviews with working mothers found many of them reporting feelings of ambivalence about earlier periods in their lives when they had been isolated at home as full-time housewives and mothers. A 'significant number of the women' had 'experienced ambivalent feelings when they were at home' (1984, p. 37), and dissatisfaction with home-centred lives had been an important factor in their decisions to seek paid work.

It could be concluded from this that gender differences in the experience of the home are a feature of certain stages of the life course, and it would be oversimple to suppose that women are uniformly restricted to the home by caring for dependants. Deem's investigation into women's leisure in Milton Keynes confirmed that 'women in their late twenties or their thirties, especially those with dependent children were least likely to be found involved in leisure outside the home' (1986, p. 29), but the presence of child-care responsibilities was not the only consideration determining leisure opportunities. In addition to responsibilities for dependent children, many women felt themselves to have their social lives constrained by domestic obligations more generally, or their 'partner's job and leisure interests' (1986, p. 36), ties which did not disappear as their children grew up. Even in later life, when the gap between the amount of time spent at home by men and women falls, the ideal of the home 'is clearly not a gender-neutral one' (Mason, 1989, p. 116), and experience of domestic life as constraining continues to be more prominent among women than it does among men.

Constraints on women's ability to achieve privacy in the home may even increase with age, since 'One effect of the husbands' tendency to begin focusing their values and their presence on the home was to compromise the wives' previously autonomous time and, to a degree, space' (Mason, 1988, p. 81). The role of 'home-making' led to the women in Mason's research being 'ambivalent about the relative benefits of the increasingly full-time company of their husbands at home' (1988, p. 82), and they reported contradictory experiences of the home as a private space shared with their husbands and yet at the same time intruded upon by them. Further evidence exists of the fact that women and men may speak about the home in the same way, for example as a private place, but do not actually experience it in the same way. Among the married couples in Aberdeen studied by Askham she found

no difference in the numbers of men and women saying they liked to get out on their own; but the impetus behind their desire appeared somewhat different. For women the impetus was often given as a desire to get away from something, i.e. the house. (1984, p. 65)

In Bristol among a sample of working-class couples Porter discovered a gulf between 'men's world' and 'women's world', captured in the different perceptions of housework: 'the husbands generally had a high regard for what their wives did at home, but when I asked the women if they thought "most men reckon what their wives do at home isn't really work" they nearly all said "yes"' (1983, p. 117).

Other researchers have argued that women do not always find it possible to express any dissatisfaction they may have with home life in an explicit fashion. Sharpe suggests that it was only because they were no longer full-time mothers at home that respondents were able to 'look back on their earlier lives, express a mixture of feelings and criticize their situation retrospectively' (1984, p. 39). A sense of being trapped might reasonably be expected to generate fatalism, as Hunt proposes in her observation that 'Dependent wives tend to accept solitude and confinement to the home as a necessary evil' (1980, p. 52). Such stoicism extended to wives in paid work in Hunt's study of the industrial village of 'Silverdale' in North Staffordshire, it being the case that all wives were 'more ideologically and practically tied to the home than their menfolk', even though 'both men and women see the family-unit as the site for the fulfilment of life-projects and consumption aspirations' (1980, pp. 187, 183). The desirability of home comforts may be agreed upon by both husbands and wives while at the same time gender differences are integral to the activities through which 'the construction of home life' (Hunt, 1989) as a relaxing environment is effected.

A further point in support of the view that women and men experience the home differently relates to the widespread but erroneous practice of treating conventional 'family' households as typical of the whole population. Among single people in the young and middle-aged groups of the population, rates of owner-occupation 'are consistently higher among men than women' (Clapham *et al.*, 1990, p. 73). More generally it can be said that 'for every family type other than married couples, women are more dependent than men on renting from the local authority' (Clapham *et al.*, 1990, p. 73), and since this dependence is not always met by adequate provision, women outside conventional households are left particularly vulnerable to homelessness (Watson with Austerberry, 1986). Lone mothers are a prominent group among those disadvantaged in the housing market (Crow and Hardey, 1991), and their limited room for manoeuvre inevitably has an adverse impact on their ability to create a satisfactory home life. Poverty is an obvious factor constraining lone mothers in their efforts to achieve domestic comfort, since 'Making a home involves the expenditure of money which for the majority of lone mothers is in short supply' (Hardey, 1989, p. 128). Elderly women living alone are another sizeable group whose poverty disadvantages them in the housing system

(Morris and Winn, 1990). In addition to economic disadvantage, women's distinct experience of the home may also be linked to other factors such as homeworking (Allen and Wolkowitz, 1987), disability (Lonsdale, 1990) and domestic violence (Pahl, 1985), all of which have specific gender dimensions, and all of which tend to be regarded as 'private' affairs, rendering them invisible to people outside the home.

It was proposed in chapter 1 that 'personal troubles' and 'public issues' are most usefully analysed together rather than separately, and discussion of the 'private' sphere of the home bears out this argument. The gendered experience of home life reflects the different economic and social positions of men and women more broadly, and also the understanding of 'home' and 'community' embodied in housing policy (Austerberry and Watson, 1985; Ungerson and Karn, 1980), architectural practice (Matrix, 1984; Roberts, 1991) and programmes of urban redevelopment (McDowell, 1983). It is also important to note that the distinction between public and private spheres which underlies these gender inequalities is an unstable one, and that important changes have taken place in conceptions of what is appropriate to each sphere. The implications of the growth of owner-occupation and the contraction of public sector housing are a matter of debate, but there are grounds for supposing that gender inequalities will become more marked as a result of the shift. It has been suggested, for example, that the sale of council house stock tends to create 'what have variously been called "sink", "residual", "ghetto" or "dump" estates' (Crow and Hardey, 1991, p. 64) on which the most vulnerable groups in the housing market such as lone mothers are disproportionately located. Such areas are associated with high crime rates, of which women are more fearful (Smith, 1989b). Owner-occupation might be expected to increase feelings of security among women, but even here it has been found that there are 'higher levels of insecurity associated with home occupancy by women' (Madigan *et al.*, 1990, p. 642).

Divergent experiences such as these translate into different senses not only of 'home' but also of 'community', where profound contradictions relating to the public/private distinction are present. According to Dominelli, 'The "community" is popularly acknowledged as women's place. Yet, work women undertake in the community, on behalf of the community, is largely invisible, making women seem part of the community, whilst being excluded from it' (1990, p. iii). Deem too found that 'Women are amongst the foremost members of community and voluntary organizations' (1986, p. 58), and notes that they are prominent as voluntary workers. Such activities challenge but do not entirely negate the ideology of a woman's place being in the home, since 'female involvement in out-of-home voluntary work is particularly likely to involve the elderly, sick and disabled' (Deem, 1986, p. 59), thereby reproducing rather than undermining women's 'caring' role. These gender differences in community involvement are also the result of the fact that women and men do not have equal access to the public sphere. The more restricted patterns of women's public lives reflect aspects of their domestic situation discussed above, but they are also the product of different experiences of and fears about violence and sexual harassment (Hanmer and Saunders, 1984; Little *et al.*, 1988; Whitehead, 1976), highlighting again the general point that women can be in the community without being able to be full members of it.

### THE CHANGING MEANING OF 'PRIVATE' AND 'PUBLIC' PROPERTY AND SPACE

The effects of the growth of home-ownership are clearly far from uniform. Watson has observed that the concept of the home 'has had, and continues to have, a quite different and shifting meaning for the working and middle classes, and for working- and middle-class women in particular' (1991, p. 138). Saunders' (1990) claim that the growth of owner-occupation at the expense of public and private renting has promoted 'ontological security' has been contested on precisely these grounds, that where poorer groups in the population buy properties they become 'marginal owners' with markedly lower levels of security than affluent home-owners (Forrest *et al.*, 1990), while changing notions of 'a home of one's own' continue to deny equal access to privacy, comfort and relaxation to all household members (Allan and Crow, 1991). The expansion of choice and opportunity which the spread of owner-occupation has undoubtedly brought for many people has to be set against the narrowing range of possibilities facing others. In this evaluation several commentators have seen fit to make use of the concept of 'polarisation' (Forrest and Murie, 1988; Pahl, 1984; Willmott and Murie, 1988), employing it to describe both the divergence of the situations of owner–occupiers and tenants and the spatial expression of widening economic positions in terms of the emergence of segregated neighbourhoods.

The changing meaning of 'public' and 'private' in the realm of housing has been due in no small part to the 'right to buy' policy of selling council houses to tenants. The sale of council houses is not a new phenomenon (Merrett with Gray, 1982), but in recent years sales have increased dramatically. This policy has had an uneven effect, since sales have been consistently higher in suburban areas than on inner-city estates (Forrest and Murie, 1988), meaning that while 'the opportunities for those who can buy have increased, those who must rent are forced to compete for a limited range of inferior and unpopular properties, an increasing proportion of which are flats' (Clapham *et al.*, 1990, p. 67). The 'residualisation' of the public rented sector has been brought about also by large-scale sales of council housing into private or housing association ownership, which again has had a differential effect. According to Morris and Winn, in areas of high housing demand such as the Docklands area of East London, 'the transfer of stock from the public to the private sector has resulted in the squeezing out of working-class communities' (1990, p. 24). While the effects of these changes on tenants who have exercised their right to buy may have been undramatic at an individual level, the overall effect of the policy has been to promote 'the transformation of the social structure of neighbourhoods and broad patterns of residential differentiation' (Forrest and Murie, 1990, p. 107). In the extreme the result is 'ghettoization, polarization, segregation and exclusion' (Forrest, 1991, p. 192) for those forced by poverty to rely on the declining housing stock of the public sector.

The implications for wider community relations of the changing character of 'public' and 'private' housing do not bear out the expectation that the spread of owner-occupation promotes the reinforcement of more privatised lifestyles. Saunders' three towns survey suggests that home-owners 'tend to go out more socially and be more satisfied with their social lives' (1990, p. 311), but it is also worth noting that council tenants in this study were almost twice as likely as owner–occupiers to think of 'home' as meaning belonging to a neighbourhood (1990, p. 273). Some of these respondents may even have been among the people in the Rosehill district of Derby whose search for identity and 'ontological security' led them to 'community' rather than to housing (Revill, 1993). This finding is at odds with the situation on an Exeter council estate which had a reputation as an undesirable place to live, where it was found that owner-occupation was seen as an expression of commitment to the local community:

> What purchasers and would-be purchasers seem to be seeking is a stake in this community – both in the sense of securing their position as residents in a period of economic uncertainty, especially over rents, and for the sake of intergenerational continuity, which is a feature of the estate. (Jordan *et al.*, 1992, p. 270)

The decision to buy is accounted for negatively as 'a reaction to the threat of housing insecurity' and more positively as producing an 'enhanced sense of belonging to the community' (1992, p. 270).

Holme also suggests that tenure preferences are based primarily on the practical matter of the relative security of renting and owning, and draws the conclusion that 'the connection between the immediate surroundings of the home and the quality of the neighbourhood relationships must be much more complex than a simple correspondence of public ownership with sociability and private ownership with exclusiveness' (1985, pp. 168–9). In the East End of London as in many other localities the changed relationship between home and community cannot be understood without considering the impact of redevelopment programmes. Large-scale clearances of old housing have made inner-city streets 'very different places from those of the 1950s' (1985, p. 169), although it is interesting to note that Cornwell's research in the same area found that gender differences persisted. Her Bethnal Green interviews included a married couple who 'do not experience "the community" in the same way as each other, so neither of them is capable of giving a fully rounded account of "community" ' (1984, p. 50). The decline of the local occupational community has meant that, for men, 'most of their sense of community comes from the atmosphere in the local pub (if they are drinkers). Women, on the other hand, occupy a much wider range of communal spaces – the shops, the street, the school gates, their relatives' houses – and they have a much wider variety of contacts' (1984, p. 50).

A third study of London's East End and the process of redevelopment there has drawn the more general conclusion that 'because women have been more deeply concerned than men with the relationships between family [and] community . . . they have been the driving force behind most community action' (Marris, 1987, p. 138). It is certainly the case, as Williams has argued, that 'Community has a particular significance for many women', representing as it does 'the point at which women's private business becomes translated into public issues' (1993, p. 33). Women's centrality to community action has given community movements a distinctive character, and the next chapter will consider the extent to which such movements have been able to influence the redevelopment process.

# 7

## REMAKING COMMUNITIES: URBAN REDEVELOPMENT AND COMMUNITY ACTION

One of the central themes linking the chapters in this book is the idea that communities are active creations. The view of communities as 'social constructions' or 'symbolic constructions' has been encountered at several points, but it is clear from these discussions that the forces behind the creation of community life are both complex and beyond easy manipulation. For example, the creation of the traditional working-class communities discussed in chapter 2 was a gradual and tentative process, as is indicated by Warwick and Littlejohn's observation that the solidarity and continuity of the traditional mining communities 'are characteristics which have had to be socially constructed onto social collectivities which were marked by heterogeneity' (1992, p. 58). Williamson too speaks of Throckley as a constructed community, 'built up as a community of miners quite deliberately by the coal company which sank the pit there in the late 1860s', although he goes on to note that the miners and their families did not passively acquiesce in this but responded by 'constructing a way of life which was theirs and not simply a reflection of the coal company's plans' (1982, p. 6). Subsequent attempts by both private and public bodies to impose particular models of community have generally met with similar resistance, if not always with comparable success.

Endeavouring to create communities is hampered by the perception of community life as 'natural' and thus antithetical to planned intervention. It appears to observers of local communities that order is only rarely 'the willed product of centralized control', it being more common to find that 'Much of what occurs seems to just happen with accidental trends becoming cumulative over time and producing results intended by nobody' (Long, 1970, pp. 303–

4). Such appearances are deceptive, of course, but they neverthe-less present a significant problem to planners charged with the responsibility of creating communities. Attempts to plan the construction of communities have a long and uneven history (Nuttgens, 1989), and were at their most ambitious in the New Towns, where the aim was the achievement of nothing less than 'balanced communities'. The official thinking of the 1940s promoted social mixing as an important policy goal: 'if the community is to be truly balanced, so long as social classes exist, all must be represented in it. A contribution is needed from every type and class of person; the community will be poorer if all are not there, able and willing to make it' (Cmd 6876, quoted in Cherry, 1988, p. 158). With hindsight such objectives may be considered utopian, and it can be argued that the project was bound to fail, since 'It is not within the ability of planning to create mixed class communities' (Lawless and Brown, 1986, p. 142). Having said this, it is also important to recognise that New Towns like Milton Keynes have become for many people 'an attractive place to live' (Deem, 1986, p. 21). Hall describes the New Towns as 'self-evidently good places to live and above all to grow up in' (1988, p. 173), even if they have as communities fallen short of their planners' high-minded ideals.

One of the broader objectives associated with the New Towns programme was to relieve pressure in Britain's inner-city areas by relocating both people and jobs away from the overcrowding and congestion which characterised older urban locations (Lawless, 1989). In the decades following the Second World War the inner areas of Britain's major cities were subjected to programmes of wholesale redevelopment, but these generated opposition on a number of fronts, so that by the mid-1970s 'it was hard to find anyone with a good word to say about planning' (Brindley *et al.*, 1989, p. 3). Planners and other 'urban managers' (as Pahl (1975) christened them) found themselves criticised for redevelopment's architectural style, even though high-rise housing had been introduced in the name of 'social responsibility' (Dunleavy, 1981). They were also criticised for the remoteness of their decision-making from ordinary people (Davies, 1972; Dennis, 1970). There was nothing particularly new in the class difference between the managers of the urban system and their electors, since 'Historically Britain's local government has always been dominated by people drawn from a higher social class than the majority of those they represent' (Saunders, 1979, p. 210). What was seen as having changed was the evolution of new forms of community movements (Lowe, 1986) which sought to impress upon policy-makers 'that working-class communities should not be ruthlessly broken up to satisfy administrative convenience' (Rex, 1988, p. 60). The period since the mid-1970s has witnessed changes described in dramatic terms as 'planning turned upside down' (Hall, 1988, p. 343) and planning 'remade' (Brindley *et al.*, 1989).

The changed nature of planning and the potential of community action to influence the pattern of redevelopment have been examined most extensively in relation to the experience of London's Docklands (Ambrose, 1986; Colenutt, 1991; Deakin and Edwards, 1993; Goodwin, 1991; Marris, 1987), but the typicality of this case is questionable. Equally insightful are studies of attempts at urban regeneration and community development in Glasgow (Donnison and Middleton, 1987), on Tyneside (Byrne, 1989) and in a number of other localities where initiatives by local state bodies aimed at revitalising economic and social life have been pursued (Carley, 1990; Deakin and Edwards, 1993; Harloe *et al.*, 1990). The power of community groups to influence these processes of redevelopment has varied significantly from case to case. On Tyneside Byrne found that 'in a relatively ethnically homogeneous community ... with a high level of residential stability, familial and quasi-familial bonds matter a good deal for social action' (1989, p. 160). Liverpool's local politics in the 1980s were characterised by a more confrontational style, and 'The council's negative attitude to various voluntary associations, and especially to cooperatives, meant that considerable local support evaporated', although it was also discovered that ' "community" could not be simply ignored or obliterated' (Urry, 1990, p. 196). The dislocation caused by redevelopment in areas such as Manchester's Moss Side has had a long-lasting and negative effect on the ability of local people to realise the potential which 'community' offers as a political resource (Parry *et al.*, 1987), although even in such unfavourable circumstances, 'community' has proved to be a potent symbol in the mobilisation of minority ethnic groups (Gilroy, 1987). We start this chapter by examining the development of new communities, focusing especially on the importance planners traditionally attached to social 'balance'.

From this, we proceed to examine the changed role of planners and other urban managers in the post-war period, and the modes of community response and opposition which have resulted.

The attempt to achieve social balance in the New Towns in the decades after 1945 drew much of its inspiration from the long-established tradition of thought which identified single-class settlements as socially undesirable and politically dangerous (Heraud, 1975). The New Towns were in many ways the successors to Ebenezer Howard and the quest for community embodied in the garden city movement which had flourished earlier in the century (Hall, 1988; Thorns, 1976), although there were some important differences between them, not least over the role to be played by the state in the creation of the new communities. Social balance was understood by the New Towns planners primarily in class terms, it being 'assumed that new towns would not replicate the single, working-class communities typical of some inter-war peripheral estates. ... They would instead accommodate social groups roughly in proportions approximating to national averages' (Lawless and Brown, 1986, pp. 137–8). The implication of this goal for housing policy was that it would be necessary to provide 'a variety of housing types, sizes and tenures' (Aldridge, 1979, p. 107). Balance was also understood to involve self-containment and economic self-sufficiency, requiring that enough jobs would be created 'for all the population of working age, that there should be a wide variety of jobs to accommodate different skills, tastes, ages and circumstances and that the industrial base should be diverse, so that the town would not be dependent on one industry' (Aldridge, 1979, p. 106). The objective of the New Towns becoming 'a microcosm of contemporary British society' (Aldridge, 1979, p. 106) meant that in several respects they were envisaged as the antithesis of the traditional working-class communities discussed in chapter 2.

The outcomes of this attempt to create balanced communities in the New Towns are important in themselves but are also instructive in relation to broader debates about planning and redevelopment. On the issue of balance in social class terms it quickly became clear that the people who moved to the New Towns were not a cross-section of the overall population, and the 1971 census showed that 'skilled manual workers are over-represented nearly everywhere and sometimes to a startling extent' (Aldridge, 1979, p. 120). The over- or under-representation of other social classes varied between locations, although the situation can be summed up by saying that the New Towns have tended to cater for what Pahl (1984) calls the 'middle mass' of the class structure rather than either extreme. Similar points can be made about the ways in which the inhabitants of the New Towns have been atypical in terms of age, household type and ethnicity. The age structure was skewed as a result of the fact that 'nearly all migrants have been young families' (Aldridge, 1979, p. 113), although over time this 'imbalance' has become less prominent. Along with the under-representation of unskilled and retired people, the New Towns have also been criticised for excluding lone parents and ethnic minorities, even if the relatively low rates of migration among these groups may at least in part be considered a reflection of their poverty and labour market position rather than the result of more direct discrimination.

The composition of the New Towns population thus supports the point made in chapter 4 about the selective character of the migration process. Deakin and Ungerson's study of migration out of London to the New Towns confirmed the findings of earlier studies that migrants 'were drawn from areas and social groups not predominantly in greatest need' (1977, p. 154). Thus, for example, minority ethnic groups were found to 'suffer from the same disadvantages as the rest of the Inner City population in their attempt to move out; and to the extent that a substantial proportion of them are unskilled or semi-skilled, they are blocked in the same way' (1977, p. 158). Dissatisfaction with housing conditions was often more important than dissatisfaction with inner-city neighbourhoods as a reason for wanting to migrate in Deakin and Ungerson's study area of Islington, a finding also generated in Madge and Willmott's (1981) research in Stockwell (another part of inner London) where as many as half of the respondents said they wanted to leave. Given the high levels of unmet demand which these studies indicate, it can be concluded that the New Towns have had only 'limited success in achieving their express purpose of contributing to the control and relief of the population concentration in London and the other conurbations' (Thorns, 1976, p. 89). More negatively the selective pattern of migration may be seen as having actively contributed to the worsening of inner-city problems by increasing the concentration of disadvantaged groups there.

There are several further bases on which the success of the New Towns as 'experiments in social engineering' (Cherry, 1988, p. 161) can be judged. The objective of creating balanced communities was pursued in a somewhat mechanical way, as for example when 'efforts were made to mix social classes at the local street level by building public housing alongside private dwellings', and patterns of segregation tended to re-emerge as 'ultimately particular neighbourhoods became in effect either working-class or middle-class residential localities' (Lawless and Brown, 1986, p. 142). A good deal can be learned about the minds of the New Towns planners from the expectation that 'the overall size of a neighbourhood would be dictated by the maximum walking distance for a woman with a pram' (Nuttgens, 1989, p. 46). Physical proximity does not guarantee that a sense of community will emerge, and even where it does, it will not necessarily conform to the planners' image of it. As Thorns has observed, 'planners have not succeeded in fulfilling their declared objectives principally because the individuals who migrated to the new towns have not shared their conception of what the new community should look like and be' (1976, p. 89). The individuals who live in New Towns do not form an 'ideological community', but rather hold 'separate and often conflicting ideas about the nature of the ideal community, which leads to many different patterns of activity within any one residential area' (1976, p. 90). Put another way, people come to be involved in local social networks via a number of 'pathways', to use Finnegan's (1989) term, and it is sociologically naive to presume that these will all converge on one point.

The conception of community as shared activities and common identity emerging spontaneously among people living and working together in a conducive physical environment has rightly been criticised for its architectural determinism and also for its anti-urbanism and nostalgic romanticism (Dennis, 1968; Glass, 1989; Heraud, 1975; Thorns, 1976). Community life cannot be created in such a formulistic fashion, since new settlements are bound to be marked out as different simply by virtue of their newness and their unique employment structure. As Finnegan has noted, 'it would be misleading to assume that, say, a recently-built housing estate in a new British town will have the same strong neighbourhood ties and sense of community identity as those where people have lived for generations following much the same trade' (1985, p. 167). It would be equally wrong, however, to conclude that community ties are a characteristic only of long-established settlements, for 'though localities certainly vary, there *are* localities in modern urban contexts where informal network and support-systems are still an important resource, and others in which they play some part without necessarily pervading the whole locality' (1985, p. 167; emphasis in original). As was noted in chapter 1, the various meanings of community in terms of territory, interest and attachment do not always coincide, and the implication of this is that the boundaries of community cannot be set in concrete.

Finnegan's own research into the internal ties among groups of amateur musicians in Milton Keynes bears out the point that social networks are unlikely to be coincidental with the hard physical boundaries of neighbourhoods as the New Towns planners conceived them. She found that

Local music-making was not typically practised within a neighbourhood-based 'community' in the traditional sense . . . of a collectivity of people living together in a specific territorial area bound together by inter-personal ties or a sense of belonging together. (1989, p. 300)

Musical associations across the whole range of types of music were only rarely 'made up predominantly of people from the same neighbourhood', the norm being that 'People *travelled* to join with others in the practice of music' (1989, p. 301; emphasis in original). Finnegan argues that the 'pathways in urban living' which these connections within local music-making represented were neither all-embracing nor random and anonymous, thus challenging both the 'nostalgic quasi-spiritual sense' (1989, p. 299) of community and the alternative interpretation of modern city life as impersonal and unconnected. These 'pathways' had an intermediate status between the extremes in that 'They were not all-encompassing or always clearly known to outsiders, but settings in which relationships could be forged, interests shared, and a continuity of meaning achieved in the context of urban living' (1989, p. 306). The musicians were united not only by common symbols but also by the collective experience of acting together, and the fact that they were 'linked not just by shared views or emotions but by social *practices*' meant that they could 'see themselves as somehow representing and enhancing the whole "community" at public events' (1989, pp. 305, 56; emphasis in original) despite being drawn from a wider area than the immediate neighbourhood.

The implications of Finnegan's study of the 'hidden musicians' of Milton Keynes go far beyond the immediate worlds of brass bands, folk groups, choirs and orchestras. Finnegan demonstrates that the neighbourhood pattern of community was not to be found in Milton Keynes, and suggests that searching for 'community' in such a preconceived sense is likely to prove a fruitless exercise. Thus 'Even the new planned neighbourhoods, each with its own type of housing, environment and likely social profile, could not easily be designated as "communities" as far as music went – or perhaps for other purposes either' (1989, p. 300). For many of the musicians in Finnegan's study the world of music offered the opportunity to express themselves as individuals, and through his or her musical activities 'An individual could make a mark free from the otherwise limiting constraints of occupation, bureaucracy or education' (1989, p. 307). As the creation of the local performers themselves, the musical groups did not conform to the neighbourhood patterns of sociability intended by the New Towns planners, illustrating the point that there are limits to how far social life can be shaped by planning. A similar conclusion could be drawn from Deem's (1986) study of women's leisure in Milton Keynes, although Deem does argue that planners can make an important contribution to widening women's choices by creating a safer and more accessible environment for their leisure.

It should not be concluded from the above discussion that the New Towns were concerned solely with social objectives. In the broad perspective of the original planners the goal of making socially balanced communities was seen as running in tandem with the objective of economic self-containment, but in more specific terms the New Towns have suffered from 'a regrettable lack of clarity about what objective or objectives were being pursued' (Aldridge, 1979, p. 185). In some New Towns such as Corby the prime concern seemed to be 'to meet existing industry's demand for housing' (Aldridge, 1979, p. 108), leading to 'imbalanced development' (Grieco, 1987a, p. 138) which had disastrous consequences when that industry went into decline. More generally the lack of clarity about the precise meanings of social balance and self-containment came to matter increasingly as the changing national economic and political context forced those responsible for running the New Towns to make difficult choices about priorities. By the 1970s official thinking was turning against publicly rented housing, and self-containment had been tacitly abandoned (Aldridge, 1979; Mullan, 1980). These changes raised numerous questions about planning and decision-making in the New Towns and the limited extent of public participation there. In the minds of the original New Towns planners neighbourhood structures were conceived in terms of a particular vision of social order and control. In Crawley, for example, 'mixing different social groups as housing was allocated was thought to encourage "community" leadership by the middle class', a plan which hinged on 'a number of assumptions about gender, family and class relations which were essentially status-quo in character' (Dickens *et al.*, 1985, p. 223). In practice, here as elsewhere, the reality was to prove somewhat different.

URBAN MANAGERIALISM AND BEYOND

While the achievements of the New Towns planners have come over time to be seen as simply prosaic rather than revolutionary, in other contexts planners have acquired a more negative image. Porteus (1989) speaks of 'The annihilation of a place called Howdendyke', a small village port on Humberside which was 'planned to death', and Marris (1987) notes how redevelopment in Docklands was experienced by many people as a form of loss over which they grieved. Both Porteus and Marris are keen to stress, however, that the power of planners should not be exaggerated, and that 'planner-bashing' (Porteus, 1989, p. 195) diverts attention away from the politicians, corporations and private individuals who also have responsibility for the ways in which redevelopment has been undertaken. Put another way, planners are tied in to a much wider urban system containing a number of competing groups with conflicting interests. Marxist analyses of this system highlight the ways in which there are 'processes of community construction and community empowerment that integrate only too well into the dynamics of capital accumulation' and that this 'capitalist form of community' (Harvey, 1989, pp. 236–7) is linked to residential differentiation and segregation along class lines. Marris (1987) adds to this picture the further dimensions of gender and racial inequalities being reproduced through redevelopment, doubting that class interests alone are a sufficient basis on which to build a challenge to the exercise of power. In general there is widespread agreement that it is necessary to drop the assumption of planners' neutrality and to ask Pahl's (1975) celebrated question, 'Whose city?'

Pahl's answer to his own question shifted over time. His earlier focus on the power which was exercised by 'urban managers' (such as planners and housing officials) over the allocation of resources gave way to a greater acknowledgement of the structural constraints within which they operated, in particular 'the constraints of capitalism' (Pahl, 1975, p. 268). Various empirical investigations confirmed the strength of the restrictions which limited the ability of urban managers to exert an independent influence on the distribution of resources such as housing and land. Mullan's investigation into the development of Stevenage, the first New Town, found decision-making there 'largely determined by industrial "needs" ', indicating the power of industrialists which had the effect of reducing the Corporation 'to a position of handmaiden' (1980, pp. 257, 259). The power of Stevenage's urban managers was also constrained by the activities of community groups, although here Mullan was tempted to conclude 'that the participatory process, and in particular the struggles of the protest groups, was merely ritualistic' (1980, p. 286). The community groups were hampered by the fact that the majority of the members of the Board of Stevenage Corporation 'had interests more akin to those of management, ownership, and professional life than to those of employee interests' (1980, p. 258). They were also socially diverse and politically inexperienced, both of which undermined their claims to represent 'community' interests.

Concern with the ideologies and motives of urban managers needs to be complemented by an analysis of the factors which restrict their ability to achieve objectives such as the creation of balanced communities. Saunders has identified 'three major sets of constraints operating to limit the autonomy of the managers of the local state . . . [which] can be summarized as ecological, political and economic forces' (1979, p. 189). In his study of urban development in the South London borough of Croydon, Saunders found that middle-class owner–occupiers were a formidable force, their residents' associations constituting 'a highly articulate and effective political group' (1979, p. 206). In contrast community action was much less reliable as a means of securing objectives for the working-class residents of the borough, it being the case that 'working class interests are generally excluded from social policy-making', not least because 'they lack the organizational base which is necessary if they are to mobilize effectively' (1979, p. 206). The outcomes of housing and commercial property developments tended to suit middle-class residents and business interests, and to frustrate the less well articulated aspirations of the working-class residents. Victories for middle-class groups (where, for example, they successfully opposed housing developments in the south of the borough) were 'at the expense of primarily working class groups who are obliged to live at higher densities and with fewer social provisions' (1979, p. 272). The role of urban managers in Croydon's development tended to reinforce existing inequalities among the local population both in terms of their material resources and their access to decision-making processes.

Without playing down the significance of the various forces constraining the activities of Croydon's urban managers in the 1970s, it is nevertheless appropriate to suppose that 'the freedom of action of a local council would be much less in a depressed area or in an economic recession' (Pahl *et al.*, 1983, p. 139). Meegan's study of Liverpool's outer estates offers the opportunity to test this proposition, since it is an investigation of a disadvantaged area which has suffered from declining economic activity in recent decades. The plans for Merseyside's economic and social restruc-turing in the period following 1945 revolved around the dispersal of both jobs and people to outer areas. The emphasis placed on the relocation of 'those in "housing need" in the old working class areas of the inner city' meant that the new settlements like Kirkby had very different class profiles from the New Towns where 'balanced communities' had been pursued as an objective. Mersey-side's outer estates were 'predominantly "one class" townships:

working class, with a marked bias towards semi-skilled and unskilled manual workers' (1989, p. 202). This 'overspill' population experienced relocation as traumatic, since their 'long-standing, tightly knit communities were broken up and extended family and kinship networks ruptured as families and neighbours were scattered in the different outlying estates' (1989, p. 203). Hopes of healthier housing conditions and better-paid and more secure work had to be set against this loss.

Meegan's account notes that planners enjoyed some success in attaining housing and employment targets in the 'boom' years of the 1950s and 1960s, but that subsequently Liverpool's outer estates have suffered rising levels of unemployment and impoverishment. In the context of parts of Kirkby having over 80 per cent of tenants in receipt of housing benefit the promised 'paradise' has had to be postponed. The 'new role for Merseyside' envisaged by planners failed to materialise, leaving a situation of 'community under siege' in which there is a 'pronounced degree of mistrust . . . towards "outsiders" ' but also 'resilience and resistance' (1989, pp. 217, 224–6). Economic adversity has coincided with a revival of a sense of community in the locality, which Meegan explains in terms of 'the remaking over time of the family support networks that were broken by the initial population dispersal from the inner city' (1989, p. 227). The majority of Kirkby households had close relatives living nearby, and these emergent networks have contributed to the identification with the locality and its people, including a concern for those who are unemployed. This resilience of community identity is expressed 'in a number of "bottom up" initiatives in which local people have joined together to try to improve their living standards and quality of life' (1989, p. 226), and these community groups have proved remarkably effective in their efforts to influence local government despite the financial restrictions imposed on it by central government and declining local resources. Merseyside's outer estates are just the sort of segregated working-class neighbourhoods which the 'balanced communities' of the New Towns were intended not to be, and they have duly produced a very different style of 'community politics'. By 'building up the confidence of local people in their ability to plan for their own locality' (Meegan, 1990, p. 105), such community groups frequently come into conflict with local urban managers and place further constraints on them.

The finding of Meegan's Merseyside research that social, spatial and tenurial polarisation has the potential to strengthen rather than weaken community action is echoed in Byrne's (1989) study of Tyneside. The planned relocation of housing and jobs from Newcastle and the surrounding area included the construction in the 1960s and 1970s of the 'created community' (1989, p. 54) of Cramlington which had many of the characteristics of a New Town without being formally designated as such. In addition to creating employment through the establishment of a diversified industrial base it was the intention of the planners to provide the new residents who moved to the area with housing, shopping and leisure facilities which would be sufficiently attractive to make the town 'free-standing'. Although initially successful in attaining some of these objectives, many people who moved to Cramlington continued to travel to Newcastle to work, and clear differences in the town's population emerged quite quickly. Even in 1981 there were definite signs of significant socio-spatial segregation in Cramlington, with the town's population falling into three clusters. Owner–occupiers in households with high levels of predominantly non-local and non-manual employment and high rates of car-ownership made up just over half the town's population. At the other end of the polarisation process was a cluster of local authority and housing association tenants among whom there was a six times higher rate of male unemployment and the likelihood of not being car-owners. The proportion of lone-parent households was over six times greater in this cluster, which accounted for approximately one seventh of Cramlington's people. The remaining third of the town's population fell into an intermediate position in terms of housing tenure and labour market position, although the profile of this group bore more of a resemblance to the second of the above clusters than it did to the first (Byrne, 1989, p. 105).

Planning in the case of Cramlington had not only failed to achieve a balanced community, in some ways it had actively contributed to the process of social polarisation by failing to establish a viable industrial base for the town. Local clusters of deprivation reflected 'the way in which a population was assembled for manufacturing work which has disappeared' (Byrne, 1989, p. 108). Parts of the new town were subject to patterns of social disadvantage which, although less extreme, nevertheless resembled those of certain inner-city Tyneside districts such as the Meadowell Estate in North Shields, and overall Byrne concluded that Cramlington was 'just as polarized as the Metropolitan Borough' (1989, p. 108). In the Cramlington sub-locality of Shankhouse 'nearly 70% of households were in receipt of housing benefit and only 42% of household heads were in employment of any kind' while in South Meadowell 'over 85% of households are in receipt of housing benefit, 47% of households are headed by single parents and the unemployment rate is over 80%' (1989, p. 110). Urban managers appear to have had a direct influence through their housing allocation procedures in bringing about this latter intensification of disadvantage, because 'the general lettings policy of the local authority since 1974 but, more particularly, in the 1980s ... has resulted in a concentration of "difficult" households (including many very young single parents) in the area from all over North Tyneside' (1989, p. 112). Such policies can be considered as a geographical expression of the widening gap between households dependent on state benefits and multi-earner households which Pahl's (1984) theory of polarisation discussed in chapter 3 attempted to explain.

Byrne's account of the unfolding of local social polarisation on Tyneside comes to conclusions which are somewhat different from those arrived at by Pahl in his Sheppey study. Contrary to the widely held belief that social polarisation threatens 'the breakdown of social order', Byrne's

Interviews with housing managers, social workers, community workers, elected representatives and residents in various areas in northern Tyneside, but particularly in North Shields and Cramlington, all give a picture of a considerable degree of survival of traditional community institutions and values in severely deprived locales. (1989, pp. 110–11)

Whereas Pahl's research led him to envisage the progressive exclusion of households without access to labour market opportunities, Byrne argues that such an 'underclass' is unlikely to emerge on Tyneside because the area's culture is against it. He claims that much of the traditional working-class culture generated in the period when the area was dominated by mining villages and occupational communities based on industries such as shipbuilding has survived down to the present. Further, 'The point is that this culture is *inclusive*. It is based on a unitary non-exclusionary conception of communal interest which traditionally was closed only above to capital and not below to an ethnically or religiously distinctive excluded group' (1989, p. 161; emphasis in original). Byrne believes that in such a context community work among poor people has potential to empower rather than control them, provided that at the same time 'the non-poor can be organized around common interests with the poor' (1989, p. 161) through, for example, strategies to modernise the local economic base and thereby create more secure employment prospects.

Byrne notes that such a programme may be undermined by pessimism on the part of local urban managers who have become cynical about their ability to act autonomously, but in his analysis the actions of urban managers have to be seen alongside the actions of community work practitioners. It is this group which has the closest contact with ordinary people and through this the opportunity to harness the collective energies of local communities. Community workers operate as a point of contact between the local state and community groups, and can play a pivotal role in a broad campaign for social change. That economic adversity in North Shields has not led to social fragmentation is due in no small part to the fact that the area has a number of community groups which 'include locale-based tenants' organizations concerned with the quality of housing provision and housing services, women's groups concerned particularly with health services, local consumer co-ops in the form of a credit union and food co-op, and youth and childcare provision organizations' (1989, p. 163). The experience of working with these groups leads most community workers 'to identify with those whom they serve', and to have little in common with those urban managers who in the past typically 'regarded working-class residential communities as moveable pieces in the development game' (1989, pp. 165, 87). If MacGregor (1990) is correct in her characterisation of the inner-city as a 'battlefield', then Byrne's analysis suggests that urban managers are in danger of losing control over their front-line troops.

### THE BASES OF COMMUNITY ACTION

Byrne's account of the prospects for community action is founded not only on his analysis of the effects of social polarisation on

Tyneside but also on his practical experiences in community work with the North Tyneside Community Development Project. Detailed assessments of the various Community Development Projects which were set up in twelve localities in the late 1960s and early 1970s to revitalise community structures are mixed (Higgins, 1978; Lawless and Brown, 1986; Loney, 1983), but there is general agreement that these 'experiments' disproved the simplistic assumptions about community action with which their originators operated. Founded on the anticipation that community workers would promote more effective liaison between agencies working in disadvantaged neighbourhoods and further 'encourage traditions of mutual support' (Marris, 1987, p. 17), their actual effect was to create 'a group of workers who transformed the scheme into a more radical critique of official policy and practice' (Short, 1984, p. 138). In doing so they took up the position of 'community against government' (Loney, 1983), and the image of the various agencies of the state, community workers and local people jointly waging a British version of the American 'war on poverty' was displaced by one in which community groups were more likely to find themselves in opposition to the state. It is a key characteristic of most urban social movements that they 'exist as a result of opposition to some aspect of local policy' (Lowe, 1986, p. 58), although there is less common ground in terms of the strategies and tactics employed in pursuit of their objectives. This in turn reflects the diversity of those objectives.

Community action is frequently a response to a perceived common threat, and examples of this type of community action are legion in the literature on urban redevelopment. It was noted above that the case of London's Docklands has been the subject of extensive research, due partly to the ambitiousness of the re-development there and partly to the strength of community organisations which have been mobilised to defend local interests. Development proposals since the early 1970s have taken several forms as planners have addressed the fundamental problem of how to revitalise an area which had seen the collapse of the local labour market with the disappearance of jobs in the docks and related industries and massive out-migration (Brindley *et al.*, 1989; Hall, 1988). While Docklands appeared to planners to be 'the largest redevelopment opportunity in Europe' (Ambrose, 1986, p. 221), to the local population redevelopment was experienced more in terms of insecurity (Marris, 1987), and the various development plans have met with considerable resistance. The area is one in which 'The sense of community . . . is still a force to be reckoned with', rooted as it is 'in a tradition of shared involvement in dock-based economic activities and a militant and articulate labour movement' (Ambrose, 1986, p. 214). The ensuing 'battle for docklands' (Hall, 1988, p. 351), referred to by Ambrose in dramatic terms as 'the second London blitz' (1986, p. 214), has proved to be an important test case in the strengths and weaknesses of community action.

The case of London's Docklands poses in a particularly acute form the question of whose interests redevelopment is intended to serve. In Docklands as elsewhere redevelopment has meant 'conflicts of local against regional control, of working class against middle class, of capital against labour' (Marris, 1987, p. 63). What this meant in more concrete terms was that the people of Docklands

saw themselves threatened by office developers, by an invasion of homeless families herded into huge, impersonal Greater London Council estates, by the conversion of the riverside into fashionable, luxury hotels and apartments; and by main roads slashing through what was left of their disintegrating, blighted and economically marginal communities. (Marris, 1987, pp. 63–4)

Throughout the 1970s attempts were made by planners and politicians to consult the local population about their wishes and interests, but such consultation discovered important divisions in local opinion. One of these divisions arose over the question of employment, with loyalties being 'divided between those who welcomed *any* development, including office blocks, because it meant jobs, and those who wished to maintain an employment structure closer to the industrial traditions of the area' (Ambrose, 1986, pp. 221–2; emphasis in original). Housing was another issue which divided local opinion, since 'there was conflict between those who wanted much more speculative private development to produce a more "normal" tenure balance and those who wanted more low-rent, local authority housing' (Ambrose, 1986, p. 222). In the context of these and other disputes, democratically elected representatives and leaders of community groups both laid claim to being the more authentic voice of local people, although they were subsequently to share the experience of being bypassed as central government set up an Urban Development Corporation to oversee the area's redevelopment.

The London Docklands Development Corporation (LDDC) appointed in 1981 'has made no secret of the fact that it seeks not just economic development but also changes in the local community itself' (Goodwin, 1991, p. 255), aiming to bring about radical shifts in the local employment and housing markets by promoting service sector occupations in place of industrial ones and owner-occupation in place of local authority property. In this plan the arrival of new types of work and new middle-class residents was expected to benefit the existing local population through the process of 'trickle down' (Colenutt, 1991), but interim assessments suggest that such effects have been limited. In the sphere of employment, 'while a small proportion of local residents obtain jobs in firms new to Docklands, the incoming firms have had minimal impact on those most in need, such as young people in low-paid "dead-end" and insecure jobs, and on the long-term unemployed' (Church and Hall, 1989, p. 363). With respect to housing, 'policies to encourage private housebuilding in an area almost totally dominated by council housing at the time of the 1981 Census have not alleviated housing hardship in the constituent east London boroughs' (Church and Hall, 1989, pp. 363–4). While acknowledging that the LDDC 'did get a lot done' (Hall, 1988, p. 355), redevelopment in Docklands can still be interpreted as a policy of 'replacing a surplus population' (Goodwin, 1991), and there is evidence that working-class tenants are being displaced to other areas (Morris and Winn, 1990).

On the basis of his extensive involvement in local community action in Docklands, Colenutt interprets claims by the LDDC to be 'working for the community' (1991, p. 37) as largely a public relations exercise. His explanation of why there has been so little community benefit from the redevelopment of Docklands is framed in terms of the insensitivity of central government and market forces to the needs and wishes of the local population, it being his view that 'direction and control must come from local democratic structures, both in local government and in the community' (1991, p. 41). The history of community action in Docklands before and since the appointment of the LDDC does not unambiguously endorse the viability of this strategy. While the

LDDC may be criticised for operating with an excessively wide 'definition of the "community" which should benefit from the regeneration of Docklands' (Brindley *et al.*, 1989, p. 118) by reference to national and global interests, it is an unresolved issue just how narrowly 'community' should be defined. The simple dichotomy of 'locals versus newcomers' may be an understandable reaction in the context of 'The social exclusiveness of the new houses and offices' (Brindley *et al.*, 1989, pp. 117, 120), but it breaks down when the range of local residents' interests is examined more closely. Redevelopment can be seen as a process which encourages competition rather than co-operation between neighbouring communities (Gillespie *et al.*, 1992), and Ambrose suggests that

In an area with a large and diverse population, and more than its fair share of individualists, it would be foolish to assert that all local residents want the same outcome from the redevelopment process . . . On many issues the diversity of views is as broad as it could possibly be. (1986, p. 241)

The presence of women's organisations, community groups with religious or ethnic affiliations, trade-union bodies and a range of more explicitly political movements testifies to the complexity of the local situation and to the difficulties inherent in identifying local community interests.

It could be suggested that the population of inner-city areas such as London's Docklands have come together as a community force most effectively through their opposition to redevelopment plans and the more general management of the urban system, but it would be wrong to portray community action as only reactive and backward-looking. While urban social movements can be characterised as 'the retreat of city dwellers into their local communities, as a defensive mechanism against corporate and state power' (Lowe, 1986, p. 193), it is also important to recognise that 'community' has the potential to inspire more positive visions of the future based on broad, inclusive alliances. Marris's study concludes that the logic of community action is 'to draw together community issues of housing, amenities and services with broader economic issues' and that this is likely to involve a coalition of diverse forces including 'feminism, movements of racial equality, ecological and environmental movements, together with liberal and socialist traditions' in the pursuit of 'a different kind of society' (1987, pp. 161–3). If the attempt 'to improve, rather than replace, existing housing and employment activities, and to aim these improvements at local people' (Goodwin, 1991, p. 261) embodied in the 1976 London Docklands Strategic Plan ultimately came to nothing, it is still noteworthy that the attempt was made to go beyond preserving the status quo. The Plan in many ways embodied the spirit which had inspired the early New Towns planners, and criticism of it as economically unrealistic illustrates the extent to which policy-making has shifted in the intervening period.

The experience of redevelopment may have made community groups and state bodies wary of close association with each other, but the situation is a long way from that of the 1940s when, typically, 'the public at large played little part in the planning process' (Hasegawa, 1992, p. 134). Community politics has posed a significant 'challenge from below' (Cochrane, 1986, p. 53) to the managers of the urban system which it has been impossible to ignore. One response to this challenge has been for urban managers actively to court community groups, as Donnison discovered in inner Glasgow, where 'Politicians and officials are trying harder to get alongside the groups they serve, to listen to their perception of the problems, and to give them some control over the resources available for solving them' (1987, p. 287). A similar picture emerges from some of Glasgow's outer estates, where Carley found a basic assumption of neighbourhood renewal to be 'that nothing lasting or significant can be achieved without the local community eventually taking over ownership and leadership of the process' (1990, p. 153). An alternative response has been for urban managers to regard community groups and their inner-city constituencies as essentially a problem of social control, and Mellor has suggested that it is 'tempting to see inner Manchester in this way – as one local resident called it, an "open concentration camp" ' (1985, p. 119). Mellor goes on to make the point, however, that it would be mistaken 'to overestimate the capacity of state agencies, especially the local authorities, to manage' (1985, p. 119), not least because of restrictions on their resources.

The conclusion which Mellor draws about inner-city areas such as Manchester's Moss Side is that a segmented and divided population is 'a weak political force' (1985, p. 120). Economic and social marginality have compounded the effects of urban redevelopment in these areas to erode the bases which sustain a sense of shared identity and the community action which is associated with it. Parry and his co-researchers found some evidence of divisions along ethnic lines on Moss Side, but noted that 'The most striking cleavage, remarked upon again and again ... was between young and old' (1987, p. 227), due in part at least to the high rates of unemployment among the young people of the area. They also found an enduring 'legacy of bitterness' over the way in which local redevelopment had disrupted 'the old networks of family and kinship' (1987, pp. 229–30) without providing the material basis on which the creation of new community ties could occur. In such an unfavourable environment, it is perhaps not surprising that local discontent should have been expressed in the violent and dramatic form of the 1981 riots. It is also important to note that some of those involved in the inner-city disturbances of the 1980s explained their actions by reference to their own interpretation of 'community' (Gilroy, 1987). In the institutions of the local state one response to these disturbances has been a renewed effort to increase the involvement of local community groups in decision-making (Parry *et al.*, 1987), although the continued elusiveness of the concept of community in discussions of local political accountability, consultation and participation (Deakin and Edwards, 1993) means that such initiatives remain highly contentious.

# 8

## COMMUNITY AND SOCIAL POLICY: CARE AND CONTROL

As has been discussed earlier in this book, the concept of 'community' is one which is sufficiently vague to allow it to be used in a variety of different ways for different purposes. Nowhere is this more apparent than in everyday political rhetoric, as social and political commentators of different persuasions seek to convey their image of the social problems facing society and the solutions they are suggesting. By its nature, such public discourse encompasses those core dilemmas within the idea of 'community' which have been the focus of much of this book. Thus one frequently finds a tension between, on the one hand, the benefits for social order of community integration and, on the other, the high value placed on individual freedom and choice. Equally, there is clearly ambiguity between the supposed 'naturalness' of community solidarity and the need for regular vigilance in guarding community integrity from the threats posed by contemporary forms of social organisation.

This view has become more entrenched as social conditions in modern society appear to undermine the traditional bases of community solidarity. At the same time as 'community' has become more problematic, the efforts made to draw upon the supposed strengths of the community have become more overt. Perhaps this is simply because they can no longer be taken for granted. Certainly it would seem that the state at different levels now incorporates community initiatives into its social policies more actively than in previous eras. Willmott (1989), for example, argues that the concept of community has come to the fore in British social policy in the latter half of the twentieth century. While he says it is too early to judge whether this represents a

154

'rhetorical exploitation of high-minded ambiguity' or a 'genuine change in ways of organising our collective life' (1989, p. 1), the growth of community approaches to policy issues is apparent in such areas as community care, community work, community policing, community development, community education, community politics, and the like. The same point is made by Cochrane: 'Today governments seem to use "community" as if it were an aerosol can, to be sprayed on any social programme, giving it a more progressive and sympathetic cachet' (1986, p. 51).

In many respects the incorporation of the language and concerns of community into policy initiatives tends to reflect a predominantly conservative, or at least anti-modernist, analysis of contemporary social problems. By this we do not mean that the programmes developed cannot be radical within their own context – the development of new towns and communities, for example, or of community policing can be recognised as significant departures from the existing dominant practices in these fields – or in their consequences. Rather we mean that by their reference to community, the solutions envisaged involve a rejection of modes of practice based upon the bureaucratic and large-scale in favour of more participatory and responsive modes. Often within this lies a progressive concern for democracy, but equally it usually entails a sense that the appropriate balance, or even rhythm, of social life has been disrupted by the impersonality and scale of contemporary organisation. Through being community-orientated, policies can begin to redress this balance and return to more socially integrative, and consequently more rewarding and successful, methods of operation.

Community care is undoubtedly the policy which has had the highest profile amongst recent initiatives which embrace a community dimension. A large part of this chapter will be concerned with the development of community care for elderly and other people needing support and with discussing the extent to which such policies are based on an appropriate analysis of contemporary community organisation. Community care is a particularly good example to use here, not just because of its social significance but also because it highlights the contradictions faced by policy-makers. On the one hand, it represents an attempt by state bureaucracies to build on the set of informal relationships occurring 'naturally' in local communities; on the other, it seeks to foster and strengthen these networks when they are lacking, as they now so often seemingly are for reasons to do with the imputed social malaise of modern society.

Before turning to the issues raised by community care, however, the chapter will first focus on other social policies which have encompassed a community perspective. In doing this, it is necessary to be selective. Some policies, like the New Town developments discussed in the previous chapter, are explicitly concerned with community issues and have a strong element of community deliberately built into them. Here a particular vision of community, one which emphasised balance and social mix, came to dominate, though with hindsight the model of social solidarity it entailed was questionable. Many other policies have an impact on community matters without this ever being an explicit aim. A number of examples of this have been given in this book already. The economic restructuring which took place in the 1980s is an obvious case in point. Here the desire to privatise public enterprises and reduce public expenditure, including industrial subsidies, resulted in a rapid decline in manufacturing in the early 1980s and led to historically high levels of unemployment. This economic 'rationalisation' had direct implications for community life in the localities most affected, not least those heavily dependent on nationalised production for their well-being (see chapter 3).

Whilst recognising the pertinence of these latter policies for shaping people's experience of community, the first section of this chapter will only be concerned with policies which aim explicitly to draw on or shape patterns of community involvement. In this, though, it is important to recognise that there is no single, monolithic model of community informing these policies. Community remains a contested notion and this is reflected in policy initiatives which attempt to mobilise it. Some policies, like community care, are premised on an essentially integrative and altruistic model of community in which networks of co-operating and benevolent individuals are seen as willing to help one another, though their efforts may need a degree of co-ordination and back-up by specialist services. At other times, for example when urban crime is high on the political agenda, a quite divergent model of community comes to the fore. Here the emphasis is not on cohesion and solidarity, but on breakdown and the need for more effective control to be exercised. It is the model of paradise lost, of 'broken' families, of parents no longer exerting discipline over children, of community disintegration and social disorder.

One other point to emphasise here, as we have elsewhere in the book, is that people do not all experience the same 'community' as one another and are not necessarily affected by policy initiatives in the same way. Not only are networks of relationships within localities discrete, so that many people have no involvement – direct or indirect – with one another, but more importantly people living in the same area can experience that area quite differently. There is not just one Stoke Newington or one Islington, one Didcot or one Cheadle Hulme. Nor for that matter is there just one 'black community' or one 'medical community'. Individuals can be involved and incorporated into the same 'community' to very different extents, depending amongst other things on their access to material and relational resources within and without it. Policy developments can play a significant part in this at a variety of levels. More specifically, political intervention in the management and distribution of resources, including those under the direct control of local and national state agencies, has a bearing on the patterns of relationships which emerge in any community.

## ENGINEERING THE COMMUNITY

In formulating 'top–down' community initiatives – that is, ones sponsored by policy-makers rather than those arising from grass-roots movements (Willmott, 1989) – policy-makers often attempt to retain the more successful aspects of existing forms of community involvement whilst altering those features which, with changing standards and expectations, are no longer socially acceptable. Like much planning and policy development, community initiatives are a form of social engineering. Redesign this element or strengthen that one, but do so in a way that maintains the essential properties of the original edifice. On the surface there seems little wrong with such a strategy: keep the good bits, modify those that are not working well; re-evaluate the whole and continue the iteration.

Two difficulties arise, however. The first is whether the pictures which policy-makers have of past, or indeed of current, communities are sufficiently accurate to enable them to shape or engineer practice successfully. As we have seen, ideological elements are so incorporated into notions of community that visions of what might be are frequently coloured by one-sided or romantic images of what was or is. While social research over the last forty years has begun to dispel some of the dominant myths, especially of working-class community life, it often seems that the more utopian paradigms linger long in the imagination of planners and policy-makers. 'Community' continues to be seen as a solution to social dilemmas whose roots lie far outside the locality in much broader structural attributes. Moreover, the model of community implicitly drawn on is one governed by consensus with little recognition of conflict and competing interests.

A second difficulty with the 'engineering' strategy is its assumption that the parts can be altered without this influencing the whole. It may be that a bridge or other mechanical venture can have particular elements strengthened or replaced without fundamentally changing its functionality. The same is less true of more 'organic' arrangements. Change in one component is likely to produce unintended consequences in other areas of the structure. This is certainly an issue as far as community change is concerned. Communities are dynamic rather than static, organic rather than passive. They develop, grow, decline, shift and alter in response to external initiatives as well as internal tensions, in terms of both their infrastructure and the varied sets of relationships which are maintained within them. Consequently in seeking to modify a particular element of community life, for example the adequacy of people's housing conditions, there is always a possibility that this will unintentionally undermine other more valued aspects of community experience, such as people's sense of commitment and solidarity, even though the policy aim is to sustain these other conditions. This dilemma arises from the interactive, dynamic character of communities, and the continuous tension existing between the elements which make up the complex 'whole'.

As an illustration of these processes, consider again Newby's (1980) analysis of the impact which state efforts to preserve the quality of community life in rural areas has had on the solidarities and commitment of different sections of the population, especially in villages within commuting distance of large conurbations. In a good number of these localities, the desire to protect rural ambience has meant an absence of industrial development and restricted house-building programmes. In the context of increased agricultural efficiency – that is, fewer jobs available in farming – the choices facing young working-class adults living in these areas have been quite limited. The absence of local employment, combined with commuter-led house price inflation, the release of tied cottages to the owner-occupied market and the lack of new rental housing provision have systematically undermined the level of social and economic commitment these young adults have to the village community.

The issue is not whether these people would have chosen to migrate anyway, but rather the impact that housing and employment policies have had on the options generally open to them, and consequently on the nature of the 'community' they and others experience. As Newby demonstrates so clearly, against the background of the wider changes occurring within society, these attempts to protect rural community life have themselves contributed to quite significant changes in the social relationships developed within the localities. In particular, whereas previously, for better or worse, most of those who lived in these villages were, through their employment, housing and social activities, dependent principally upon others living in the locality and thus tied to the local economy and social structure, this is no longer the case. Increasingly people moving to the villages because of their rural appeal are people whose style of life depends on employment in nearby urban centres, who are not dependent on local services and who, as a consequence, are not structurally embedded in the locality to anything like the same degree. They live in the village but are not fully 'of' it. In turn, as a result of these socio-economic shifts, the overall character of local solidarities and conflicts takes on quite a different pattern to those occurring previously in the communities.

Similarly, with post-war reconstruction and slum clearance, the state's attempts at improving housing stock resulted in significant shifts in the solidarities that were evidenced in different working-class localities. As we discussed in chapter 2, traditional working-class communities, to the extent they existed in the manner usually portrayed, were based upon overlapping networks of kin and other contacts which in quite large part derived from families living in the area for more than one generation. The dominant form of housing tenure – privately rented – also encouraged geographical stability at a time of housing need as access to housing depended on one's reputation with the landlord or rent collector. In addition though, the poor quality of housing, with its shared facilities and inadequate insulation, made privacy hard to maintain and encouraged a mutual dependence. Whatever else this did, it led to greater potential for involvement between local kin and neighbours, no matter what the balance between co-operation and conflict was in practice. It was this involvement, together with local knowledge of social relations accruing from common heritage, which generated the sense of solidarity which is now retrospectively celebrated.

As we discussed in chapter 4, new housing developments on urban peripheries altered much of this. To begin with, the allocation methods used for council housing were quite distinct from that used by private landlords. With some measure of need replacing local reputation, the estates tended to be populated by people at a common phase of their life course who had little previous knowledge of one another. The result was that kinship could no longer play the role in social life it had in the previous localities. Moreover, the far higher internal specification of this new housing meant that the degree of involvement of neighbours with one another was reduced. There was less knowledge of one another, less need for co-operation and less opportunity for conflict. Thus by improving housing standards and changing allocation procedures the underlying basis of social solidarity in these localities was altered with quite distinct patterns being generated from those reported in 'traditional' communities.

This indicates very well how the 'engineering' model of change is suspect. Particular elements within the whole cannot be modified without the whole itself being changed. It was sometimes suggested that given time the old solidarities would re-emerge. People would once again come to share a common heritage and re-establish local kinship networks. With hindsight it is evident that this has only happened to a limited degree. Whatever their intention and no matter how carefully they designed their estates' layout, the planners could never reproduce the 'community' they were relocating. By improving housing and providing the conditions for greater domestic privacy, they undermined one of the previous cornerstones for solidarity in a fashion that meant it could only re-emerge if their policies were to fail. Equally, of course, changes in the provision of housing were themselves part of a wider movement in social and economic matters which influenced the nature of the dependencies existing in different localities. Increased geographical mobility, the growth of owner-occupation, including transfers from the council sector through 'right-to-buy' policies, and the development of private transport systems have all played a part here. The central point remains: particular aspects of community existence cannot be modified in isolation; change in one sphere will have uncertain, and possibly undesired, repercussions in others.

COMMUNITY CONTROL

In the 1960s and 1970s, even state-sponsored community initiatives appeared to have a radical, transformative potential, especially those which were orientated towards the developing domain of community work. In the United States, the Model Cities Program provided a new source of funding for community-based organisations and projects, many of which were openly oppositional to established political structures and hierarchies. Likewise in the 1970s in Britain, the Community Development Projects sponsored by the Home Office generated analyses and initiatives which were highly critical of existing policies. While created to provide low-cost, 'self-help' models for regenerating localities facing economic decline, they tended to be at the forefront of the critiques which community work practice as a genre was developing at this time. Moreover writers like Castells (1977, 1978) were suggesting that, as a result of economic contradictions within the urban sphere, radical political action was more likely to arise from grass-roots concerns about community provision than from workplace antagonisms as predicted by classical Marxism.

Since this time, though, 'top–down' policies which incorporate elements of community participation have become less open to radical subversion, being framed more around a conservative concern for consolidating social order through drawing on existing elements of community solidarity. Writing about community politics, Cochrane suggests: 'The aim is to involve people in decision-making to commit them to decisions and to generate independent activity which is not threatening but supportive and – ultimately – subordinate rather than complementary' (1986, p. 59). In this light, the attraction of community involvement within contemporary policy-making is less about democratic self-determination and more about managing social tensions and assisting state bureaucracies to accomplish their objectives.

As an example, consider the drive towards community policing which developed in the 1980s. This embraced a range of initiatives, including more local beat patrols, neighbourhood watch and local crime prevention schemes, all endeavouring to build a stronger partnership between the police and local communities in order to reduce crime levels. Unfortunately, as Willmott (1989) notes after reviewing the evidence so far available, there is little sign that these developments have been particularly successful in this. Indeed, after pointing out that schemes like neighbourhood watch are most popular in affluent suburban areas 'where residential burglary is least likely to occur', Hudson suggests that they may lead 'more to near-neurotic preoccupation with the risk of burglary than to any reduction in its actual incidence' (1987, p. 85). Willmott recognises that cynics might well conclude that 'community policing represents little more than a public relations exercise' (1989, p. 73).

It could be argued that, in part, this lack of success stems from the short time which community policing has had to establish itself within a police culture still dominated by more traditional forms of policing. Yet, as Smith (1987) argues, the tensions within community policing run deeper than this. First of all there are issues about the nature of policing itself. Community policing calls for flexibility and sensitivity to local patterns, which in turn means responding to the same behaviour in different ways depending on circumstances. To some degree this necessarily runs counter to the need to uphold the law in a consistent and fair fashion. Secondly, and more importantly for the present discussion, there are clear problems with the idea of community within these approaches. In essence, community policing seeks to build on the consensus that exists within a community in order to combat crime. Yet in practice that consensus cannot be taken for granted, not least in those localities where the police tend to be most active. They are faced with conflict between different groups within the locality, each having somewhat different values and interests (see, for example, Foster, 1990). Furthermore, by the nature of their function, the police will be perceived (usually correctly) as having more sympathy with socially dominant values than oppositional ones.

There is no doubt that people are now far more aware of the possibilities of their being directly affected by criminal activity than they were a generation or two ago. Much publicity has been given to the significant rises in official crime statistics occurring in recent years. While some part of this may be to do with changed patterns of crime reporting, the increased incidence of crimes like theft, burglary and personal assault has resulted in much greater public concern and vigilance. Recent years have seen a large increase in private security measures – burglar, rape and car alarms, window locks, infra-red security lights, etc. – as well as changes in policing practice and the growth of community anti-theft initiatives like neighbourhood watch schemes.

Much of the public debate on crime implies that the people most at risk are those who are most affluent. The reality is rather different. As the quote from Hudson given above indicates, it is those living in poorer neighbourhoods who are most likely to be victims, and not people living in the better-off areas. While Britain is still a long way 'behind' the United States, where Sampson reports 'the lifetime risk of being murdered is as high as 1 in 21 for black males' (compared to 1 in 132 for white males) (1993, p. 259), none the less inner-city areas and urban council estates characterised by high levels of multi-deprivation are, statistically, far more dangerous places to live than owner-occupied suburban districts. In Downes' words:

As we now know from victim surveys, to the long list of regressive taxes to which the most deprived are subject, we must now add crime and its control. For those living in the worst housing estates and privately rented sectors are both under-protected and over-controlled by the authorities. (1989, p. 239)

There is also an important gender element here, for there are differences in the extent to which men and women feel safe engaging in different activities. In their book *Well-Founded Fear:*

*A community study of violence to women*, Hanmer and Saunders (1984) address this issue by focusing on the problems women face in using public spaces at different times of the day. Their study, which is based on a survey of women living in a small area of Leeds in the early 1980s, reveals the extent to which many women's fear of harassment, or worse, figures in their decisions about their activities outside the home, especially at night. While the study took place at a time when public awareness of the issues had been heightened by the 'Yorkshire Ripper' murders, their research indicates how concerns over personal safety commonly structure the ease with which women feel free to participate in different public activities.

Using self-definitions, almost half of the 129 women interviewed in the study reported experiencing or witnessing during the previous year one or more incidents outside the home which they considered violent (1984, p. 37). These included sexual harassment, threats and physical violence. Only a small minority of these events were reported to the police, including only two of the ten crimes categorised as major by the authors in which the respondents were the victim (1984, ch. 4). The authors emphasise how knowledge of such experiences results in many women routinely taking precautionary steps so as not to put themselves at risk of attack or abuse. Some, like this elderly woman, were cautious about venturing out of their homes: 'Of course if it was safe I would go out. I'm 75. So I don't go out at all after dark. In winter, as soon as it's dark I stay in. You're not safe even in your own homes. What else can we do?' (1984, p. 18). Others made sure they avoided certain areas or did not go out alone. In this sense, the public space of 'community' existing outside their home was less theirs than it was some other people's. 'Each woman works out, possibly only semi-consciously, the places, times and means governing her use of public space' (1984, p. 65).

The answer to some of these problems may lie in different or more responsive police practices, though it is difficult to believe that community policing or neighbourhood watch schemes really have much relevance to the problems faced by those living in the more run-down and hazardous areas. The issues that increased crime rates raise are more structural than this, notwithstanding the claims of some in positions of influence that individual wickedness lies at their roots. In particular, the late twentieth century has seen increased social and economic polarisation in many countries in the Western world, including Britain. The major line of cleavage is between those who have access to secure and better-paid employment, and through this to better-quality housing, education and health care, and those who are excluded from the labour market, trapped in long-term dependence on state benefits and poverty, and effectively denied full rights of citizenship.

There is clearly a 'community' dimension to this polarisation, through both the differential impact of unemployment and the operation of housing markets. These processes are being exacerbated by the 'residualisation' of the council house sector, particularly with respect to some of the large and now shabby public housing estates built in the post-war period. The concentration of families with high levels of deprivation and need in unpopular and poorly serviced estates has become an established feature of the urban landscape. Like some parts of the inner city, they have turned into a 'trap of urban squalor for the old, the sick, the unemployed and the unsuccessful ethnic minorities' (Halsey, 1989, p. 230). In the words of the Archbishop of Canterbury's Commission on Urban Priority Areas, the process is

one of deprived people being left in the Urban Priority Areas as the successful move out to middle Britain. The former have decreasing wealth, health, services, income, investment and amenity: the latter have rising affluence, opportunity, power, and advantage: in one ugly word – polarization. (1985, p. 23)

We are a long way from properly understanding the links which exist between urban poverty, unemployment, social deprivation and crime, and it is all too easy to derive false 'explanations' from simple correlations (Bulmer, 1989). Within public discourse, the notion of an 'underclass' has attracted much attention, though there are competing views about its adequacy and what its implications are for social policy. None the less the way in which Wilson's (1987) study draws on the concept in analysing the profound structural changes experienced by ghetto communities in the United States is persuasive and has a degree of resonance with the situation in some parts of Britain's cities. For no matter what the conceptual framework used, it is evident that parts of urban Britain are experiencing social and economic transformations which are extremely damaging to their social fabric. The urban disturbances and riots in cities like Liverpool, London, Bristol, Manchester and Newcastle-upon-Tyne during the 1980s and 1990s provide a symbol of these transformations, though once they are contained, continuing public neglect is a more typical response.

Indeed it is increasingly apparent that much current social policy actually contributes to the problems suffered in these urban communities rather than providing solutions to them (Hope and Shaw, 1988). In recent years, changes in housing policies, employment policies, social security policies and educational policies have all encouraged rather than discouraged social and economic polarisation. Moreover the 1980s demonstrated, as Halsey amongst others has recognised, that the 'public and political consequences [of polarisation] can be neutralized in a democracy' (1989, p. 231). He paints a picture of 'social containment by minimum state welfare, police and burglar alarms with individualised failure, anomie and apathy made public only fitfully by occasional urban riot' (Halsey, 1989, p. 232). We are here a long way from the image of traditional working-class communities discussed in chapter 2. Whether the experience of such levels of poverty and disadvantage will generate new patterns of community solidarity, and what these patterns might be, are moot points. However, if current trends in these areas continue, fuelling social dislocation and providing people with little commitment to dominant social interests, increased social conflict both within and outside these localities seems inevitable.

THE COMMUNITY IN COMMUNITY CARE

We will now turn to a rather different issue of policy concern: that of community care. All societies face the problem of how to provide adequate support for those of its members who are unable to care properly for themselves. This issue has become of increasing concern in technologically advanced societies because of the demographic shifts which have accompanied industrial development. Two issues are particularly prominent, both a consequence of increasing life expectancy. Firstly, through changes in medical and related intervention, the number of people with disabling physical and mental conditions who need quite high levels of support has increased significantly. Not only are more people surviving disabilities that in previous eras would have resulted in infant or childhood death, but also those who reach maturity are living longer. Secondly, and in demographic terms more importantly, life expectancy in general has increased, with more people than previously experiencing longer periods of infirmity at the end of their lives. It is not just that there are more elderly people – in Britain some 800,000 over the age of 85 in 1991 compared to fewer than 100,000 in 1901 – but that there are more who have a disabling condition who require substantial levels of personal support.

Estimating the numbers of people needing some form of personal care is not an easy task, partly because of the difficulty of defining what counts as need for personal support over and above the routine exchanges of everyday life. For example, when does shopping for someone, such as an elderly father, become a form of personal support rather than just an expression of solidarity? Using the General Household Survey as a basis, OPCS (1992) has estimated that, excluding standard child-care, some 6.8 million people in Great Britain are involved in providing informal care for others. Of these, a quarter are providing care for more than twenty hours per week. In addition there are 300,000 people living in residential units of one sort or another, often requiring substantial amounts of personal support (Higgins, 1989). It is within this demographic context that policy initiatives about the need for community care have developed.

At a general, and rather crude, level, community care is often portrayed as providing a middle path between institutional resolutions of personal support needs and informal, more privatised ones. For different reasons and to differing degrees, both of these models are now seen as inadequate to the care dilemmas to which policy currently needs to respond. Examining how the state has reacted to these care dilemmas reveals some of the tensions and ambiguities within official thinking about the ways in which individuals become incorporated into community networks and organisations. It thereby allows us to address aspects of community integration which we have so far not considered. We will begin by commenting briefly on the two traditional forms of care provision from which current policy has developed, the institutional and the informal.

Traditionally institutional care involved social segregation and attempted economies of scale through the use of relatively large, asylum-type accommodation. Provision tended to be 'total' in Goffman's (1963) sense, whether it was for psychiatric patients in mental hospitals, elderly people in local authority homes or people with learning difficulties in mental-handicap institutions. That is, residents lived their lives almost fully within the institution, generally following standard routines and timetables laid down for administrative convenience and having little opportunity for participation within mainstream social life. Thus the community to which residents belonged within this form of care provision was very clearly the community of the institution. While staff, professionals, visitors and some others entered the institution and so to a small degree brought in the outside world, the residents themselves tended to have relatively little involvement with people unconnected with the institution. Isolation and social segregation were more prominent features of their experiences than wider social or communal participation, even where the geographical location of the institution meant that the local economy was reliant upon its existence.

Important though institutional care is, most care provision has always been informal, taking place in ordinary domestic households. This is true of those whose needs are acute and temporary, as well as of those who have chronic infirmities and disabilities. Sometimes, of course, people in need receive relatively little support, either because of their own sense of independence and desire to remain autonomous for as long as possible, or because informal support is not available. However, despite media representations which highlight the plight of those who are left alone to manage, this is by no means a typical picture. Most people in need do receive informal support from others, particularly from those living in the same household but sometimes from those living elsewhere. We have already seen that, on the basis of General Household Survey data, it has been estimated that 1½ million people provide at least twenty hours' worth of care per week (OPCS, 1992). Of these, three-quarters live in the same household as the person for whom they care. Typically these carers are spouses, mothers or resident children. In addition, though, as elderly parents become infirm, non-resident daughters (or daughters-in-law) are especially likely to be drawn into care provision.

Increasingly it has been recognised that caring for someone with chronic infirmity can be extremely burdensome. Numerous reports have shown how long the hours can be and how onerous some of the tasks, such as lifting and carrying, are, especially for people who may not themselves be as fit as they were. (It is worth noting that Green (1988) reports that 26 per cent of people in the General Household Survey claiming to provide twenty or more hours of care per week were over sixty-five.) In addition, many of those providing extensive care do so over a long period without much chance of respite, sometimes with their sleep patterns being systematically disrupted by night-time demands. This and the constancy of their caring responsibilities can leave some carers with little time or energy for sustaining other interests and activities. Caring comes to be the major focus of their lives, dominating their sense of self as well as their lifestyle. Under these circumstances, caring is a highly privatised activity, providing relatively few opportunities for significant involvement with others outside the household (see, for example, Briggs and Oliver, 1985; Cecil *et al.*, 1987; Glendinning, 1983; Nissel and Bonnerjea, 1982).

Over the last twenty or so years the main way in which social policy has responded to these different dilemmas in care provision has been by encouraging the development of community care initiatives. Broadly speaking, there have been two main strands to this. They can be quite neatly summarised as *care in the community* and *care by the community*. The emphasis placed on these is patterned to some degree by the reason why support is needed. For infirm elderly people the emphasis has been more on care by the community, whereas for other groups, especially those where health bureaucracies rather than social services ones have been dominant, more emphasis has been given to care in the community, at least for those people who are not living with relatives.

However, it would be wrong to demarcate these two forms of community care too strongly. From the early 1980s they were being elided and seen as complementary, a process in no small way encouraged by the desire to reduce public expenditure. This was

neatly captured by Patrick Jenkin, one time Secretary of State for
Social Services, in his oft-quoted remark:

My colleagues and I have been seeking to argue the case that care in the
community must mean care by the community . . . we have stressed the
key role of family, of friends and of neighbours. We have sought to
persuade social service departments to try to build partnerships with
voluntary agencies and with informal caring networks. (Sinclair and
Thomas, 1983, p. ii)

As this indicates, the policy thrust of care by the community is
on informal care more than professional, paid care, though formal
services often have an important supporting role to play. Here care
and support are provided within the home, either the individual's
own home or the home they share with members of their close
family. Put simply, the aim is to maintain people's level of
independence and autonomy as fully as possible for as long as
possible – hence the emphasis on being in their own home, with all
the ideological connotations this carries – and to share whatever
support is needed between a network of informal carers, abetted as
appropriate by those with specialist skills and expertise. This
network of carers may at times need mobilising through the efforts
of professionals, though in most instances it is assumed that such
networks occur naturally within communities. In drawing on
them, policy can encourage continued social involvement, promote
individual freedom rather than the dominance of professional
regimes and limit the costs of service provision.

The policy thrust of care in the community is rather different.
Broadly, this often involves people with similar types of disability
living in group homes of one form or another, in established
residential areas. The actual scale and organisation of these homes
varies a good deal. Some are relatively small, having, say, four or
five residents; others are rather larger. Some are organised and
supported by statutory or voluntary organisations; others are
privately run. Some provide high levels of housekeeping and care;
others offer only limited amounts of support (Watson and Cooper,
1992). None the less they differ significantly in their rationale
from the older asylum-style institutions, whether they are catering
for people with learning difficulties, for elderly people or for
younger people with physical disabilities.

The perceived advantages for the individuals involved of this shift to smaller residential units include a less regimented lifestyle in which individual rather than organisational concerns are given priority. Ideally each resident should be able to exercise a degree of control and choice over their actions and schedules which was not feasible in the larger units. A strong element within this is the recognition that the unit is the residents' home, and that 'home' here should be interpreted in the domestic sense and not the institutional one – '*my* home' rather than '*a* home'. As far as possible efforts should be made to provide the same freedoms and privacies as people normally expect to exercise in their own homes.

Equally, within this model there is the idea that people should not be socially segregated from mainstream community involvement. Rather, the aim is to use local resources to normalise lifestyles as far as possible and encourage integration with the surrounding community. Instead of generating strong boundaries in the way that traditional institutions did, integration with the local community should be fostered. Thus, to the extent their disabilities allow, residents make use of local services – doctors, post offices, shops, churches, etc. – rather than having them specially provided. In the process, it is held, such routine involvement in community life can generate informal contacts with others living in the area. In this sense the home offers a base within the community rather than being a community in itself.

The reality of both care by the community and care in the community tends to be rather different from these models. In part this is because the rhetoric of political ideology has not been matched by adequate resources. But also important is the mismatch between the character of much community life and the assumptions upon which these policies are built. If we consider care by the community first, many of the difficulties discussed earlier with the informal mode continue to operate. In particular, there is very little evidence that informal networks of care actually do develop to any significant degree, whether or not agencies attempt to foster them. As we have seen, the organisation of much informal care limits opportunities for social participation and is consequently ill-equipped to build on community solidarities. Indeed the activities of caring – the demands it makes and the time it involves – will tend to be disruptive of relationships and exclude carers from community involvement. Importantly too, people generally try to maintain a degree of reciprocity and balance within the social ties they have. With neighbours and friends in particular, there is usually a reluctance at becoming too dependent or too indebted, unless there are ways of reciprocating the help received. Of itself this tends to limit the support given by and accepted from friends and neighbours, both to those who are in need of support and to those who are acting as carers.

We also need to be conscious of the normative and moral boundaries that are conventionally placed around caring and of the sense of privacy which is central to many people's conception of how home and family life should be ordered. Put bluntly, it is one thing to accept help from a neighbour with shopping or cutting the lawn, but another to have them come in and help with, say, matters of personal hygiene. Some activities are seen as far more appropriate for family (however that is defined) or professionals than for relationships constructed on other bases. Consequently, the more extensive the care and support required, the less likely it is that effective informal networks of non-kin carers are likely to evolve. Moreover there appears to be a tendency for neighbours and other people outside the household to become more careful about 'interfering' with someone's care needs when family members are providing support. This appears especially marked when the care is being given to a close relative in the carer's own home, for example to an infirm parent or a disabled child.

Finch and Mason (1993) have argued that kinship cannot be understood properly in terms of a set of standard kinship norms. None the less a hierarchy of obligation and responsibility does seem to operate with respect to care provision. One study that brings this out particularly clearly is Qureshi and Walker's (1989) examination of the support given to elderly people in Sheffield. Although allowance needs to be made for factors like health, employment and proximity, their data indicate that categories of most likely carer tend to be ordered as follows: spouse; relative in lifelong household; daughter; daughter-in-law; son; other relative; non-relative (1989, ch. 5). Other research supports this finding, and likewise indicates that in those cases where there is co-operation in caring, it is other relatives who are most likely to be involved rather than non-family. Often, indeed, studies have reported that the burden of care falls most heavily on one particular individual with other family members playing a comparatively small part. This is so in studies of families with a disabled child (see, for example, Glendinning, 1983; Wilkin, 1979) and also in cases where an infirm parent needs support. Overall the idea that community care policies can build upon effective informal caring networks, spontaneous or otherwise, seems optimistic. The routine organisation of relationships within contemporary communities is not obviously compatible with such a policy goal.

When we turn to care in the community, the issues raised about the role of the community are rather different. The key question concerns the extent to which different people in need of support are accepted as legitimate members of the community and adequately integrated into its routine life. As we have discussed earlier, from one perspective communities can be viewed as networks of inclusion and exclusion. What matters here then is the extent to which those people who are being provided with forms of support and care within the community are able to participate with others in different types of activity rather than being excluded and treated as different. How welcoming are those others within existing networks? How easily and to what degree do those needing support become included? What is the social basis upon which solidarity develops?

Clearly the answer to these questions depends on many factors, including the individual's history of involvement with others in the locality and the reason why support is required. For example, someone moving into a home for elderly people after a lifetime in the locality is likely to have very different experiences from someone who has been rehoused from a psychiatric hospital to a group home in an area with which they have little previous connection. Crucially though, integration into networks and communities depends not simply on living in an area, but on having shared interests – in both senses of this term – and consequently a basis for developing solidarities. Put simply, the process here can be conceived as involving three linked elements: *presence*, *opportunity* and *acceptance*.

As was noted above, a major difference between the asylum model of care and care in the community is the extent to which residents make use of services existing within the locality. Whereas people in large institutions tend to be invisible as individuals to those outside, once they use local shops and other agencies their presence within the locality is much more evident. Of itself, this can have a number of benefits, both in terms of the freedom, autonomy and control the individual can exercise and as a way of increasing public awareness. However, it does not necessarily result in significant personal relationships developing. Drawing on Wirth's famous phrase, the contacts that are made may actually be 'impersonal, superficial, transitory and segmental' (1938, p. 12), those very properties which tend to be taken as indicative of social distance rather than solidarity within modern societies. In addition, of course, some of those receiving support in the community, for example many frail older people living in residential or nursing homes, rely on local services coming to them rather than the other way round. Because of their infirmity, the chances of their being able to develop informal relations, as it were, 'naturally' within the locality are quite restricted.

This raises the second concern: the opportunity people have to develop more significant personal relationships. Here the issue is not just the degree to which they come across others in their daily routines, but more the extent to which the contexts of the interaction are such as to encourage a fuller solidarity developing. It is again difficult to generalise about this as people's circumstances vary so much. Indeed for some it may be that simply being recognised by others, regularly being greeted in the street or shops, is sufficient to give a sense of involvement or participation. Yet this is a rather minimal notion of community; for most people, social participation involves something more. At the community level, it usually entails being incorporated into a complex network of different relationships, some being of considerable personal significance to us, others less so. It is this combination of interlocking and different solidarities – kin, friends, workmates, neighbours – which generally provides a sense of participation. Thus the issue here is the extent to which different people receiving care in the community, and especially those living in forms of group home, really are sufficiently integrated in the routines of (local) social and economic activity to be able to develop personal solidarities of a significant type.

This in turn is linked to the third issue: the extent to which people receiving support are accepted by others as part of their social networks, and at what level. It is one thing to say that care will be organised within a locality, but another as to whether the unit providing care, and the people involved, will be welcomed there. This may not be too much of a problem with respect to residential homes for elderly people, though even here some may be concerned with changes to the character of their neighbourhood. It is a more central issue when the unit is catering for more stigmatised groups. At one level this is seen in the opposition which is sometimes mobilised against plans to develop forms of supported housing. More directly, there is the question of how the social identities of residents are constructed by other people within the locality and whether these are, in Goffman's (1963) terms, sufficiently 'spoiled' to affect the forms of interaction which arise. For example, people with learning difficulties, or with known mental-health problems, may be sympathetically treated by some living nearby but be deliberately excluded and avoided by others. Indeed, 'sympathetic' treatment can itself be a stigmatising action to the degree it represents a notion of difference and marks people off as distinct from the normal. In these instances, it is unlikely that those involved will be incorporated easily into routine networks of personal relationships in the same manner and to the same degree as those who are not stigmatised.

To conclude this section, it can be seen that different policies on community care have attempted to build on aspects of community life so as to generate more appropriate, as well as more cost-effective, mechanisms for providing support for those less able to care for themselves. However, it is certainly questionable whether these policies are likely to achieve their full aims because they are premised on a rather simplistic notion of community solidarity and integration. Living in a neighbourhood does not of itself result in relationships of a tending or caring form developing. As we have seen, by the nature of their dependency many of those in need of support often have less opportunity than others to become socially integrated. And many of the relationships which they are able to develop in the locality are framed in ways that make active caring unlikely, just as they are for people who are not in need of support. This is a key issue: attempts to build upon informal relationships occurring 'naturally' in the community are not likely to succeed if in the process they require that the routine construction of such relationships is modified and distorted. In addition, though, contemporary community life, with its inter-locking networks of differentiated relationships, is as much about division and exclusion as it is about integration and inclusion. Importantly, the social identity of some of those requiring support is sufficiently stigmatised to result in their being systematically excluded from the social mainstream in a way which runs counter to the intentions of community care policies.

# 9

## CONCLUSIONS:
## THE CONTINUING IMPORTANCE OF
## THE SOCIOLOGY OF COMMUNITY

This book has been concerned with examining some of the key processes and debates addressed in recent research into community relationships. Only a minority of the studies we have discussed explicitly describe themselves as 'community studies', but all are concerned with the ways in which individuals are embedded into sets of personal relationships which are based outside the household. By taking a quite catholic stance on what should be contained under the rubric of 'community', we hope we have shown that a community focus remains of theoretical as well as substantive interest for those concerned with understanding solidarity and conflict, identification and distance, in social life. In this final chapter we do not intend to summarise the arguments of previous chapters in turn. Instead we want to conclude by focusing on three different issues which highlight the complexity and contested character of the idea of community in sociological analysis.

Throughout the book we have emphasised the 'boundary' and 'closure' problems inherent in the concept of community as it is generally used in sociology. In particular, where community is taken as having a geographical reference, one's analytical gaze tends to be focused inwards onto relationships within the locality irrespective of the relevance of other ties lying outside this domain. One approach that has attempted to overcome this difficulty is network analysis. In theory at least, network analysis allows the examination of a wider range of relationships, irrespective of their geographical base. Precisely because it is apparently analytically free-floating and independent of specific contexts and institutional settings, a network approach is often taken as offering the prospect of a more objective, less evaluative analysis than is possible using a conventional community framework. Although we do not discuss these claims in depth, the first section of this chapter will examine critically some of the advantages of looking at community issues from a network perspective.

Building on this, the second section of the chapter focuses on the relationship between social identity and participation in different forms of community. In particular, we return to questions we raised in earlier chapters about the extent to which different people are embedded to different degrees in sets of local or non-local relationships which inform their sense of self and play a part in locating them socially. Here we again consider, though not exclusively, the model of traditional working-class communities which has formed a backdrop to much of the discussion in this book. By doing so we hope to highlight the complexities of community solidarity, and in the process indicate the social basis of division and conflict within the different forms of community that develop in contemporary society.

The final section of the chapter considers the continuing relevance of community studies for sociology. As we have seen, a number of writers have questioned whether a community approach is sufficiently rigorous to aid the development of satisfactory social analysis. Some have stressed definitional and conceptual difficulties; others have been concerned with methodological problems. It is clear that these issues are here to stay. No standard definition of community is going to emerge, nor are the methodological dilemmas going to be resolved to everyone's satisfaction. This does not mean, however, that sociology will be better for jettisoning its concerns with community issues, nor that a community studies approach to understanding social relations has little to offer. As we hope to have shown in the body of this text, research into community life, interpreted widely, has provided a rich vein of ideas and analysis which are central to current debates within sociology. Our understanding of social life would be far the poorer if such research were to cease.

## NETWORK PERSPECTIVES

We started off this book by referring to communities as 'inter-locking social networks of neighbourhood, kinship and friendship'. This is a theme we want now to develop further, as a social network perspective has often been seen as offering solutions to some of the dilemmas the concept of 'community' entails. As is well known, the idea of social network was first introduced into the anthropological and sociological literature, at least in its current form, by Barnes in 1954. He found that the then conventional language of social anthropology did not allow him to analyse the character of social ties and conflicts evident within the Norwegian parish in which he was conducting fieldwork. The concept of social network gained further prominence with the publication of Bott's (1957) influential study of the impact of social network structure on marital relations. Building on Barnes's work, Bott indicated how analysing the specific constellation of connections within an individual's social network could explain patterns of behaviour which at first sight seemed a long way removed from the details of network structure. Moreover if the division of labour within marriage was closely related to the mutual involvement of others within the couple's social circle, it seemed feasible that many other forms of social action might also be shaped by the distinct network of informal relationships which each individual maintained.

The social network perspective quickly captured the imagination of sociologists and others concerned with studying communities (Frankenberg, 1969), for it seemed to provide a way of resolving some of the classical problems faced by community sociology. First of all, it was quite explicitly focused on those informal, largely non-institutionalised relationships which were at the heart of community solidarity and conflict. Whereas previous approaches were well able to analyse more formal, enduring aspects of social structure, they were noticeably weak in handling the more pliable and apparently idiosyncratic web of personal ties. The network approach explicitly aimed to bring informal relationships, whether of kinship, friendship or locality, to the centre of the analytical framework and demonstrate the significance they had not just emotionally for the individual but for patterns of social organisation more widely. Moreover it did this in a way which was not dependent on any notion of locality or place. Rather than closing the question of community down to issues of what types of relationship emerged in particular geographical locations, be they 'traditional' working-class areas, new housing estates or whatever, a network conception opened up the analysis and allowed the researcher to focus on the much wider and potentially more revealing totality of informal relationships any individual maintained.

Second, it did this in a rigorous and concrete manner. Instead of referring loosely to community relations or degrees of community solidarity, it provided a means of mapping out the full set of informal relations to which any individual was party and then linking the connections between these others. Once this was done, the structural characteristics of the network could be ascertained. That is, rather than just being a set of linked individuals, the detailed pattern of any network's configuration could be examined and subsequently contrasted with those occurring in other networks. The dominant mode of analysing network structure was through what Bott (1957, p. 59) first termed 'connectedness', but which later came to be reformulated as network density – essentially the ratio of actual ties existing in the network to the potential number which would exist if all those involved knew one another. Over the years much effort was put into developing ways of measuring this and other structural properties of complex networks, often drawing on quite complex mathematical theory (Holland and Leinhardt, 1979; Scott, 1991; White *et al.*, 1976). As with Bott's work, the purpose of much of this effort was to find correlations between different types of social or economic activity and some specific characteristic(s) of network structure, though in reality there have been few studies which have attained the elegant simplicity of Bott's early formulation.

In recent years, the most influential researcher concerned with understanding community life through network approaches has been Wellman. He and his colleagues at the University of Toronto have been concerned to argue, first, that the traditional approach to communities of treating a geographical area as though necessarily of sociological relevance is mistaken; and second, that network analysis provides a means of connecting informal ties to those 'macro' structural concerns which have dominated sociological analysis. Wellman's work is based on studies of East York, an area of Toronto first settled between the wars, principally by British emigrants, but which in recent years had been developed further with 'many high-rise apartment towers looking down on the older red brick homes' (Wellman *et al.*, 1988, p. 136) providing housing for a new wave of southern European and Asian Canadians.

On the basis of qualitative research as well as a larger-scale survey, Wellman demonstrates the 'fuzzy reality' (Wellman *et al.*, 1988, p. 137) which typifies the boundaries of most people's personal networks. This refers, in part, to the difficulty of specifying precisely who should be included in any network, but more importantly here also to the geographical spread of each individual's contacts. Rather than being contained neatly within clearly bounded neighbourhoods, informal ties of solidarity, including those of kinship and friendship, occur over such a wide area that geographical conceptions of community lose any power they may have had to explain people's incorporation into the social realm. Wellman argues that whatever the sociological status of 'traditional' working-class communities in Britain or North America, under contemporary conditions of modernity, locality no longer has the significance assigned it by the more established theories of community. He is here echoing in different language Stacey's (1969) arguments that we need concepts and theories which focus our gaze as much outwards from localities as inwards. With the possibility of network analysis providing an appropriate framework for doing this, it becomes feasible to link personal and informal worlds with organisational and structural transformations.

This is no small claim, but is very much in line with the concerns which have dominated the sociology of community since its development towards the end of the last century. Indeed it was conventional theorising about the harmful consequences of capitalism and industrial urbanism on apparently well-integrated and solidaristic rural communities that coloured many of the post-war empirical projects which focused on urban community integration. As we discussed in chapter 2, these studies 're-discovered' patterns of community solidarity which many thought had been irretrievably lost. Wellman's argument is that these studies of so-called traditional communities 'overgilded' the lily. In particular, they implied a homogeneity of experience and a containment of social activity which, in line with the inherent connotations of the term 'community', resulted in much consequent research becoming too concerned with matters of local cohesion and solidarity. As a result they failed to recognise or address properly the different and varied levels of commitment and exchange which most people sustain within their networks.

This in turn resulted in inadequate theorising about the roles of different informal relationships within the complexity of social organisation. Wellman and his colleagues' analysis is important here for drawing attention to the significance of 'little networks in a big world' (Wellman *et al.*, 1988, p. 174) and indicating how informal ties 'are important to the routine operations of households, crucial to the management of crises, and sometimes instrumental in helping respondents change their situations' (Wellman and Wortley, 1990, p. 583). More specifically they discuss how the East Yorkers' networks provide them with '*havens*: a sense of being wanted and belonging, and readily available companionship . . . "*band-aids*": emotional aid and small services. . . . *ladders* to change their situations . . . and *levers* . . . to change the world' (Wellman *et al.*, 1988, p. 174; emphases in original). Although Wellman and his colleagues do not explicitly refer here to the writings of C. Wright Mills, their approach to networks as 'personal communities' which have none of the sharp boundaries of planners' and politicians' conceptions of community echoes Mills' point about the disjuncture between personal and public domains which was discussed in chapter 1.

Wellman emphasises how different people provide these different services. There is no sense of any individual's relationships being homogeneous or interchangeable with one another. They have their own distinct exchange basis and are used as appropriate for different ends. By implication Wellman argues that this is the character of much contemporary 'community' life. It is not that 'community-style' ties are absent; most individuals actively maintain a small number of significant informal bonds and regularly draw on these to help solve life's contingencies, small or large. However, these ties are rarely located exclusively within an immediate or bounded neighbourhood, and nor are they necessarily close-knit or dense in the way that the traditional model of community suggests. So too Wellman points out that the character of people's personal networks, and the use to which they put them, vary depending on the structural location of those involved. In particular, he has shown how an individual's work situation, itself shaped by such issues as gender, ethnicity and class, can pattern the character of informal relationships and thus the forms which personal networks take. For example, women with domestic responsibilities and no employment tend to be involved in quite different sets of relationships from men in secure and full-time employment (Allan, 1989; Wellman, 1985).

While we are not convinced that a network perspective of itself solves the range of problems associated with the sociology of community, or indeed that analysing community life inevitably leads one to overemphasise local solidaristic ties at the expense of antagonistic or more distant ones, the issues which a network approach brings to the fore are important ones. Here we want to emphasise two related matters which we have addressed in earlier chapters. The first is that there clearly is no such single thing as community. Community has many meanings; it involves different sets of experience for different groups of people, and indeed for the same people at different times in their lives. Bulmer's (1989, p. 253) term 'intermediary structures' highlights the function which community institutions serve of connecting the individual to the wider society, echoing Wellman *et al.*'s (1988, p. 131) suggestion that the network approach helps to locate people 'in small-scale social structures, and links them to large-scale institutions'. Parker *et al.*'s study of drug-users in the Wirral provides an interesting example of the value of a network approach. Using it, they are able 'to map out the informal social structure of the "heroin community"' (1988, p. 69) and assess the extent of what was to official agencies very much a hidden phenomenon.

Yet how 'community' (or, for that matter, a personal network) acts in this way, and the extent to which it does so, depends upon people's overall social location, which of course varies from one individual to another. In other words, community is never experienced in identical ways by everybody involved, and any conceptualisation which fails to recognise this is bound to be, at best, partial. Each individual's structural location, their material circumstances, their position within the division of labour, their gender, age, ethnic identity, the obligations and responsibilities they have for others, etc., will all influence their incorporation into community-relevant relationships, and do so in ways not easily specified or predicted. Much of this book has been concerned with unravelling the interplay of these different factors.

The second issue to emphasise here is the dynamic character of all forms of community. Wellman is right to criticise those approaches which derive a fixed model of community existence from an imagined past and then attempt to contrast contemporary patterns against this as a lack. Communities are never static, though the rapidity of change occurring within them does obviously vary. As we saw in earlier chapters, shifts in the economic environment, be this expansion or contraction, will have some impact on the nature and quality of social solidarities occurring within the area. So too an influx of migrants, whether caused by housing and job opportunities or by some other factor, is likely to have a bearing on the patterns of conflict and social division which emerge within the locality. Indeed time itself, even if there were no other changes, will impinge on local relationships as each section of the community ages, takes on different responsibilities and attempts to protect its current interests.

### COMMUNITY BOUNDARIES AND SOCIAL IDENTITIES

One of the dominant meanings of the concept of community is that those who are members of it, those who belong to it, have something in common which marks them off from outsiders who do not belong and/or are not allowed to belong. What that commonality consists of can vary. Most often when we use the term 'community', we think of locality and neighbourhood. People who belong to the local community are those who live there, whose lives are to some degree built around activities and relationships which are developed within it. But other forms of community exist with different bases of membership. Increasingly, it seems, appeals to different forms of solidarity are made through the language of community. For instance, the term 'black community' is now widely used, and it is also common for specific minority ethnic groups to be identified and to identify themselves as a community. Bhachu's study of the East African Sikh community in Britain, for example, describes it as 'an established community' (1985, p. 30) despite its dispersed character, due to the strength of the communications network which exists between members. Similarly, within universities people refer to the 'student community' and sometimes to the 'community of scholars'; and phrases like the 'legal community' or the 'scientific community' are often used in the media.

If the applicability and relevance of these terms is to do with common membership and a sense of belonging and shared identity, then it is pertinent to ask about the nature of the solidarities entailed and the level of commitment there is to the community in question. At one extreme of popular (and sociological) imagination, there seems to be either the traditional urban working-class community or else the small, relatively isolated rural community; at the other, there is a much looser network of individuals who share some specific element of their lives, such as an occupation, in common. The issue in question here is not simply what unites these different groupings all labelled 'community', but also how the commitments individuals have to these communities are patterned and shaped, and how much divergence there is within them.

Once again it is useful here to start by considering the character of 'traditional' urban, working-class communities. As we discussed in chapter 2, one common strand in the imagery of these communities is the sense that all those who belonged to them were in roughly the same situation as one another. Their lives were patterned by the same broad complex of forces over which they exercised relatively little control. Their work was arduous, their pay quite low; their housing, rented from private landlords, was of poor quality; and education, health and social services provided them with little support. They were bound together through high-density kin and neighbour networks which could be mobilised to provide emotional and material aid as it was needed. To use Abrams's graphic metaphor, within these communities:

three circumstances impel the growth of neighbourhood care: *extreme social homogeneity* because in every respect everyone is in the same awful boat; *permanence* because there is no prospect of anyone around you getting into any other boat; and *threat* because the waves and winds could overturn and drown the whole lot of you two minutes from now, tomorrow, next week, anytime. (1980, pp. 14–15, emphases in original)

Of course, this image is only partial. The solidarity that was experienced was real enough. People living in an area did feel a degree of loyalty to it; they were embedded in local economic and social relationships which structured their lives and which quite effectively tied them to the 'community'. Yet at the same time, not everybody was fully incorporated into close-knit social networks;

for example, not everybody had kin who could provide support. Think here of the people whom Townsend (1957) interviewed living in Bethnal Green's local authority homes for the elderly. Disproportionately these were people without children available to provide them with routine support as they became infirm, and who consequently were largely excluded from community involvement in their old age. More generally, the networks in which people were involved were never uniform. Some people had fuller networks than others; some less dense ones. Some people strove hard to protect their privacy and to keep personal and family matters confidential, perhaps remaining a little aloof from their neighbours in order to limit channels of gossip. Others had a more communal orientation and valued social participation more highly.

In an important sense, there was no single, homogeneous community. People were embedded in local relationships to different degrees and in different ways. Sometimes this was concealed by the social and economic decline which was affecting many of these localities. The sense of solidarity in many instances increased as the population shrank through out-migration exceeding in-migration; with few jobs available and poor housing, there were few reasons for outsiders to choose to move in to these areas, and strong 'push' factors encouraging the more mobile among the local population to leave. Through their shared histories, those who remained often did have more knowledge of one another than people living in other types of areas, and tended to be comparatively well integrated as a result. Yet equally, the manner in which people were incorporated was shaped by their own circumstances and social identities. The experience of community was radically different for men and women. It was different for young and old; and different again for those with more secure or more precarious household incomes. As we have discussed, there were important differences in the social standing of different families, with divisions, often contested, between the rough and the respectable. Within the communities fine gradations separated those whom outsiders looking in at the community might tend to lump together.

In terms of community embeddedness, it should also be remembered that some individuals and households were 'trapped' more completely than others into these localities, either by their housing or by the particular occupational skills they had acquired.

Thus the post-war development of council housing, often built on the fringes of existing urban areas, allowed some people – typically families with relatively young children – the opportunity to 'escape' from the community in which they had grown up. Whether or not the social consequences of this were entirely welcome is less important here than the very fact of movement and change. To echo the point made earlier, there are not only variations in the extent to which different sections of the population are embedded into local social and economic structures, but as importantly this varies over time as the opportunities and constraints open to people are modified by external developments.

So here we can ask the question of what it means to 'belong' to such a community. The answer has to be different things to different people, depending on their 'commitment' not in the sense of emotional attachment but rather on the basis of the extent of their social and economic incorporation into sets of activities and relationships which are grounded in the particular locality. So too when we pose questions about the borders constructed around these communities, Wallman's powerful image of boundaries being like tea-bags, rather than balloons, is particularly germane. There is flow over time – of individuals, households and groups – into and out of the locality, but more importantly into and out of relationships which can be seen as 'embedding'. There is, to use Wellman's term again, a 'fuzziness' about who belongs and about what belonging entails. The barriers are permeable, though conversely the extent to which they are so is itself a reflection of the emergent character of any community.

These same issues are evident from a different vantage point in the other form of community regularly idealised in popular culture – the settled rural village. Of course, such communities are rarely as 'settled' as the dominant imagery would suggest. Agricultural processes have been altering and productivity increasing, with the consequence that rural depopulation due to out-migration of farmworkers has been recognised as a public issue for at least a century. During the course of the present century significant portions of many rural villages have come to be populated by people who have little, if any, direct involvement with farming or the wider agricultural economy. As well as what might be termed the rural 'service sector' – teachers, mechanics, clerics, veterinary surgeons, local administrators, doctors, etc. – there are increasing numbers of people whose lifestyle is dependent on commuting to jobs in urban centres. As we have seen, these latter people are tied in to the local social and economic system in quite different ways to those who are directly reliant on the local economy.

Yet even if we stay with the image of a rural area populated by people whose lifestyles are built upon their close links to agricultural production, we can recognise that the sets of relationships they maintain will by no means all be equivalent. Certainly they are all likely to have a commitment to the area and a sense of belonging to the community, but this does not mean that they all experience this in the same way or have corresponding interests in its future development. As all the classic rural community studies demonstrated, economic and social hierarchy played as large a part in these localities as in any others, with class and status divisions readily apparent (see for example, Frankenberg, 1969; Littlejohn, 1963; Williams, 1956). Indeed such divisions are generally more noticeable in these communities because direct, cross-class contact tends to be built into the routine of everyday interaction. That is, whereas housing segregation tends to foster a degree of class and status 'insulation' in urban areas, the smaller scale of village existence means that people from different class locations are more likely to have a personal involvement with one another.

This has repercussions for the social management of class and status differences. Newby (1977) has been especially influential in augmenting the analysis of earlier rural community studies by examining the patterns of deference and antagonism which prevail between different groups in such circumstances. Recognising that deference derives from power (rather than being its source), his concept of the 'deferential dialectic' highlights the tension between differentiation and identification within hierarchical, personal relationships such as those arising in rural communities (see also Bell and Newby, 1976). Here the recognition of social boundaries remains important, for identification – an appreciation of (some) shared interests and common membership – must not become overidentification if the hierarchy is to be successfully managed.

Thus friendship patterns, for example, and sociability tend to mirror social divisions. Those who spend time together and mix most freely are likely to occupy similar social positions. Interestingly too, Whitehead (1976) and Hunt and Satterlee (1986) have separately shown how village pubs – often taken as a key arena for the symbolic expression of community solidarity – tend to be differentiated either in their clientele or by the cliques which develop. There may be camaraderie and bantering between the array of people who drink there, but not far beneath the surface the social distances maintained between different sectors of the community are made manifest in ways which contrast with the egalitarianism Oxley (1974) describes as typical of drinking bars in small-town Australia.

As with traditional working-class communities, this raises issues about what belonging to a community entails. Just how embedded within community life do you need to be to be regarded as a member? And what aspects of community life count for this? Given the importance of the social divisions that are maintained within these localities, in what sense is it sensible to talk of a single community? As before, what these issues force us to recognise is the inappropriateness of conceptualising communities in terms of firm boundaries, fixed membership and rigid patterns of inclusion and exclusion. The social reality of community life is simply not like this, even in those localities which seem to match most closely popular images of what 'real' communities comprise. Instead what is needed is a much more fluid, much more dynamic notion of community, one which recognises that some people are more embedded or entrapped in those relationships pertinent to the form of community in question, be this a locality or some non-geographical interest. The interesting questions are not framed around whether this or that neighbourhood, this or that occupational grouping, is a community in some rigidly delineated manner, but rather what is the character of the commitments that tie people in their differing degrees to a specific social environment.

Following on from this discussion of traditional working-class and rural communities, we can pose the question of whether higher levels of community solidarity develop in more homogeneous or in socially diverse neighbourhoods. Traditional working-class communities are characterised by similarity: as we have already said, broadly speaking those living in them share the same life-chances and lifestyles. Rural communities, in contrast, are much more differentiated; there you have variation rather than correspondence. Yet while both these configurations can quite legitimately be characterised as communities, when planners have attempted to use either as a blueprint for re-creating communities, their efforts have been largely unsuccessful, as was seen in chapter 7. Willmott's general sense is that, 'contrary to the common impression, a *mixture* of classes in a neighbourhood tends to work against the development of community ties and sentiments, which flourish more in a homogeneous setting' (1986, p. 93; emphasis in original). A similar conclusion was reached by Karn, whose research among people who had retired to seaside towns dominated by older people threw 'considerable doubt on the widely held view that "balanced communities" provide the best setting for social contacts' (1977, p. 96). Yet while Pahl is right to argue that 'The idea that it is good for people to be mixed-up socially has received well-deserved criticism over the years' (Pahl, 1975, p. 50), it is also the case that socially homogeneous groupings cannot be guaranteed to constitute sustainable 'communities'. Common residence and immobility may create what Bauman has called 'communities by inertia' (1992, p. xix), but the social networks found in such 'traditional' communities are difficult to reproduce once the basis of their continuity is removed, as it has been in the modern era.

The pursuit of 'balanced communities' once again highlights the inadequacy of treating communities as static entities. There is no simple logarithm that will reveal the mysteries of community for there is no such single thing as community in the first place. There are many different forms of community, and generating solidarity between people who live near to one another depends not simply on social balance or commonality, but rather on the sets of social exchange, conflict, interdependency, antagonism and the like which people generate in their relationships with those others involved. These social relationships also occur within specific local cultural and historical contexts, with infinite variations of detail. Certainly different social and economic circumstances will lead to different patterns emerging, but those who seek to develop a particular form of community solidarity are rarely, if ever, in a position to exercise sufficient control over the varied range of processes which fashion these outcomes.

Many criticisms have been directed at the concept of 'community' and at its use within sociology and social science more generally. Building on Stacey's (1969, p. 134) statement that 'it is doubtful whether the concept "community" refers to a useful abstraction', Halsey (1974, p. 130) remarks that community 'Unfortunately . . . has so many meanings as to be meaningless.' In particular, we can identify three major difficulties which confront any attempt to be more specific about the meaning or content of 'community'. First, there is the problem of locality. Although, as we have seen, the idea of community has been applied to social groupings based on criteria other than geography, this remains by far the most common referent for the term. One of the concept's major attractions within both social science and everyday talk is its embodiment of the idea that living in an area provides a potential basis for mutual participation and involvement with others also residing there.

If this is principally taken as an opportunity to investigate the nature of relationships of solidarity, indifference and discord within a specified locality or neighbourhood, then the issues are in essence no more complex than studying any other administrative or organisational unit, be it an industrial plant, a religious sect or a prison. One needs to be conscious of the dangers of 'closure', of concentrating solely on what goes on within the delineated area and paying insufficient heed to outside influences, but that applies equally to these other research topics. Relations within an industrial plant are as much premised on factors emanating from the wider social and economic formation as those within a locality. The fact that, say, housing associations or educational establishments are not 'in command of their own economic or political fate' (Bulmer, 1985, p. 432) does not render their study uninteresting or unimportant; nor does it make the study of localities misguided. However, difficulties emerge if any locality is analysed as though it were structurally isolated and unaffected by social and economic processes occurring at a non-local level; or indeed if too simplistic or too deterministic a theory about the relationship between environmental form and social relationships is posited.

Second, there is the problem of the normative and evaluative connotations of the term 'community'. As we have seen, the vagueness of the term is overlaid with positive resonances about its social desirability. Within social and political discourse, community is rarely, if ever, used in a negative fashion. As R. Williams (1983, p. 76) points out, this is not as true of other concepts of social collectivity, such as state, bureaucracy or even family. In Plant *et al.*'s (1980, p. 206) words, community 'is used not only to describe or to refer to a range of features in social life but also to put into a favourable perspective those features. Community is a valued and valuable achievement.' However, as Plant and his colleagues argue, it is not simply the normative colouring of community that creates difficulty for the social analyst, rather it is the overlay of this colouring on the different, and often incompatible, descriptive meanings that the term has. 'While there is formal consensus that to talk about "community" is to talk in a commendatory way, there is no such consensus about what precisely is being commended' (Plant *et al.*, 1980, p. 207).

This brings us to the third issue, which is also explicated clearly in the work of Plant and his colleagues. It is the essential contestability of the notion of 'community'. Part of this lies in the different meaning of elements associated with community, including locality, solidarity, shared beliefs and moral perspectives, common traditions and allied interests. There is little agreement about the relative weightings to be given these different elements, and indeed over which empirical cases, historical or contemporary, best capture the 'real essence' of community. Plant *et al.* (1980, pp. 210–15) discuss the value of trying to reduce these elements to a 'core descriptive meaning' in the way that Clark (1973) does. In Clark's view, the fundamental elements of community are 'a sense of solidarity' and 'a sense of significance' (1973, p. 404). As Plant *et al.* argue, this is all very well but, even assuming agreement that these are the core elements, without further specification of what these elements themselves entail, they are not in practice very useful for social analysis. Yet once an attempt is made to put flesh on them and operationalise them, they once again become contestable.

Formal and consensus concepts have to be transformed into debatable and contestable conceptions before they can be used in social science, but once this transformation occurs it is difficult to see how ideology, in the sense of a basic set of normative preferences, can be avoided. (Plant *et al.*, 1980, p. 213)

If this is accepted, we are left with the problem of whether the concept of community can ever be of benefit for understanding social processes. To put this slightly differently, is there any value for sociology of taking a 'community' approach and doing community studies? As we have tried to show in the different chapters of this book, we believe the answer is 'yes'. To begin with, one has to be struck by the very richness of the term, which is of course the positive side of its being so hard to define and imbued with normative connotation. The concept is constantly drawn on by people in everyday discourse to express both descriptively and evaluatively aspects of their social experience. As we noted earlier, people do have an understanding of community organisation, community action, community policing, community nursing, community work, community schooling and the like. Their understandings may differ and be ill-specified and extremely difficult to operationalise and measure. They certainly lack the precision commonly expected of scientific terms but, like 'family', they exist and their received meanings are lived out and acted upon. It is in this way that it makes sense to speak of 'the community' as an actor, as Roberts *et al.* (1992) do in their analysis of how the residents of a Glasgow housing scheme took action to try to improve their estate's poor record relating to child accidents, coming together as a community to press for the implementation of accident prevention schemes.

As argued earlier, a significant reason why the notion of community does have a salience for people is that it represents a term of social organisation which mediates between the personal and the institutional, between household and familial issues which many feel they have a degree of control over and the large-scale social and economic structures which are dominated by events and processes outside ordinary people's influence. This, of course, by itself does not make the term 'community' valid for social analysis. Yet if it did not exist, it would surely need to be invented. How else can one explain the continued use of a term which has received so much conceptual abuse? It does address an element or level of social experience which cannot be ignored or done away with. Other terms like 'local social system', 'locality' or 'social network' may augment that of 'community', but despite the efforts that have gone into their refinement, it is noticeable that they have not managed to replace 'community' as a major construct within social analysis and discourse. Arguably what they have done is allow the dimensions or elements of 'community' to be specified a little more clearly.

So too, although the 'old' tradition of community studies went out of fashion in British sociology towards the end of the 1960s amid a welter of criticism about their methodological and theoretical flaws, such studies are re-emerging in one form or another as appropriate vehicles for generating a fuller understanding of the routine organisation of social life. Certainly the analytical limitations of such studies need to be recognised. It is, for example, quite evident that research centred on communities as local social systems can never provide a total analysis of the processes impacting on their development – many political and economic decisions, for instance, are simply not made at the community level. But equally the converse is true. Examining capitalism as a world-wide social and economic system, or analysing the development of new geo-political conflicts tells us very little about the everyday routines, passions, worries, solidarities and divisions of people living aspects of their lives in different settings.

We have cited many studies in this book which are concerned with ordinary people's everyday lives. Some of these have been termed community studies by their authors; some neighbourhood studies; some locality studies. Others have been categorised under other terms: industrial or workplace studies; household studies; political studies; or whatever. The terminology here seems to us relatively unimportant. What matters is the range of research that continues to focus on issues pertinent to a community level of analysis; that is, a level above that of individual and household, of greater scope than family or kin grouping, yet one which is located and consequently contextualised within Wellman *et al.*'s (1988) relatively 'small-scale social structures'.

There is one other issue to raise here, concerning a common criticism made about community studies in the past. This is that by their very method they are unscientific. In particular, being based as they so often are on participant observation or, in its more recent guise, ethnography, questions have long been asked about both the reliability and validity of the approach. One is mindful here of the classic examples of community re-studies reaching quite different conclusions to the originals despite a relatively short passage of time – see Redfield (1930) and Lewis (1951) on Tepoztlan in Mexico; Lynd and Lynd (1929, 1937) on Muncie in the United States; for a full discussion, see Bell and Newby (1971, ch. 3). Similar points could be made about the 're-studies' of Bethnal Green by Cornwell (1984), Holme (1985) and others, the findings of which have cast considerable doubts on the original, classic study by Young and Willmott (1957). Such concerns have been expressed more generally in the criticism that community studies are not cumulative. Each 'community' study, whether locality-based or otherwise, is its own special case. What one researcher discovers may not be matched in the findings of a different researcher. Furthermore it is extremely difficult to know which communities can properly be compared with one another; when like is being compared to like. To put this another way, what features are general characteristics of communities like this one, whatever this is taken to be, and which are more specific?

If by cumulative science is meant the idea that through multiple research projects a once-and-for-all understanding of the organisation of a set of phenomena can be established, in line with the common-sense model of scientific development, then it is true that community studies have not been cumulative. But then no area of social science – and few within natural science - has actually progressed in such a neat and tidy fashion. The conflicts and disagreements there are over class theory or the construction of gendered work, for example, generate no more of a monolithic model than the study of community matters. Moreover, the methods used for collecting data in the better contemporary studies of community living are as sophisticated as any within sociology. Consider, for example, the extensive fieldwork, involving a range of different methods over a considerable period of time, that Pahl (1984) and Wallace (1987) used for their study of Sheppey in Kent. The theoretical sophistication of the analysis of their data by themselves and others stands as some sort of evidence that 'community'-type research has much to contribute to the discipline of sociology more generally.

The description of Pahl's Sheppey research as 'an admittedly important locality study in a rather unusual place' (Byrne, 1989, p. 24) is a somewhat unfair one, since every locality has its peculiarities. As Saunders has noted, it is not possible to find 'any particular towns or areas which could be taken as "microcosms" of the wider society, for every town has its own unique history and character. There is no such place as "Middletown" ' (1990, p. 45). What matters in community research is not the search for some elusive 'typicality', but the study of ordinary people's everyday lives in the full variety of contexts. Finnegan's awareness of the fact that Milton Keynes is not typical of all English towns did not stop her from studying music-making there, and social science is the richer for her commitment to the investigation of 'a *real* place which contains real people experiencing and creating musical forms which they themselves value and to which they are prepared to commit a great deal of their lives' (1989, pp. xi–xii; emphasis in original). Without the study of diverse places, people and social institutions and relationships, a genuinely comparative social science would not be possible.

We rather hope this book has indicated the cumulative possibilities of community research. We have drawn throughout on many different studies. They have by no means all been in agreement with each other over the impact of specific social processes or the dominant characteristics of collective organisation. None the less what we have tried to do is draw on the different studies to illustrate the debates there are and to consolidate the knowledge which has accumulated about different aspects of community order and conflict. We have been able to show that it is possible for community studies to build on one another, though the process for doing this is rarely a straightforward replication, but more a constant chiselling away at different aspects of community living, partly in response to the findings and arguments of other, earlier pieces of research. As we hope we have demonstrated in the preceding chapters, the study of community is important within sociology: it can reveal a good deal about the way in which people's everyday lives are fashioned; and it does allow connections to be made between the individual's lifestyle and the more immediate social and economic contexts in which they develop. Provided the sociological gaze is turned outwards as well as inwards, these in turn can be linked to social and economic processes which occur well beyond the orbit of any individual's own experience. It is for these reasons as much as any that, despite all the criticisms made, the study of community so frequently captures the imagination of sociologists. Long may it be so.

# REFERENCES

Abercrombie, N., Warde, A., with Soothill, K., Urry, J. and Walby, S. (1988), *Contemporary British Society*, Cambridge: Polity.

Abrams, P. (1978), 'Introduction: Social facts and sociological analysis', in P. Abrams (ed.) *Work, Urbanism and Inequality: U.K. society today*, London: Weidenfeld and Nicolson, pp. 1–16.

Abrams, P. (1980), 'Social change, social networks and neighbourhood care', *Social Work Service* 22, pp. 12–23.

Aldrich, H., Cater, J., Jones, T. and McEvoy, D. (1981), 'Business development and self-segregation: Asian enterprise in three British cities', in C. Peach, V. Robinson and S. Smith (eds) *Ethnic Segregation in Cities*, London: Croom Helm, pp. 170–90.

Aldridge, M. (1979), *The British New Towns: A programme without a policy*, London: Routledge and Kegan Paul.

Allan, G. (1979), *A Sociology of Friendship and Kinship*, London: George Allen and Unwin.

Allan, G. (1989), *Friendship: Developing a sociological perspective*, Hemel Hempstead: Harvester Wheatsheaf.

Allan, G. and Crow, G. (1989), 'Introduction', in G. Allan and G. Crow (eds) *Home and Family: Creating the domestic sphere*, London and Basingstoke: Macmillan, pp. 1–13.

Allan, G. and Crow, G. (1991), 'Privatization, home-centredness and leisure', *Leisure Studies* 10, pp. 19–32.

Allatt, P. and Yeandle, S. (1992), *Youth Unemployment and the Family: Voices of disordered times*, London: Routledge.

Allcorn, D. and Marsh, C. (1975), 'Occupational communities – communities of what?', in M. Bulmer (ed.) *Working-Class Images of Society*, London: Routledge and Kegan Paul, pp. 206–18.

Allen, J. (1990), 'Localities and social change', in J. Anderson and M. Ricci (eds) *Society and Social Science: A reader*, Milton Keynes: The Open University, pp. 192–5.

Allen, S. and Wolkowitz, C. (1987), *Homeworking: Myths and realities*, London and Basingstoke: Macmillan.

Ambrose, P. (1986), *Whatever Happened to Planning?*, London: Methuen.

Anderson, B. (1991), *Imagined Communities: Reflections on the origin and spread of nationalism*, London: Verso.

Anwar, M. (1985), *Pakistanis in Britain: A sociological study*, London: New Century.

Anwar, M. (1986), *Race and Politics: Ethnic minorities and the British political system*, London: Tavistock.

Archbishop of Canterbury's Commission on Urban Priority Areas (1985), *Faith in the City: A call for action by church and nation*, London: Church House.

Askham, J. (1984), *Identity and Stability in Marriage*, Cambridge: Cambridge University Press.

Austerberry, H. and Watson, S. (1985), 'A woman's place: A feminist approach to housing in Britain', in C. Ungerson (ed.) *Women and Social Policy*, London and Basingstoke: Macmillan, pp. 91–108.

Ayres, P. (1990), 'The hidden economy of dockland families: Liverpool in the 1930s', in P. Hudson and W. R. Lee (eds) *Women's Work and the Family Economy in Historical Perspective*, Manchester: Manchester University Press, pp. 271–90.

Bagguley, P. (1991), *From Protest to Acquiescence? Political movements of the unemployed*, London and Basingstoke: Macmillan.

Bagguley, P., Mark-Lawson, J., Shapiro, D., Urry, J., Walby, S. and Warde, A. (1990), *Restructuring: Place, class and gender*, London: Sage.

Bailey, J. (1980), *Ideas and Intervention: Social theory for practice*, London: Routledge and Kegan Paul.

Ballard, C. (1979), 'Conflict, continuity and change: Second generation South Asians', in V. Saifullah Khan (ed.) *Minority Families in Britain: Support and stress*, London and Basingstoke: Macmillan, pp. 109–29.

Ballard, R. (1982), 'South Asian families', in R. N. Rapoport, M. Fogarty and R. Rapoport (eds) *Families in Britain*, London: Routledge and Kegan Paul, pp. 179–204.

Ballard, R. and Ballard, C. (1977), 'The Sikhs: The development of South Asian settlements in Britain', in J. Watson (ed.) *Between Two Cultures: Migrants and minorities in Britain*, Oxford: Basil Blackwell, pp. 21–56.

Barnes, J. (1954), 'Class and committees in a Norwegian island parish', *Human Relations* 7 (1), pp. 39–58.

Bassett, K., Boddy, M., Harloe, M. and Lovering, J (1989), 'Living in the fast lane: Economic and social change in Swindon', in P. Cooke (ed.)

*Localities: The changing face of urban Britain*, London: Unwin Hyman, pp. 45–85.

Bauman, Z. (1990) *Thinking Sociologically*, Oxford: Basil Blackwell.

Bauman, Z. (1992), *Intimations of Postmodernity*, London: Routledge.

Baxter, S. and Raw, G. (1988), 'Fast food, fettered work: Chinese women in the ethnic catering industry', in S. Westwood and P. Bhachu (eds) *Enterprising Women: Ethnicity, economy and gender relations*, London: Routledge, pp. 58–75.

Bell, C. (1977), 'Reflections on the Banbury restudy', in C. Bell and H. Newby (eds) *Doing Sociological Research*, London: George Allen and Unwin, pp. 47–62.

Bell, C. and Newby, H. (1971) *Community Studies: An introduction to the sociology of the local community*, London: George Allen and Unwin.

Bell, C. and Newby, H. (1976), 'Husbands and wives: The dynamics of the deferential dialectic', in D. L. Barker and S. Allen (eds) *Dependence and Exploitation in Work and Marriage*, London: Longman, pp. 152–68.

Bellaby, P. (1987), 'The perpetuation of a folk model of the life cycle and kinship in a pottery factory', in A. Bryman, B. Bytheway, P. Allatt and T. Keil (eds) *Rethinking the Life Cycle*, London and Basingstoke: Macmillan, pp. 53–71.

Beynon, H., Hudson, R., Lewis, J., Sadler, D. and Townsend, A. (1989), ' "It's all falling apart here": Coming to terms with the future in Teesside', in P. Cooke (ed.) *Localities: The changing face of urban Britain*, London: Unwin Hyman, pp. 267–95.

Bhachu, P. (1985), *Twice Migrants: East African Sikh settlers in Britain*, London: Tavistock.

Binns, D. and Mars, G. (1984), 'Family, community and unemployment: A study in change', *Sociological Review* 32 (4), pp. 662–95.

Bondi, L. (1991), 'Women, gender relations and the inner city', in M. Keith and A. Rogers (eds) *Hollow Promises: Rhetoric and reality in the inner city*, London: Mansell, pp. 110–26.

Bornat, J. (1993), 'Representations of community', in J. Bornat, C. Pereira, D. Pilgrim and F. Williams (eds) *Community Care: A reader*, London and Basingstoke: Macmillan, pp. 21–32.

Bostyn, A.M. and Wight, D. (1987), 'Inside a community: Values associated with money and time', in S. Fineman (ed.) *Unemployment: Personal and social consequences*, London: Tavistock, pp. 138–54.

Bott, E. (1957), *Family and Social Network*, London: Tavistock.

Brah, A. (1986), 'Unemployment and racism: Asian youth on the dole', in S. Allen, A. Waton, K. Purcell and S. Wood (eds) *The Experience of Unemployment*, London and Basingstoke: Macmillan, pp. 61–78.

Briggs, A. and Oliver, J. (eds) (1985), *Caring: Experiences of looking after disabled relatives*, London: Routledge and Kegan Paul.

Brindley, T., Rydin, Y. and Stoker, G. (1989), *Remaking Planning: The politics of urban change in the Thatcher years*, London: Unwin Hyman.

Brody, H. (1973), *Inishkillane: Change and decline in the west of Ireland*, London: Allen Lane.

Brooks, D. and Singh, K. (1979), 'Pivots and presents: Asian brokers in British foundries', in S. Wallman (ed.) *Ethnicity at Work*, London and Basingstoke: Macmillan, pp. 93–112.

Buck, N., Gordon, C., Pickvance, C. and Taylor-Gooby, P. (1989), 'The Isle of Thanet: Restructuring and municipal conservatism', in P. Cooke (ed.) *Localities: The changing face of urban Britain*, London: Unwin Hyman, pp. 166–97.

Bulmer, M. (1975), 'Sociological models of the mining community', *Sociological Review* 23, pp. 61–92.

Bulmer, M. (1978a), 'Social structure and social change in the twentieth century', in M. Bulmer (ed.) *Mining and Social Change: Durham county in the twentieth century*, London: Croom Helm, pp. 15–48.

Bulmer, M. (ed.) (1978b), *Mining and Social Change: Durham county in the twentieth century*, London: Croom Helm.

Bulmer, M. (1984), *The Chicago School of Sociology: Institutionalization, Diversity, and the Rise of Sociological Research*, Chicago: University of Chicago Press.

Bulmer, M. (1985), 'The rejuvenation of community studies? Neighbours, networks and policy', *Sociological Review* 33, pp. 430–48.

Bulmer, M. (1986), *Neighbours: The work of Philip Abrams*, Cambridge: Cambridge University Press.

Bulmer, M. (1987), *The Social Bases of Community Care*, London: Allen and Unwin.

Bulmer, M. (1989), 'The underclass, empowerment and public policy', in M. Bulmer, J. Lewis and D. Piachaud (eds) *The Goals of Social Policy*, London: Unwin Hyman, pp. 245–57.

Burke, P. (1992), *History and Social Theory*, Cambridge: Polity.

Byrne, D. (1989), *Beyond the Inner City*, Milton Keynes: Open University Press.

Calhoun, C. (1983), 'Community: Toward a variable conceptualization for comparative research', in R. S. Neale (ed.) *History and Class: Essential readings in theory and interpretation*, Oxford: Basil Blackwell, pp. 86–110.

Carley, M. (1990), *Housing and Neighbourhood Renewal: Britain's new urban challenge*, London: Policy Studies Institute.

Cashmore, E. and Troyna, B. (1983), *Introduction to Race Relations*, London: Routledge and Kegan Paul.

Castells, M. (1977), *The Urban Question: A Marxist approach*, London: Arnold.

Castells, M. (1978), *City, Class and Power*, London: Macmillan.

Cecil, R., Offer, J. and St Leger, F. (1987), *Informal Welfare: A sociological study of care in Northern Ireland*, Aldershot: Gower.

Cherry, G. (1988), *Cities and Plans: The shaping of urban Britain in the nineteenth and twentieth centuries*, London: Edward Arnold.

Chinn, C. (1988), *They Worked all their Lives: Women of the urban poor in England, 1880–1939*, Manchester: Manchester University Press.

Church, A. and Hall, J. (1989), 'Local initiatives for economic regeneration', in D. Herbert and D. Smith (eds) *Social Problems and the City: New perspectives*, Oxford: Oxford University Press, pp. 345–69.

Clapham, D., Kemp, P. and Smith, S. (1990), *Housing and Social Policy*, London and Basingstoke: Macmillan.

Clark, D. B. (1973), 'The concept of community: A re-examination', *Sociological Review* 21 (3), pp. 397–416.

Clark, D. Y. (1987), 'Families facing redundancy', in S. Fineman (ed.) *Unemployment: Personal and social consequences*, London: Tavistock, pp. 97–117.

Clark, D. and Taylor, R. (1988), 'Partings and reunions: Marriage and offshore employment in the British North Sea', in J. Lewis, M. Porter and M. Shrimpton (eds) *Women, Work and Family in the British, Canadian and Norwegian Offshore Oilfields*, London and Basingstoke: Macmillan, pp. 112–39.

Cochrane, A. (1986), 'Community politics and democracy', in D. Held and C. Pollitt (eds) *New Forms of Democracy*, London: Sage, pp. 51–77.

Cockburn, C. (1977), *The Local State: Management of cities and people*, London: Pluto.

Coffield, F., Borrill, C. and Marshall, S. (1986), *Growing up at the Margins: Young adults in the north east*, Milton Keynes: Open University Press.

Cohen, A. (ed.) (1982), *Belonging: Identity and social organisation in British rural cultures*, Manchester: Manchester University Press.

Cohen, A. (1985), *The Symbolic Construction of Community*, London: Tavistock.

Cohen, A. (1986), 'Of symbols and boundaries, or, Does Ertie's greatcoat hold the key?', in A. Cohen (ed.) *Symbolising Boundaries: Identity and diversity in British cultures*, Manchester: Manchester University Press, pp. 1–19.

Cohen, A. (1987), *Whalsay: Symbol, segment and boundary in a Shetland Island community*, Manchester: Manchester University Press.

Cohen, P. (1984), 'Subcultural conflict and working-class community', in E. Butterworth and D. Weir (eds) *The New Sociology of Modern Britain*, London: Fontana, pp. 109–17.

Colenutt, B. (1991), 'The London Docklands Development Corporation: Has the community benefited?', in M. Keith and A. Rogers (eds) *Hollow Promises: Rhetoric and reality in the inner city*, London: Mansell, pp. 31–41.

Connell, J. (1978), *The End of Tradition: Country life in central Surrey*, London: Routledge and Kegan Paul.

Cooke, P. (ed.) (1989), *Localities: The changing face of urban Britain*, London: Unwin Hyman.

Cooke, P. (1990) *Back to the Future: Modernity, postmodernity and locality*, London: Unwin Hyman.

Cornwell, J. (1984), *Hard-Earned Lives: Accounts of health and illness from East London*, London: Tavistock.

Coser, L. (1974), *Greedy Institutions: Patterns of undivided commitment*, New York: Free Press.

Couper, M. and Brindley, T. (1975), 'Housing classes and housing values', *Sociological Review* 23, pp. 563–76.

Cousins, J. and Brown, R. (1975), 'Patterns of paradox: Shipbuilding workers' images of society', in M. Bulmer (ed.) *Working-Class Images of Society*, London: Routledge and Kegan Paul, pp. 55–82.

Critcher, C. (1979), 'Sociology, cultural studies and the post war working class', in J. Clarke, C. Critcher and R. Johnson (eds) *Working-Class Culture: Studies in history and theory*, London: Hutchinson, pp. 13–40.

Crow, G. (1989a), 'The post-war development of the modern domestic ideal', in G. Allan and G. Crow (eds) *Home and Family: Creating the domestic sphere*, London and Basingstoke: Macmillan, pp. 14–32.

Crow, G. (1989b), 'The use of the concept of "strategy" in recent sociological literature', *Sociology* 23 (1), pp. 1–24.

Crow, G. (1993), 'The traditional working-class community revisited', in C. Critcher, D. Waddington and M. Wykes (eds) *Proceedings of the Coal, Culture and Community Conference, Sheffield, 1991*, Sheffield: Pavic Press.

Crow, G. and Allan, G. (1990), 'Constructing the domestic sphere: The emergence of the modern home in post-war Britain', in H. Corr and L. Jamieson (eds) *Politics of Everyday Life: Continuity and change in work and the family*, London and Basingstoke: Macmillan, pp. 11–36.

Crow, G. and Hardey, M. (1991), 'The housing strategies of lone parents', in M. Hardey and G. Crow (eds) *Lone Parenthood: Coping with constraints and making opportunities*, Hemel Hempstead: Harvester Wheatsheaf, pp. 47–65.

Crow, G., Marsden, T. and Winter, M. (1990), 'Recent British rural sociology', in P. Lowe and M. Bodiguel (eds) *Rural Studies in Britain and France*, London: Belhaven Press, pp. 248–62.

Dahya, B. (1974), 'The nature of Pakistani ethnicity in industrial cities in Britain', in A. Cohen (ed.) *Urban Ethnicity*, London: Tavistock, pp. 77–118.

Dalglish, C. (1989), *Refugees from Vietnam*, London and Basingstoke: Macmillan.

Dalley, G. (1988), *Ideologies of Caring: Rethinking community and collectivism*, London and Basingstoke: Macmillan.

Damer, S. (1989), *From Moorepark to 'Wine Alley': The rise and fall of a Glasgow housing scheme*, Edinburgh: Edinburgh University Press.

Damer, S. (1990), *Glasgow: Going for a song*, London: Lawrence and Wishart.

Daunton, M. (1987), *A Property-Owning Democracy? Housing in Britain*, London: Faber and Faber.

Davidoff, L. (1976), 'The rationalization of housework', in D. Barker and S. Allen (eds) *Dependence and Exploitation in Work and Marriage*, London: Longman, pp. 121–51.

Davidoff, L. and Westover, B. (1986), ' "From Queen Victoria to the Jazz Age": Women's world in England, 1880–1939', in L. Davidoff and B. Westover (eds), *Our Work, Our Lives, Our Words: Women's history and women's work*, London and Basingstoke: Macmillan, pp. 1–35.

Davies, A. (1992), *Leisure, Gender and Poverty: Working-class culture in Salford and Manchester, 1900–1939*, Buckingham: Open University Press.

Davies, J. G. (1972), *The Evangelistic Bureaucrat: A study of a planning exercise in Newcastle upon Tyne*, London: Tavistock.

Davies, J. G. and Taylor, J. (1970), 'Race, community and no conflict', *New Society* 9 (July), pp. 67–9.

Davis, H. (1979), *Beyond Class Images: Explorations in the structure of social consciousness*, London: Croom Helm.

Day, G. and Murdoch, J. (1993), 'Locality and community: Coming to terms with place', *Sociological Review* 41 (1), pp. 82–111.

Deakin, N. and Edwards, J. (1993), *The Enterprise Culture and the Inner City*, London: Routledge.

Deakin, N. and Ungerson, C. (1977), *Leaving London: Planned mobility and the inner city*, London: Heinemann.

Deem, R. (1986), *All Work and no Play? The sociology of women and leisure*, Milton Keynes: Open University Press.

Delamont, S. (1980), *The Sociology of Women: An introduction*, London: George Allen and Unwin.

Dennis, F. (1993), 'Tiger Bay: A rainbow estate', in J. Bornat, C. Pereira, D. Pilgrim and F. Williams (eds) *Community Care: A reader*, London and Basingstoke: Macmillan, p. 9.

Dennis, N. (1968), 'The popularity of the neighbourhood community idea', in R. Pahl (ed.) *Readings in Urban Sociology*, Oxford: Pergamon Press, pp. 74–92.

Dennis, N. (1970), *People and Planning: The sociology of housing in Sunderland*, London: Faber and Faber.

Dennis, N., Henriques, F. and Slaughter, C. (1969), *Coal is our Life: An analysis of a Yorkshire mining community*, London: Tavistock.

Devine, F. (1989), 'Privatised families and their homes', in G. Allan and G. Crow (eds) *Home and Family: Creating the domestic sphere*, London and Basingstoke: Macmillan, pp. 82–101.

Devine, F. (1992), *Affluent Workers Revisited: Privatism and the working class*, Edinburgh: Edinburgh University Press.

Dhooge, Y. (1982), 'Livelihood II: Local involvement', in S. Wallman and associates *Living in South London*, Aldershot: Gower, pp. 103–27.

Dickens, P. (1988), *One Nation? Social change and the politics of locality*, London: Pluto.

Dickens, P. (1990), *Urban Sociology: Society, locality and human nature*, Hemel Hempstead: Harvester Wheatsheaf.

Dickens, P., Duncan, S., Goodwin, M. and Gray, F. (1985), *Housing, States and Localities*, London: Methuen.

Dominelli, L. (1990), *Women and Community Action*, Birmingham: Venture Press.

Donnison, D. (1987) 'Conclusions', in D. Donnison and A. Middleton (eds) *Regenerating the Inner City: Glasgow's experience*, London: Routledge and Kegan Paul, pp. 272–91.

Donnison, D. and Middleton, A. (eds) (1987), *Regenerating the Inner City: Glasgow's experience*, London: Routledge and Kegan Paul.

Downes, D. (1989), 'Only disconnect: Law and order, social policy and the community', in M. Bulmer, J. Lewis and D. Piachaud (eds) *The Goals of Social Policy*, London: Unwin Hyman, pp. 234–44.

Dunleavy, P. (1981), *The Politics of Mass Housing in Britain 1945–1975: A study of corporate power and professional influence in the welfare state*, Oxford: Clarendon Press.

Eade, J. (1989), *The Politics of Community: The Bangladeshi community in East London*, Aldershot: Avebury.

Edgell, S. (1980), *Middle-Class Couples: A study of segregation, domination and inequality in marriage*, London: George Allen and Unwin.

Eldridge, J. (1980), *Recent British Sociology*, London and Basingstoke: Macmillan.

Eldridge, J. (1984), 'Foreword', in G. Giarchi, *Between McAlpine and Polaris*, London: Routledge and Kegan Paul, pp. xi–xii.

Elias, N. (1974) 'Foreword – towards a theory of communities', in C. Bell and H. Newby (eds) *The Sociology of Community: A selection of readings*, London: Frank Cass, pp. ix–xii.

Elias, N. and Scotson, J. (1965), *The Established and the Outsiders*, London: Frank Cass.

Elliott, B. and McCrone, D. (1982), *The City: Patterns of domination and conflict*, London and Basingstoke: Macmillan.

Emmett, I. (1982), 'Place, community and bilingualism in Blaenau Ffestiniog', in A. Cohen (ed.) *Belonging: Identity and social organisation in British rural cultures*, Manchester: Manchester University Press, pp. 202–21.

Evason, E. (1985), *On the Edge: A study of poverty and long-term unemployment in Northern Ireland*, London: Child Poverty Action Group.

Ferris, J. (1985), 'Citizenship and the crisis of the welfare state', in P. Bean, J. Ferris and D. Whynes (eds) *In Defence of Welfare*, London: Tavistock, pp. 46–73.

Finch, J. (1989), *Family Obligations and Social Change*, Cambridge: Polity.

Finch, J. and Mason, J. (1993), *Negotiating Family Responsibilities*, London: Routledge.

Finnegan, R. (1985), 'Working outside formal employment', in R. Deem and G. Salaman (eds) *Work, Culture and Society*, Milton Keynes: Open University Press, pp. 150–78.

Finnegan, R. (1989), *The Hidden Musicians: Music-making in an English town*, Cambridge: Cambridge University Press.

Flett, H. (1979), 'Bureaucracy and ethnicity: Notions of eligibility to public housing', in S. Wallman (ed.) *Ethnicity at Work*, London and Basingstoke: Macmillan, pp. 135–52.

Ford, J. (1988), *The Indebted Society: Credit and default in the 1980s*, London: Routledge.

Forman, C. (1979), *Industrial Town: Self-portrait of St Helens in the 1920s*, London: Paladin.

Forrest, R. (1991), 'The privatization of collective consumption', in M. Gottdiener and C. Pickvance (eds) *Urban Life in Transition*, London: Sage, pp. 169–95.

Forrest, R. and Murie, A. (1987), 'The affluent homeowner: Labour market position and the shaping of housing histories', in N. Thrift and P. Williams (eds) *Class and Space: The making of urban society*, London: Routledge and Kegan Paul, pp. 30–59.

Forrest, R. and Murie, A. (1988), *Selling the Welfare State: The privatisation of public housing*, London: Routledge.

Forrest, R. and Murie, A. (1990), *Moving the Housing Market: Council estates, social change and privatization*, Aldershot: Avebury.

Forrest, R., Murie, A. and Williams, P. (1990), *Home Ownership: Differentiation and fragmentation*, London: Unwin Hyman.

Foster, J. (1990), *Villains: Crime and community in the inner city*, London: Routledge.

Fox, R. (1978), *The Tory Islanders: A people of the Celtic fringe*, Cambridge: Cambridge University Press.

Frankenberg, R. (1957), *Village on the Border: A social study of religion, politics and football in a North Wales community*, London: Cohen and West.

Frankenberg, R. (1969), *Communities in Britain: Social life in town and country*, Harmondsworth: Penguin.

Frankenberg, R. (1976), 'In the production of their lives, men (?) . . . sex and gender in British community studies', in D. Leonard Barker and S. Allen (eds) *Sexual Divisions and Society: Process and change*, London: Tavistock, pp. 25–51.

Gallie, D. (1985), 'Directions for the future', in B. Roberts, R. Finnegan and D. Gallie (eds) *New Approaches to Economic Life: Economic restructuring, unemployment and the social division of labour*, Manchester: Manchester University Press, pp. 512–30.

Giarchi, G. (1984), *Between McAlpine and Polaris*, London: Routledge and Kegan Paul.

Gilbert, D. (1992), *Class, Community and Collective Action: Social change in two British coalfields, 1850–1926*, Oxford: Clarendon Press.

Gillespie, N., Lovett, T. and Garner, W. (1992), *Youth Work and Working Class Youth Culture: Rules and resistance in West Belfast*, Buckingham: Open University Press.

Gilligan, J. H. (1984), 'The rural labour process: A case study of a Cornish town', in T. Bradley and P. Lowe (eds) *Locality and rurality: Economy and society in rural regions*, Norwich: Geo Books, pp. 91–112.

Gilligan, J. H. (1987), 'Visitors, tourists and outsiders in a Cornish town', in M. Bouquet and M. Winter (eds) *Who from their Labours Rest? Conflict and practice in rural tourism*, Aldershot: Avebury, pp. 65–82.

Gilligan, J. H. (1990), 'Padstow: Economic and social change in a Cornish town', in C. C. Harris (ed.) *Family, Economy and Community*, Cardiff: University of Wales Press, pp. 165–85.

Gilligan, J. H. and Harris, C. C. (1989), 'Community and community studies: Studying local social life', in R. Burgess (ed.) *Investigating Society*, London: Longman, pp. 12–31.

Gilroy, P. (1987), *There ain't no Black in the Union Jack: The cultural politics of race and nation*, London: Hutchinson.

Gittins, D. (1982), *Fair Sex: Family size and structure, 1900–39*, London: Hutchinson.

Gittins, D. (1985), *The Family in Question: Changing households and familiar ideologies*, London and Basingstoke: Macmillan.

Gittins, D. (1986), 'Marital status, work and kinship, 1850–1930', in J. Lewis (ed.) *Labour and Love: Women's experience of home and family, 1850–1940*, Oxford: Basil Blackwell, pp. 249–67.

Glass, R. (1989), *Clichés of Urban Doom and Other Essays*, Oxford: Basil Blackwell.

Glendinning, C. (1983), *Unshared Care: Parents and their disabled children*, London: Routledge and Kegan Paul.

Glyptis, S. (1989), *Leisure and Unemployment*, Milton Keynes: Open University Press.

Goffman, E. (1959), *The Presentation of Self in Everyday Life*, Garden City, New York: Doubleday Anchor.

Goffman, E. (1963), *Stigma: Notes on the management of spoilt identity*, Englewood Cliffs, N.J.: Prentice Hall.

Goldthorpe, J.H., Lockwood, D., Bechhofer, F. and Platt, J. (1969), *The Affluent Worker in the Class Structure*, Cambridge: Cambridge University Press.

Goodin, R. (1985), *Protecting the Vulnerable: A reanalysis of our social responsibilities*, Chicago: University of Chicago Press.

Goodwin, M. (1991), 'Replacing a surplus population: The policies of the London Docklands Development Corporation', in J. Allen and C. Hamnett (eds) *Housing and Labour Markets: Building the connections*, London: Unwin Hyman, pp. 254–75.

Gordon, E. and Brietenbach, E. (eds) (1990), *The World is Ill Divided: Women's work in Scotland in the nineteenth and early twentieth centuries*, Edinburgh: Edinburgh University Press.

Graham, H. (1983), 'Caring: A labour of love', in J. Finch and D. Groves (eds) *A Labour of Love: Women, work and caring*, London: Routledge and Kegan Paul, pp. 13–30.

Grant, L. (1990), 'Women in a car town: Coventry, 1920–45', in P. Hudson and W. R. Lee (eds) *Women's Work and the Family Economy in Historical Perspective*, Manchester: Manchester University Press, pp. 220–46.

Gray, F. (1989), 'Class and stratification', in M. Ball, F. Gray and L. McDowell, *The Transformation of Britain: Contemporary social and economic change*, London: Fontana, pp. 424–58.

Green, H. (1988), *Informal Carers* (OPCS Series GH5 no.15 Supplement A), London: HMSO.

Greer, S. (1991), 'The community of limited liability', in P. Worsley (ed.) *The New Modern Sociology: Readings*, Harmondsworth: Penguin, pp. 309–12.

Grieco, M. (1987a), *Keeping it in the Family: Social networks and employment chance*, London: Tavistock.

Grieco, M. (1987b), 'Family networks and the closure of employment', in G. Lee and R. Loveridge (eds) *The Manufacture of Disadvantage: Stigma and social closure*, Milton Keynes: Open University Press, pp. 33–44.

Hall, P. (1988), *Cities of Tomorrow: An intellectual history of urban planning and design in the twentieth century*, Oxford: Basil Blackwell.

Halsey, A. H. (1974), 'Government against poverty in school and community', in D. Wedderburn (ed.) *Poverty, Inequality and Class Structure*, Cambridge: Cambridge University Press, pp. 123–40.

Halsey, A. H. (1989), 'Social polarization, the inner city and community', in M. Bulmer, J. Lewis and D. Piachaud (eds) *The Goals of Social Policy*, London: Unwin Hyman, pp. 228–33.

Hanmer, J. and Saunders, S. (1984), *Well-Founded Fear: A community study of violence to women*, London: Hutchinson.

Hardey, M. (1989), 'Lone parents and the home', in G. Allan and G. Crow (eds) *Home and Family: Creating the domestic sphere*, London and Basingstoke: Macmillan, pp. 122–40.

Harloe, M., Pickvance, C. and Urry, J. (eds) (1990), *Place, Policy and Politics: Do localities matter?*, London: Unwin Hyman.

Harper, D. (1992), 'Small N's and community case studies', in C. Ragin and H. Becker (eds) *What is a case? Exploring the foundations of social inquiry*, Cambridge: Cambridge University Press, pp. 139–58.

Harris, C. C. (1983), 'Introduction', in C. Rosser and C. C. Harris *The Family and Social Change: A study of family and kinship in a South Wales town*, London: Routledge and Kegan Paul.

Harris, C. C. (1987), *Redundancy and Recession in South Wales*, Oxford: Basil Blackwell.

Harris, C. C. (1990), 'Reflections on family, economy and community', in C. C. Harris (ed.) *Family, Economy and Community*, Cardiff: University of Wales Press, pp. 187–213.

Harris, C. and Morris, L. (1986), 'Households, labour markets and the position of women', in R. Crompton and M. Mann (eds) *Gender and Stratification*, Cambridge: Polity, pp. 86–96.

Harris, R. (1972), *Prejudice and Tolerance in Ulster: A study of neighbours and 'strangers' in a border community*, Manchester: Manchester University Press.

Harvey, D. (1989), *The Urban Experience*, Oxford: Basil Blackwell.

Harvey, L. (1987), *Myths of the Chicago School of Sociology*, Aldershot: Avebury.

Hasegawa, J. (1992), *Replanning the Blitzed City Centre: A comparative study of Bristol, Coventry and Southampton 1941–1950*, Buckingham: Open University Press.

Hebron, S. and Wykes, M. (1991), 'Gender and patriarchy in mining communities', in M. Cross and G. Payne (eds) *Work and the Enterprise Culture*, London: Falmer, pp. 160–72.

Heller, A. (1984), *Everyday Life*, London: Routledge and Kegan Paul.

Henderson, J. and Karn, V. (1987), *Race, Class and State Housing: Inequality and the allocation of public housing in Britain*, Aldershot: Gower.

Heraud, B. (1975), 'The New Towns: A philosophy of community', in P. Leonard (ed.) *The Sociology of Community Action*, Keele: Sociological Review Monographs, pp. 39–55.

Higgins, J. (1978), *The Poverty Business in Britain and America*, Oxford: Basil Blackwell.

Higgins, J. (1989), 'Homes and institutions', in G. Allan and G. Crow (eds) *Home and Family: Creating the domestic sphere*, London and Basingstoke: Macmillan, pp. 159–73.

Hill, S. (1976), *The Dockers: Class and tradition in London*, London: Heinemann.

Hobbs, D. (1989), *Doing the Business: Entrepreneurs, the working class, and detectives in the East End of London*, Oxford: Oxford University Press.

Hoggart, R. (1958), *The Uses of Literacy: Aspects of working class life with special reference to publications and entertainments*, Harmondsworth: Penguin.

Holland, P. and Leinhardt, S. (1979), *Perspectives on Social Network Research*, London: Academic Press.

Holme, A. (1985), *Housing and Young Families in East London*, London: Routledge and Kegan Paul.

Hope, T. and Shaw, M. (1988), *Communities and Crime Reduction*, London: HMSO.

Howe, L. (1990), *Being Unemployed in Northern Ireland: An ethnographic study*, Cambridge: Cambridge University Press.

Hudson, B. (1987), *Justice through Punishment: A critique of the 'justice' model of corrections*, London: Macmillan.

Hudson, R. and Williams, A. (1989), *Divided Britain*, London: Belhaven Press.

Humphries, S. (1981), *Hooligans or Rebels? An oral history of working-class childhood and youth 1889–1939*, Oxford: Basil Blackwell.

Hunt, G. and Satterlee, S. (1986), 'Cohesion and division: drinking in an English village', *Man* 21(3), 521–37.

Hunt, P. (1980), *Gender and Class Consciousness*, London and Basingstoke: Macmillan.

Hunt, P. (1989), 'Gender and the construction of home life', in G. Allan and G. Crow (eds) *Home and Family: Creating the domestic sphere*, London and Basingstoke: Macmillan, pp. 66–81.

Hutson, S. and Jenkins, R. (1989), *Taking the Strain: Families, unemployment and the transition to adulthood*, Milton Keynes: Open University Press.

Jackson, B. (1968), *Working Class Community: Some general notions raised by a series of studies in northern England*, London: Routledge and Kegan Paul.

Janowitz, M. (1967), *The Community Press in an Urban Setting*, 2nd edn, Chicago: University of Chicago Press.

Jenkins, R. (1983), *Lads, Citizens and Ordinary Kids: Working-class youth life-styles in Belfast*, London: Routledge and Kegan Paul.

Jordan, B., James, S., Kay, H. and Redley, M. (1992), *Trapped in Poverty? Labour-market decisions in low-income households*, London: Routledge.

Karn, V. (1977), *Retiring to the seaside*, London: Routledge and Kegan Paul.

Karn, V. and Henderson, J. (1983), 'Housing atypical households: Understanding the practices of local government housing departments', in A. W. Franklin (ed.) *Family Matters: Perspectives on the family and social policy*, Oxford: Pergamon, pp. 71–86.

Karn, V., Kemeny, J. and Williams, P. (1985), *Home Ownership in the Inner City: Salvation or despair?* Aldershot: Gower.

Kemeny, J. (1981), *The Myth of Home Ownership: Private versus public choices in housing tenure*, London: Routledge and Kegan Paul.

Kent, R. (1981), *A History of British Empirical Sociology*, Aldershot: Gower.

Klein, J. (1965), *Samples from English Cultures*, vol. I, London: Routledge and Kegan Paul.

Lawless, P. (1989), *Britain's Inner Cities*, 2nd edn, London: Paul Chapman.

Lawless, P. and Brown, F. (1986), *Urban Growth and Change in Britain: An introduction*, London: Harper and Row.

Lee, D. and Newby, H. (1983), *The Problem of Sociology*, London: Hutchinson.

Lewis, J. (1986), 'Introduction: Reconstructing women's experience of home and family', in J. Lewis (ed.) *Home and Family: Women's experience of home and family, 1850–1940*, Oxford: Basil Blackwell, pp. 1–24.

Lewis, J. and Meredith, B. (1988), *Daughters Who Care: Daughters caring for mothers at home*, London: Routledge.

Lewis, O. (1951), *Life in a Mexican Village: Tepoztlan restudied*, Urbana: University of Illinois Press.

Little, J., Peake, L. and Richardson, P. (eds) (1988), *Women in Cities: Gender and the urban environment*, London and Basingstoke: Macmillan.

Littlejohn, J. (1963), *Westrigg: The sociology of a Cheviot parish*, London: Routledge and Kegan Paul.

Lockwood, D. (1975), 'Sources of variation in working-class images of society', in M. Bulmer (ed.) *Working-Class Images of Society*, London: Routledge and Kegan Paul, pp. 16–31.

Loney, M. (1983), *Community against Government: The British Community Development Project, 1968–78 – a study of government incompetence*, London: Heinemann.

Long, N. (1970), 'The local community as an ecology of games', in P. Worsley (ed.) *Modern Sociology*, Harmondsworth: Penguin, pp. 303–6.

Lonsdale, S. (1990), *Women and Disability: The experience of physical disability among women*, London and Basingstoke: Macmillan.

Lowe, S. (1986), *Urban Social Movements: The city after Castells*, London and Basingstoke: Macmillan.

Lowe, S. (1988), 'New patterns of wealth: The growth of owner occupation', in R. Walker and G. Parker (eds) *Money Matters: Income, wealth and financial welfare*, London: Sage, pp. 149–65.

Lummis, T. (1985), *Occupation and Society: The East Anglian fishermen 1880–1914*, Cambridge: Cambridge University Press.

Lynd, R. and Lynd, H. (1929), *Middletown*, New York: Harcourt Brace.

Lynd, R. and Lynd, H. (1937), *Middletown in Transition*, New York: Harcourt Brace.

McDowell, L. (1983), 'City and home: Urban housing and the sexual division of space', in M. Evans and C. Ungerson (eds) *Sexual Divisions: Patterns and processes*, London: Tavistock, pp. 142–63.

Macfarlane, A. (1977), *Reconstructing Historical Communities*, Cambridge: Cambridge University Press.

MacGregor, S. (1990), 'The inner-city battlefield: Politics, ideology, and social relations', in S. MacGregor and B. Pimlott (eds) *Tackling the Inner Cities: The 1980s reviewed, prospects for the 1990s*, Oxford: Oxford University Press, pp. 64–92.

McKee, L. (1987), 'Households during unemployment: The resourcefulness of the unemployed', in J. Brannen and G. Wilson (eds) *Give and Take in Families: Studies in resource distribution*, London: Allen and Unwin, pp. 96–116.

McKee, L. and Bell, C. (1986), 'His unemployment, her problem: The domestic and marital consequences of male unemployment', in S. Allen, A. Waton, K. Purcell and S. Wood (eds) *The Experience of Unemployment*, London and Basingstoke: Macmillan, pp. 134–49.

Madge, C. and Willmott, P. (1981), *Inner City Poverty in Paris and London*, London: Routledge and Kegan Paul.

Madge, J. (1970), *The Origins of Scientific Sociology*, London: Tavistock.

Madigan, R., Munro, M. and Smith, S. (1990), 'Gender and the meaning of the home', *International Journal of Urban and Regional Research* 14 (4), pp. 625–47.

Mann, M. (1973), *Workers on the Move: The sociology of relocation*, Cambridge: Cambridge University Press.

Marris, P. (1987), *Meaning and Action: Community planning and conceptions of change*, London: Routledge and Kegan Paul.

Mars, G. (1982), *Cheats at Work: An anthropology of workplace crime*, London: George Allen and Unwin.

Marshall, G. (1990), *In Praise of Sociology*, London: Unwin Hyman.

Mason, J. (1988), ' "No peace for the wicked": Older married women and leisure', in E. Wimbush and M. Talbot (eds) *Relative Freedoms: Women and leisure*, Milton Keynes: Open University Press, pp. 75–85.

Mason, J. (1989), 'Reconstructing the public and the private: The home and marriage in later life', in G. Allan and G. Crow (eds) *Home and Family: Creating the domestic sphere*, London and Basingstoke: Macmillan, pp. 102–21.

Matrix (1984), *Making Space: Women and the man-made environment*, London: Pluto Press.

Meacham, S. (1977), *A Life Apart: The English working class 1890–1914*, London: Thames and Hudson.

Meegan, R. (1989), 'Paradise postponed: The growth and decline of Merseyside's outer estates', in P. Cooke (ed.) *Localities: The changing face of urban Britain*, London: Unwin Hyman, pp. 198–234.

Meegan, R. (1990), 'Merseyside in crisis and in conflict', in M. Harloe, C. Pickvance and J. Urry (eds) *Place, Policy and Politics: Do localities matter?*, London: Unwin Hyman, pp. 87–107.

Mellor, R. (1977), *Urban Sociology in an Urbanized Society*, London: Routledge and Kegan Paul.

Mellor, R. (1985), 'Manchester's inner city: The management of the periphery', in H. Newby, J. Bujra, P. Littlewood, G. Rees and T. Rees (eds) *Restructuring Capital: Recession and reorganization in industrial society*, London and Basingstoke: Macmillan, pp. 105–23.

Merrett, S. with Gray, F. (1982), *Owner-Occupation in Britain*, London: Routledge and Kegan Paul.

Middleton, A. (1987), 'Glasgow and its east end', in D. Donnison and A. Middleton (eds) *Regenerating the Inner City: Glasgow's experience*, London: Routledge and Kegan Paul, pp. 3–33.

Mills, C. Wright (1959), *The Sociological Imagination*, London: Oxford University Press.

Moore, R. (1974), *Pit-Men, Preachers and Politics: The effects of Methodism in a Durham mining community*, Cambridge: Cambridge University Press.

Moore, R. (1975), 'Religion as a source of variation in working class images of society', in M. Bulmer (ed.) *Working-Class Images of Society*, London: Routledge and Kegan Paul, pp. 35–54.

Moore, R. (1977), 'Becoming a sociologist in Sparkbrook', in C. Bell and H. Newby (eds) *Doing Sociological Research*, London: George Allen and Unwin, pp. 87–107.

Moore, R. (1982), *The Social Impact of Oil: The case of Peterhead*, London: Routledge and Kegan Paul.

Morris, J. and Winn, M. (1990), *Housing and Social Inequality*, London: Hilary Shipman.

Morris, L. (1990a), *The Workings of the Household: A US–UK comparison*, Cambridge: Polity.

Morris, L. (1990b), 'The household and the labour market', in C. C. Harris (ed.) *Family, Economy and Community*, Cardiff: University of Wales Press, pp. 79–97.

Morris, L. and Irwin, S. (1992), 'Unemployment and informal support: Dependency, exclusion, or participation?', *Work, Employment and Society* 6 (2), pp. 185–207.

Morris, R. and Mogey, J. (1965), *The Sociology of Housing: Studies at Berinsfield*, London: Routledge and Kegan Paul.

Mullan, B. (1980), *Stevenage Ltd; Aspects of the planning and politics of Stevenage New Town 1945–78*, London: Routledge and Kegan Paul.

Newby, H. (1977), *The Deferential Worker: A study of farm workers in East Anglia*, London: Allen Lane.

Newby, H. (1980), *Green and Pleasant Land? Social change in rural England*, Harmondsworth: Penguin.

Newby, H., Bell, C., Rose, D. and Saunders, P. (1978), *Property, Paternalism and Power: Class and control in rural England*, London: Hutchinson.

Nissell, M. and Bonnerjea, L. (1982), *Family Care for the Handicapped Elderly: Who pays?*, London: Policy Studies Institute.

Nuttgens, P. (1989), *The Home Front: Housing the people 1840–1990*, London: BBC Books.

Oakley, A. (1992), *Social Support and Motherhood*, Oxford: Basil Blackwell.

Okely, J. (1983), *The Traveller-Gypsies*, Cambridge: Cambridge University Press.

Oldman, C. (1991), 'The myth of independence: Home-ownership in old age', in J. Hutton, S. Hutton, T. Pinch and A. Shiell (eds) *Dependency to Enterprise*, London: Routledge, pp. 141–53.

OPCS (1992), 'General household survey: Carers in 1990', *OPCS Monitor SS92/2*, London: HMSO.

Oxley, H. G. (1974), *Mateship in Local Organization*, Queensland: University of Queensland Press.

Pahl, J. (ed.) (1985), *Private Violence and Public Policy: The needs of battered women and the response of the public services*, London: Routledge and Kegan Paul.

Pahl, R. E. (1975), *Whose City? And further essays on urban society*, 2nd edn, Harmondsworth: Penguin.

Pahl, R. E. (1984), *Divisions of Labour*, Oxford: Basil Blackwell.

Pahl, R. E., Flynn, R. and Buck, N. H. (1983), *Structures and Processes of Urban Life*, 2nd edn, London: Longman.

Pahl, R. E. and Wallace, C. (1985), 'Household work strategies in economic recession', in N. Redclift and E. Mingione (eds) *Beyond Employment: Household, gender and subsistence*, Oxford: Basil Blackwell, pp. 189–227.

Pahl, R. E. and Wallace, C. D. (1988), 'Neither angels in marble nor rebels in red: privatization and working-class consciousness', in D. Rose (ed.) *Social Stratification and Economic Change*, London: Hutchinson, pp. 127–49.

Parker, H., Bakx, K. and Newcombe, R. (1988), *Living with Heroin: The impact of a drugs 'epidemic' on an English community*, Milton Keynes: Open University Press.

Parry, G., Moyser, G. and Wagstaffe, M. (1987), 'The crowd and the community: Context, content and aftermath', in G. Gaskell and R. Benewick (eds) *The Crowd in Contemporary Britain*, London: Sage, pp. 212–54.

Patterson, S. (1965), *Dark Strangers: A study of West Indians in London*, Harmondsworth: Penguin.

Peach, C. (1981), 'Conflicting interpretations of segregation', in P. Jackson and S. Smith (eds) *Social Interaction and Ethnic Segregation*, London: Academic Press, pp. 19–33.

Peach, C. and Smith, S. (1981), 'Introduction', in C. Peach, V. Robinson and S. Smith (eds) *Ethnic Segregation in Cities*, London: Croom Helm, pp. 9–22.

Pennington, S. and Westover, B. (1989), *A Hidden Workforce: Homeworkers in England, 1850–1985*, London and Basingstoke: Macmillan.

Plant, R., Lesser, H. and Taylor-Gooby, P. (1980), *Political Philosophy and Social Welfare: Essays on the normative basis of welfare provision*, London: Routledge and Kegan Paul.

Platt, J. (1971), *Social Research in Bethnal Green: An evaluation of the work of the Institute of Community Studies*, London: Macmillan.

Poplin, D. (1979), *Communities: A survey of theories and methods of research*, New York: Macmillan.

Porter, M. (1983), *Home, Work and Class Consciousness*, Manchester: Manchester University Press.

Porteus, J. D. (1989), *Planned to Death: The annihilation of a place called Howdendyke*, Manchester: Manchester University Press.

Procter, I. (1990), 'The privatisation of working-class life: A dissenting view', *British Journal of Sociology* 41 (2), pp. 157–80.

Pryce, K. (1979), *Endless Pressure: A study of West Indian life styles in Bristol*, Harmondsworth: Penguin.

Qureshi, H. and Walker, A. (1989), *The Caring Relationship: Elderly people and their families*, London: Macmillan,

Redfield, R. (1930), *Tepoztlan: A Mexican village*, Chicago: University of Chicago Press.

Rees, A. (1951), *Life in a Welsh Countryside: A social study of Llanfihangel yng Ngwynfa*, Cardiff: University of Wales Press.

Rees, G. and Thomas, M. (1991), 'From coalminers to entrepreneurs? A case study in the sociology of re-industrialization', in M. Cross and G. Payne (eds) *Work and the Enterprise Culture*, London: Falmer, pp. 57–78.

Revill, G. (1993), 'Reading "Rosehill": Community, identity and inner-city Derby', in M. Keith and S. Pile (eds) *Place and the Politics of Identity*, London: Routledge, pp. 117–40.

Rex, J. (1973), *Race, Colonialism and the City*, London: Routledge and Kegan Paul.

Rex, J. (1977), 'Sociological theory and the city', *Australian and New Zealand Journal of Sociology* 13, pp. 218–23.

Rex, J. (1988), *The Ghetto and the Underclass: Essays on race and social policy*, Aldershot: Avebury.

Rex, J. and Moore, R. (1967), *Race, Community and Conflict: A study of Sparkbrook*, London: Oxford University Press.

Rex, J. and Tomlinson, S. (1979), *Colonial Immigrants in a British City: A class analysis*, London: Routledge and Kegan Paul.

Riley, D. (1983), *War in the Nursery: Theories of the child and mother*, London: Virago.

Roberts, B., Finnegan, R. and Gallie, D. (1985), 'Introduction', in B. Roberts, R. Finnegan and D. Gallie (eds) *New Approaches to Economic*

*Life: Economic restructuring, unemployment and the social division of labour*, Manchester: Manchester University Press, pp. 1–19.

Roberts, E. (1984), *A Woman's Place: An oral history of working class women, 1890–1940*, Oxford: Basil Blackwell.

Roberts, E. (1986), 'Women's strategies, 1890–1940', in J. Lewis (ed.) *Labour and Love: Women's experience of home and family, 1850–1940*, Oxford: Basil Blackwell, pp. 223–47.

Roberts, H., Smith, S. J., and Lloyd, M. (1992), 'Safety as a social value: A community approach', in S. Scott, G. Williams, S. Platt and H. Thomas (eds), *Private Risks and Public Dangers*, Aldershot: Avebury, pp. 184–200.

Roberts, K. (1978), *The Working Class*, London: Longman.

Roberts, K. (1984), 'Youth unemployment and urban unrest', in J. Benyon (ed.) *Scarman and After: Essays reflecting on Lord Scarman's Report, the riots and their aftermath*, Oxford: Pergamon, pp. 175–83.

Roberts, M. (1991), *Living in a Man-made World: Gender assumptions in modern housing design*, London: Routledge.

Roberts, R. (1973), *The Classic Slum: Salford life in the first quarter of the century*, Harmondsworth: Penguin.

Robins, K. (1990), 'Global local times', in J. Anderson and M. Ricci (eds) *Society and Social Science: A reader*, Milton Keynes: The Open University, pp. 196–205.

Robinson, V. (1981), 'The Development of South Asian settlement in Britain and the myth of return', in C. Peach, V. Robinson and S. Smith (eds) *Ethnic Segregation in Cities*, London: Croom Helm, pp. 149–69.

Robinson, V. (1986), *Transients, Settlers and Refugees: Asians in Britain*, Oxford: Clarendon Press.

Ross, E. (1983), 'Survival networks: Women's neighbourhood sharing in London before World War One', *History Workshop* 15, pp. 4–27.

Rosser, C. and Harris, C. C. (1983), *The Family and Social Change: A study of family and kinship in a South Wales town*, abridged edn, London: Routledge and Kegan Paul.

Saifullah Khan, V. (1979a), 'Migration and social stress: Mirpuris in Bradford', in V. Saifullah Khan (ed.) *Minority Families in Britain: Support and stress*, London and Basingstoke: Macmillan, pp. 37–57.

Saifullah Khan, V. (1979b), 'Work and network: South Asian women in South London', in S. Wallman (ed.) *Ethnicity at Work*, London and Basingstoke: Macmillan, pp. 115–33.

St Leger, F. and Gillespie, N. (1991), *Informal Welfare in Belfast: Caring communities?*, Aldershot: Avebury.

Salaman, G. (1974), *Community and Occupation: An exploration of work/leisure relationships*, Cambridge: Cambridge University Press.

Salaman, G. (1986), *Working*, London: Tavistock.

Sampson, R. (1993), 'The community context of violent crime', in W. J. Wilson (ed.) *Sociology and the Public Agenda*, London: Sage, pp. 259–86.

Sanders, C. (1992), 'Bengal to Brick Lane revisited', *The Higher*, 7 February, p. 15.

Sarre, P., Phillips, D. and Skellington, R. (1989), *Ethnic Minority Housing: Explanations and policies*, Aldershot: Avebury.

Sarsby, J. (1988), *Missuses and Mouldrunners: An oral history of women pottery workers at work and at home*, Milton Keynes: Open University Press.

Saunders, P. (1979), *Urban Politics: A sociological interpretation*, London: Hutchinson.

Saunders, P. (1984), 'Beyond housing classes', *International Journal of Urban and Regional Research* 8, pp. 233–51.

Saunders, P. (1986), *Social Theory and the Urban Question*, 2nd edn, London: Hutchinson.

Saunders, P. (1990), *A Nation of Home Owners*, London: Unwin Hyman.

Scherer, J. (1972), *Contemporary Community: Sociological illusion or reality?* London: Tavistock.

Scott, J. (1991), *Social Network Analysis: A handbook*, London: Sage.

Seabrook, J. (1979), *Mother and Son: An autobiography*, London: Victor Gollancz.

Sharpe, S. (1984), *Double Identity: The lives of working mothers*, Harmondsworth: Penguin.

Shaw, A. (1988), *A Pakistani Community in Britain*, Oxford: Basil Blackwell.

Short, J. (1982), *Housing in Britain: The post-war experience*, London: Methuen.

Short, J. (1984), *The Urban Arena: Capital, state and community in contemporary Britain*, London and Basingstoke: Macmillan.

Sinclair, I. and Thomas, D. (eds) (1983), *Perspectives on Patch* (NISW Paper no. 14), London: NISW.

Smith, D. (1988), *The Chicago School: A liberal critique of capitalism*, London and Basingstoke: Macmillan.

Smith, D. (1989), ' "Not getting on, just getting by": Changing prospects in south Birmingham', in P. Cooke (ed.) *Localities: The changing face of urban Britain*, London: Unwin Hyman, pp. 235–66.

Smith, D. J. (1987), 'The police and the idea of community', in P. Willmott (ed.) *Policing and the Community*, London: Policy Studies Institute, pp. 54–67.

Smith, S. (1989a), *The Politics of 'Race' and Residence: Citizenship, segregation and white supremacy in Britain*, Cambridge: Polity.

Smith, S. (1989b), 'The challenge of urban crime', in D. Herbert and D. Smith (eds) *Social Problems and the City: New perspectives*, Oxford: Oxford University Press, pp. 271–88.

Stacey, M. (1960), *Tradition and Change: A study of Banbury*, London: Oxford University Press.

Stacey, M. (1969), 'The myth of community studies', *British Journal of Sociology*, 20(2), pp. 134–47.

Stacey, M. (1981), 'The division of labour revisited or overcoming the two Adams', in P. Abrams, R. Deem, J. Finch and P. Rock (eds) *Practice and Progress: British sociology 1950–1980*, London: George Allen and Unwin, pp. 172–90.

Stacey, M., Batstone, E., Bell, C. and Murcott, A. (1975), *Power, Persistence and Change: A second study of Banbury*, London: Routledge and Kegan Paul.

Strathern, M. (1981), *Kinship at the Core: An anthropology of Elmdon, a village in north-west Essex in the nineteen-sixties*, Cambridge: Cambridge University Press.

Stubbs, C. and Wheelock, J. (1990), *A Woman's Work in the Changing Local Economy*, Aldershot: Avebury.

Suttles, G. (1972), *The Social Construction of Communities*, Chicago: University of Chicago Press.

Taylor, R. (1979), 'Migration and the residual community', *Sociological Review* 27 (3), pp. 475–89.

Tebbutt, M. (1983), *Making Ends Meet: Pawnbroking and working class credit*, Leicester: Leicester University Press.

Thompson, E. (1968), *The Making of the English Working Class*, Harmondsworth: Penguin.

Thompson, P. with Wailey, T. and Lummis, T. (1983), *Living the Fishing*, London: Routledge and Kegan Paul.

Thorns, D. (1976), *The Quest for Community: Social aspects of residential growth*, London: George Allen and Unwin.

Tivers, J. (1985), *Women Attached: The daily lives of women with young children*, London: Croom Helm.

Tönnies, F. (1955), *Community and Association*, London: Routledge and Kegan Paul.

Townsend, P. (1957), *The Family Life of Old People*, London: Routledge and Kegan Paul.

Townsend, P., Phillimore, P. and Beattie, A. (1988), *Health and Deprivation: Inequality and the north*, London: Croom Helm.

Tunstall, J. (1962), *The Fishermen: The sociology of an extreme occupation*, London: MacGibbon and Kee.

Turner, R., Bostyn, A.M. and Wight, D. (1985), 'The work ethic in a Scottish town with declining employment', in B. Roberts, R. Finnegan